Young People, Social Media and the Law

This book critically confronts perceptions that social media has become a 'wasteland' for young people. Law has become preoccupied with privacy, intellectual property, defamation and criminal behaviour in and through social media. In the case of children and youth, this book argues, these preoccupations – whilst important – have disguised and distracted public debate away from a much broader, and more positive, consideration of the nature of social media. In particular, the legal tendency to consider social media as 'dangerous' for young people – to focus exclusively on the need to protect and control their online presence and privacy, whilst tending to suspect, or to criminalise, their use of it – has obscured the potential of social media to help young people to participate more fully as citizens in society. Drawing on sociological work on the construction of childhood, and engaging a wide range of national and international legal material, this book argues that social media may yet offer the possibility of an entirely different – and more progressive – conceptualisation of children and youth.

Brian Simpson is a Professor in the School of Law at the University of New England, Australia.

Young People, Social Media and the Law

Brian Simpson

Routledge
Taylor & Francis Group
LONDON AND NEW YORK

First published 2018
by Routledge
2 Park Square, Milton Park, Abingdon, Oxon OX14 4RN

and by Routledge
605 Third Avenue, New York, NY 10017

Routledge is an imprint of the Taylor & Francis Group, an informa business

British Library Cataloguing-in-Publication Data
A catalogue record for this book is available from the British Library

Library of Congress Cataloging-in-Publication Data
A catalog record for this book has been requested

ISBN: 978-1-138-81443-1 (hbk)
ISBN: 978-1-315-74748-4 (ebk)

Typeset in NewBaskerville
by Apex CoVantage, LLC

For Helen

Contents

Acknowledgements

In many ways, the ideas in this book are the culmination of conversations over the years with various colleagues and friends. Often those discussions have been about matters that were not directly related to the central themes of this book but yet have touched upon them in a manner that I have found important and useful. In particular, I thank Mark O'Brien, Chris Ashford, Maria Murphy, Cheryl Simpson, Lara Karaian and Kelvin Johnstone for such conversations. I also thank my colleagues at the School of Law at the University of New England for the supportive workplace they provide, as well as Dalhousie Law School in Canada where I spent part of my sabbatical during which I also worked on this book. I also thank Colin Perrin and the production team at Routledge for their support, hard work and patience.

On a personal level, I acknowledge the support of my wife Helen, who has had to endure the trials and tribulations of my project alongside me. This book is dedicated to her.

Introduction

This book is concerned with the relationship of young people, social media and the law. It draws examples of how law does, or might, construct this relationship across jurisdictions. It is not then an analysis of the applicable law in various countries but rather an exploration of how 'law' attempts to address the rapidly evolving and global practice of social media as it relates to young people. An argument in the book is that law is but part of a larger collection of narratives that construct both young people and social media. For that reason, it seemed appropriate to divide the book between 'narratives of social media present' where many of the current debates about young people, social media and the law appear to be located. The second part then deals with 'narratives of social media future' and, while overlapping with the first part of the book, offers some attempt to discern where future narratives may take us.

Throughout the book there is reference to children and young people, sometimes together and sometimes interchangeably. While to some the term 'children' suggests young children, while 'young people' refers to youths or older children, in law all people under a certain age, often eighteen, are referred to as 'children'. Thus 'children's rights' in international law usually applies to all who are under eighteen. There is rarely a reference in this context to 'young people's rights'. For the purposes of this work the focus is often on older children; however, for reasons that may be apparent in the pages that follow, to specify a particular age at which a child becomes a young person is fraught. In keeping with another theme in the work that the law often prefers vague terms where certainty is problematic or controversial, I offer no further clarity around the precise age of a young person.

Part I

Narratives of social media present

Chapter 1

Moral panics, young people, social media and the law

New forms of technology and their subsequent application have always carried with them a mix of hope and anxiety. On the one hand, new technologies can present the hope of a better tomorrow, making our lives easier or, in the case of new communication technologies, better connected. Yet at the same time as we see the positives of technological change, there can also be a fear of the change that underpins new ways of conducting our lives that may be overwhelming. Part of this fear is of the unknown, of the various unintended and unexpected consequences of such change. Thus, while we live in an age where communication technology has evolved to certainly change our lives and social interactions in ways that only a few decades ago would have been unthinkable for many people, we nevertheless find ourselves in a tense relationship with this change. 'Social media', as it has come to be known, sits centrally within this tension. It is no surprise, then, that many turn to the law to mediate this tension.

1.1 The construction of social media as a legal problem

In many ways, the notion of 'social' within the term 'social media' often receives little analysis. For many, social media is anything but 'social'. The social connection that individuals claim to feel from their use of social media does not prevent that same use being decried by others as the reason for an increasing disconnection between people. The clichéd example is the person walking along a city street looking at their phone rather than looking where they are going. Somewhat ironically, the consequences of doing this often feature in videos on social media such as YouTube, where it ends in someone falling into a fountain or hitting themselves on a wall. As some would have it, the sad fact here is that someone might be recording that person's misfortune for subsequent sharing rather than stepping in to warn the person of what is about to occur. This is given as 'another example' of the social disconnection in the age of social media.

While writing this book, the May 2017 Manchester bombing at the Manchester Arena took place. As we have all come to expect when such events occur, social media played its part in informing many of what was happening before mainstream news organisations had reported the events. Yet while such communication has enabled people to find out quickly where danger exists and whether their loved ones are safe, and more broadly made all of us in effect 'news reporters', there is also a sense of cynicism and fear that the amount of information and questions about the authenticity of this news does not mean that all is positive in the world of social media. One of the relatives of a victim, unaware that his brother was present at the concert, commented afterwards that on the night of that attack he read tweets of the attack but himself commented that already people were sending conjecture and false information about what happened. His comment would resonate with many views of social media: 'Social media is good for spreading fear and worry'.[1] Such sentiments resonate with many people – but is this the whole story of social media? Do such anecdotes themselves only gain a form of currency because they too become part of the social media morass?

If the election of Donald Trump as president of the United States in 2016 was the only benchmark of how social media is to be perceived, then the answer to that question may be rather straightforward. Trump's use of Twitter is perceived as both comedic and scary.[2] Yet in some ways the fact that a US president tweets directly to the public epitomises both the positive and the negative aspects of social media. One attraction of social media is that it can engage people directly in conversation and provide a form of access to those with power not otherwise available to the general citizenry. Populist leaders such as Trump must regard such a sense of connection as heaven sent, in part because, as Astra Taylor remarks, 'online, some speak louder than others'.[3] While social media has an appearance of being a space for all to exchange views, as she notes there are the 'followers' and the 'followed' online.[4] In that sense, social media is also a space of social hierarchies. However, this is not to say that social media readily facilitates the expression of power. The limitations of social media such as Twitter – at the moment still 140 characters per tweet – as well as the very direct and immediate nature of the interaction which is otherwise applauded, also carry with them the dangers associated with the expressing of views without reflection that may trigger a host of other problems, anxieties and longer-term credibility issues, especially so if the tweeter is the president of a superpower.

For that reason, it is not now clear how many powerful people manage their own social media. In part, this is the inherent problem with social media; it can be difficult to know whether the people that you think are engaging with you through that media are who they say they are. Social media is a managed space for many people, particularly for those with political or economic power, and authenticity treads a fine line between spin and cover-up as a consequence. While that can mean that many social media interactions are simply 'fake', this ambiguity of identity can also be manipulated to have many social media utterances re-constructed and re-interpreted by others on behalf of the person in whose name they have been made when they are later seen to be unpopular or ill-advised statements. The re-definition of the meaning of words is a well-known device in the law to accommodate changing circumstances, and social media contains many similar examples. In addition to this, it is relatively easy to question the authenticity of statements in social media on the basis that it is easy to make such statements without evidence. However, verification is not a strong hallmark of social media, and as a result many views are expressed that blur fact and opinion, truth and falsehood.

In terms, then, of how social media and its use are constructed as a legal problem, it is clear that law struggles with categorising the phenomenon so that it can place it within a traditional legal framework. The essence of social media is that it is highly disorganised (even allowing for those that attempt to manage their use of it), spontaneous and immediate. Law, on the other hand, seeks order, reflection and delay before issuing opinions. Law and social media are social phenomena that have little understanding of each other and are in an inevitable tension. This results in a legal discourse around social media that shifts between focusing on the consequences of social media that somehow relate to traditional notions of legal harm (bullying, identity fraud, loss of privacy) and giving way to a resigned recognition that social media is a 'wild west' that in an ideal world would be best avoided. If social media atomises our relationships with each other, it seems to follow that law tends to react to it on those terms rather than attempting to form a regulatory regime that overarches the whole. Social media has been part of a process that has turned the law into a reactionary device rather than an institution that seeks to provide a more general framework for human interaction.[5] One outcome of this is that when we speak of rights in relation to social media, law tends towards 'reactive' or protective rights, such as the right to privacy or to be safe from harm. It is difficult for law to create a rights discourse around social media that is proactive, other than in general terms. For example, the law may speak of a right to access social media, but on what terms and for whom becomes far too challenging for legal traditionalists to formulate.

1.2 Social media and romantic notions of children and young people: revisiting Stan Cohen in the age of the Internet and 'fake news'

These various impulses are demonstrated in law's response to young people's relationship with social media. Stan Cohen's classic work *Folk Devils and Moral Panics*[6] analyses how young people are often misunderstood, their differences amplified, and perceived problems in their behaviour presented in terms that are out of proportion to their actual threat to social order – what he termed a 'moral panic'. The need to create 'folk devils' trumps, as Cohen argues, more imaginative responses to young people's troubles. It is instructive to return to Cohen's work in the age of the Internet, as much of his analysis of moral panics relies on the manufacturing of news and the distortion of the facts, in his study of young people, to fit with the views of dominant groups within society.[7] If one reads contemporary debates about politics and social media, one would be forgiven for thinking that the age of 'fake news' is an invention of the Internet age and social media. It is why claims that social media is an effective way of spreading fear and worry resonates with many people, but it would be a mistake to think that social media began this way of manufacturing news. This is not to say that social media does not present new challenges in how news is generated and constructed. Clearly, the speed of its dissemination and the notion that anyone with a smartphone can be a reporter of the news means that social media is a different form of news in that sense. However, as Cohen's work shows, the spreading of fear and worry in the media did not commence with social media.

To some extent it seems trite to make this point, but it is fruitful to connect current concerns regarding social media and young people with Cohen's work for the simple reason that his remark that 'the intellectual poverty and total lack of imagination in our society's response to its adolescent troublemakers during the last twenty years'[8] continues to haunt debates about young people and social media. We continue to be afraid *of* young people and their use of social media because it is viewed as a means of bullying others, facilitating the committing of crime and other acts of disorder, or in more recent years encouraging acts of terrorism. At the same time, we are afraid *for* young people and their use of social media because it is associated with activities that sexualise the 'innocent' child, encourage them to focus on their body image or otherwise facilitate behaviour that takes away their childhood. To paraphrase Cohen, these fears about young people and social media demonstrate a singular lack of imagination in tackling the social problems and issues generated by social media use by youth.

The law's approach to social media and young people remains stuck in a binary conceptualisation of young people that either sees them as innocent and in need of protection from harm or regards them as to be feared and requiring to be controlled. These are longstanding analyses of childhood and youth that depend on a narrow intellectual understanding of childhood.[9] A more rigorous approach to young people and the legal response to social media would engage with the literature that has emerged in recent years that stresses more sophisticated understandings of children's rights and, in particular, the increased recognition of children and young people's right to autonomy.[10] After all, young people's use of social media is in fact an activity that empowers them – for good or bad – and whatever the law's response is to that use, the manner in which young people have taken control of their online identities and practices makes the legal response potentially irrelevant for how young people see their online world.

A recent example of this continued lack of engagement with more imaginative legal responses to social media and youth and instead one that remains stuck with the perpetuation of a narrow construction of childhood is that of the *Growing Up Digital Taskforce Report* by the Children's Commissioner for England.[11] On its face, this report suggests that at long last children might be regarded as 'digital citizens' with their own set of rights in the digital and online world. Somewhat promisingly, the report makes claims to seek a re-writing of the *United Nations Convention on the Rights of the Child* to include digital citizenship for children.[12] The notion of citizenship being used here might be regarded as something that empowers the individual and proceeds from their individual autonomy. The report in that sense hinted at a new way of locating children in debates about the online world and their participation in it.

However, the report continues to give great emphasis and some priority to the need for young people to accept certain digital responsibilities, expressing concern about the protection of children online and the need for them to in effect behave 'appropriately', even though this co-opts the language of children's rights. To a great extent, then, the problem with the report lies in its nuance. Thus, while the early part of the report refers to the aim of imparting the necessary skills to children so that they may become 'agents of their own lives',[13] in articulating the detail of what 'digital citizenship' means for children the report states this to be 'how to protect your rights online and how to respect others' rights; how to disengage as well as engage with the digital world – ultimately nothing less than how to make the online world a force for good and one which empowers and inspires children, rather than entrapping them'.[14] The flavour of this detail underpinning digital citizenship is that of an online world that is currently fraught and populated with problems and dangers, that needs to be made 'better' by 'better children' who do 'good' online.

That a report in this area can seriously use the term 'force for good' in the times within which we live is remarkable. Quite simply, whose definition of 'good' is being used here? The term's use does, however, locate the report within that discourse that romanticises children and young people and leads to certain activities being labelled as self-evidently problematic when conducted online. This is because the binary of good versus bad that so dominates discussion of children and young people also permeates discussions of online activity. Such counterpoints may make for elegant writing, but they are meaningless in the context of judgments about the value of what people do with their time. The report outlines, for example, the need to provide children and young adults with 'resilience, information and power'[15] in order to 'open up the internet to them as a place where they can be citizens not just users, creative but not addicted, open yet not vulnerable to having their personal information captured and monetised by companies'.[16] As with many discussions of children's claim for rights, they are often held to a higher standard than adults. For adults, the right to be an active citizen is something that many adults choose to do minimally, if at all. For children, the sense is that they are expected to be all these things and more, in order to justify the rights claimed on their behalf.

Clearly, an autonomous individual should be able to decide how their interactions with others should occur, with the appropriate consequences to follow. In the case of children and young people, citizenship training often revolves around the obligations of citizenship rather than rights to autonomy. What the binary discussions above reveal has more to do with fears about what children and young people (and for that matter anyone) might do if they are encouraged to make their own decisions than they have to do with a more expansive sense of children's rights. In effect, this discussion about what young people do online is rooted in the history of controlling the youth underclass. Thus, one of the central underpinnings of the report, 'digital resilience', is presented not so much as a broad empowerment of children and young people but as a pre-condition to their protection as seen from the concerns of parents. Thus, while the report does accept that parents and children differ as to what dangers exist to them online,[17] it places considerable emphasis on surveys that reveal parental concern with children's accessing 'inappropriate material', 'oversharing personal information', social media's being an 'overwhelming distraction from other activities' and 'unwanted contact by strangers'.[18] While the report then proceeds to suggest that older children should champion digital citizenship and mentor younger children in this space, it is clear that the curricula and direction is directed to the fears of adults.

While it is clearly important to guide children in the use of technology and to not assume that they have some inner resilience that can be invoked to protect themselves, it is also important to make the point that the parental fears expressed have also in common a set of normative judgments that make those fears far from self-evident. Put simply, we have to question what constitutes 'inappropriate' material, at what point does one 'overshare' information, when is a distraction 'overwhelming' and when is contact 'unwanted' (and by whom?). Rarely, if ever, mentioned in these reports are the underlying and competing ideas about childhood which provide the immediate answers to these questions for the individuals articulating these fears, but which are in no way universally and consistently held by all.

One of those parental concerns with respect to social media is the amount of time children and young people spend online. Yet time is itself a concept rarely explored in relation to childhood. The notion that children may be spending 'too much' time online prompts the question, then what should they be doing with their time? The answer lies somewhere in our understanding of childhood as a social construction. As Alison James and Alan Prout illustrate, discussion of time in childhood is either about the child's future adulthood more than any sense of their present, or based on a timeless view of childhood which connects with notions of childhood innocence.[19] The former aspect of how children and time connect has much to do with the child's preparation for adulthood. The Digital Taskforce Report frames much of its discussion around this view of the child. In this sense, the digital citizenship discussed in the report is about the future child as an adult and not a form of children's present citizenship. Hence, we see statements in the report about children's acquiring skills so that they can 'grow up as agents of their own lives'.[20] Indeed, the very title of the report – *Growing Up Digital* – speaks to the child's future adulthood, rather to in any sense children's *being* digital.

The other connection between time and childhood connects with notions of the innocent child. James and Prout make the point that romantic views of childhood innocence see childhood as a time when, citing Holt, children are 'small and weak' and need to be protected from the harshness of the world outside until they become strong and clever enough to cope with it'.[21] The point is that for many children this mythical childhood does not exist.[22] This concept of childhood underpins the Digital Taskforce Report. The tenor of that report is to prepare children for the future, to provide the skills they require to negotiate the online world which is populated with many 'good' resources but also contains 'bad' things such as bullying, sexualised messages and commercial content seeking to exploit them. In more recent times the notion that children and young people are being radicalised online to commit terrorist acts has further added to the notion that childhood innocence must be buffered against these dark aspects of the Internet. The resilient child is presumably the child who has acquired this outer skin that protects them from these bad influences – a child in a sense who is no longer truly a 'child'. The problem is that this conforms to a rather old-fashioned view of children as having no present minds of their own, but instead as being weak and vulnerable and so in need of protection from present dangers.

Within this paradigm the connection between time online and corruption of the child is a simple equation. For example, Louis Reynolds and Ralph Scott contend that 'young people in the UK spend on average more than a day a week on social media' while schools give 'minimal time to the discussion of the civic and moral questions this new digital commons throws up, or to the provision of the skills young people need to be informed, critical and effective citizens in this new context'.[23] The problem then is that insufficient time is being invested in children and young people in order to divert them towards more appropriate ways of thinking in the future. Social media thus becomes the vehicle for bad influences:

> our rapidly changing societies are confronted, increasingly aggressively, by new expressions of a much older problem – political extremism and violent radicalism. The role social media play in the recruitment and

> exploitation of young people by extremist groups, in the propagation of the narratives of violent radical organisation and in the distribution of misinformation should highlight the urgency of addressing this issue.[24]

While Reynolds and Scott do not suggest that extremism is itself created by social media, there is clearly in their discussion the sense that social media as a form of communication possesses seductive qualities that make the messages sent by those who advance extreme ideologies easier to cut through to young people. Thus, for them, new ways of protecting children and young people from that influence are required. There are clearly two matters that this argument raises. The first is the question of how one defines extremism in this context. This is an uncomfortable discussion to have for sure, but it is important for no other reason than to remind ourselves that to regard views that challenge mainstream thinking as 'extreme' is an inherently conservative political project itself. Certainly, advocating harm to others is likely to be broadly agreed as being inappropriate, but such broad consensus does not mean that it is any less a normative position. The larger question is whether advocating euthanasia or abortion by choice would be regarded as 'extreme' by some in society. If so, then the types of matters to be regulated in social media could be constantly expanded.

The second matter raised by the Reynolds and Scott discussion is whether new forms of technology are always treated with suspicion and indeed become the scapegoat for social ills with deeper or other causes. The Royal Commission on Television held in Australia before broadcasting began in 1956 was concerned about the impact television would have on family life in terms which echo many of the concerns about social media today. One recommendation of that Royal Commission, although not adopted, was to have a break in transmission in the early evening after children's programmes had ceased 'to enable younger children to be put to bed without the distraction of an absorbing television programme, and to give older children an opportunity to do their homework and read books'.[25] Prior to the arrival of terrorism as an immediate problem in relation to social media, there was much concern with providing children and young people with the skill set and resources to enable them to be protected from being exploited by media advertising, a focus that was principally on their exploitation as consumers. In effect, this constructed children as vulnerable innocents who needed to be protected from the broadcasters and corporations that seek to turn profits.[26] This also relates to the concern that children and young people may be frittering away their time on social media instead of preparing for their future as 'productive citizens'. Yet here we also see the tensions in the state's concern with children and young people. While one aim is to ensure they are protected from exploitation, the state also wants them to learn how to be good consumers, or in other words, 'the state's agenda is itself complex, as the state is keen to ensure that children develop the appropriate attitudes not just with respect to their general behaviour in the community, but also that they learn the norms of the market-place'.[27] Likewise, in encouraging young people to become 'good' digital citizens, one of the features of citizenry can also be the expression of opinions in opposition to existing norms. Innocent children may not have much of note to say, but a child or young person who is armed with knowledge transforms into either a model citizen or something to be feared.

1.3 Social media, relationships and the law's struggle to articulate new forms of respect

While the debates surrounding social media reflect many of those that occupied attention during the rise of television, there are clearly differences with that earlier technology that generate many of the anxieties today. Social media is interactive and unlike broadcasting is not so readily regulated by a central authority.[28] What this means is that the state has to renegotiate the social contract around which relationships between individuals and the state, as well as between individuals, are formed in relation to new forms of media. It is perhaps one reason why we hear the term 'respect' so often today in social media. Cultivating 'respect' is in effect a form of 'soft law', which seeks to ensure compliance with certain norms absent the capacity of the legal system to enforce them. There is of course nothing particularly remarkable about that role of law, as soft law is a well-established concept in the literature, particularly in the context of international law,[29] though it is not without its critics.[30]

Where the law struggles in this context is in defining behaviour that should be regarded as 'inappropriate' when participated in online. Of course, such definitional problems have long been a dilemma for the law. 'Bullying' in the physical world may be universally condemned, but defining precisely what constitutes it is another matter. Simply placing the word 'cyber' in front of 'bullying' may suggest that it can now take place with similar harmful effects in the online world, but it is often forgotten that importing the term into the online environment also brings with it all the definitional issues (and more) present in its real-world manifestation. The additional issues imported into online applications of the term include the problem that when conducted in and through social media, bullying will also raise issues of freedom of speech and expression which do not usually present themselves when it is conducted in more traditional physical settings. Many legal problems arise where the law must 'balance' between competing legal norms and expectations. Social media often presents law with the need to conduct such difficult balancing acts.

An example of the above is the experience in Nova Scotia, Canada, with what is claimed to be one of the first cyber-safety laws in the world. Prior to its enactment a report was prepared for the Provincial Legislature on the need for and framework within which law reform might occur in this context.[31] The catalyst for this report and subsequent legislation was a number of youth suicides in Nova Scotia,[32] although the attempted suicide and subsequent death of a local teenager after being sexually assaulted and then shamed about it online is often credited with being the major cause of the reform.[33] The report begins by analysing the social context within which young people use social media and the generational divide that exists in that space. It stresses the immersive nature of the technology and how 'for many young people "virtual reality" is their reality'.[34] The challenge for adults is to understand how the online or virtual world that young people inhabit can be more important to them than the 'natural world'.[35] This leads to an important binary constructed by the report:

> Young people growing up in today's society experience the best and the worst of civilization's evolution and innovation. The opportunities and possibilities presented by today's (and tomorrow's) technology are exciting. In the hands of some misguided people, technology can also be a powerful weapon. The underbelly of the technology beast is dark. Exploring this underside can give us insight into the new incarnation of an old problem.[36]

This binary understanding of new communication technology as a battle between 'good' and 'bad' uses of the technology in fact tells us little about the real problems facing the law and society in this area. For a start, if 'cyber-bullying' (however defined) is a 'bad' use of the technology, then what is a 'good' use? Whose judgments on these matters will prevail? And to what extent do these constructions of social media simply reflect ideas of the 'good' and 'bad' child or young person, the angelic and the demonic child or young person?

To some extent the prevalence of social media as a form of communication has arguably widened the voices that are now heard in society. The notion that everyone is a reporter or journalist is often said today as a means of understanding the far easier access that the 'ordinary' and diverse range of people globally have to report and comment on events.[37] One might expect that in a contemporary context, notions of what constitutes good and bad are themselves likely to be questioned by that diversity of opinion. If so, then are the changes brought on by new technologies being lamented not for the loss of what is 'good' but for the re-writing of what that even means?

The report then follows the above point with the statement that 'bullying behaviour is just one manifestation of a society which, in rushing to embrace technology, has challenged human relationships and possibly diminished both respect and a sense of responsibility'.[38] It also suggests that there has been 'a loss of community and less recognition of core social values' occurring as society adapts to 'the rapid pace of change'.[39] At the same time as this is occurring, the report also recognises that bullying is not itself a new phenomenon,[40] even if new technology is thought to have altered how it is engaged in, and due to its nature, technology can cause a more harmful form of bullying.[41] Under the sub-heading 'social interaction in the digital age', the report once again utilises the 'good' versus 'bad' binary in relation to social media:

> While every member of our society benefits from the efficiencies of modern technology, negative repercussions, such as deteriorating social skills, are also becoming evident. Technology promotes, and somehow makes acceptable, behaviours that previous generations would have dismissed as outrageously offensive and rude. Listening to music through headphones or reading and responding to personal messages on a smart phone during a conversation, meeting, movie, concert, or, as recently recounted to one Task Force member, a job interview, would have been completely inexcusable. Many terms and nicknames, not to mention the forms of language and spelling that are now considered entirely acceptable for electronic communication, further add to the confusion and concern.[42]

The report then proceeds to comment on the lack of 'credible adult role models' for youth as many 'famous and successful' people themselves engage in bullying of others. This combines with the marketing of sex, aggression and violence as entertainment to normalise such behaviour. This leads to the conclusion that there is a 'desperate state [in] our social relationships' that requires us to 'shift and rebuild the foundation of society'.[43]

As an underpinning narrative for legal reform in relation to cyber safety, the construction of the issues to be addressed in that regard by this report is perhaps familiar, but nevertheless problematic. As Phillip Smith et al. observe, 'The theme of growing incivility is both a commonplace and a universal of human life'.[44] As they note, an example of the way in which academics and politicians alike tend to analyse 'anti-civic individualism' narrowly is the 'Respect Agenda', which was launched in the United Kingdom in January 2006 by then-Prime Minister Tony Blair.[45] At a time when social media hardly existed, the identification of the problem then in society with respect to anti-social behaviour has an eerie resonance with the way in which the 'dark' side of social media is discussed today. As Smith et al. note, the Respect Agenda was framed around the sense that such behaviour was 'both symptom and cause of a wider and more insidious malaise in which selfishness and individualism have come to replace civic-mindedness, thus threatening the organic roots of community life'.[46] The further construction of this problem also echoes aspects of the dark side of social media notions discussed above. Tony Blair connected anti-social behaviour with areas of low social capital and, as such, as being more prevalent amongst the poor.[47] 'Good' people, in effect, were subjected to fear intimidation by an unruly minority.[48]

The legal response to this was the broadening of powers to address 'anti-social behaviour' by using definitions that were vague to say the least. The Crime and Disorder Act 1998 set up a system of anti-social behaviour orders that could be imposed on a person aged 10 or more who acted

> in an anti-social manner, that is to say, in a manner that caused or was likely to cause harassment, alarm or distress to one or more persons not of the same household as himself.[49]

When enacted, this provision was squarely directed towards public order matters, as in regulating how people behaved in physical public spaces. This is reflected in the law's own terms as it included provisions for such matters as 'dispersal powers'[50] and 'public spaces protection orders'.[51] By 2014, the law had been amended to replace anti-social behaviour orders with criminal behaviour orders that can be imposed when a person has been convicted of an offence and a court then is satisfied that 'the offender has engaged in behaviour that caused or was likely to cause harassment, alarm or distress to any person' and that such an order is considered to help prevent that behaviour from continuing.[52]

It is the breadth of the terms used in such legislation that is remarkable and worrying. Enacted to address so-called 'anti-social behaviour' in the physical world, one can see the possibility for a wider application with new forms of incivility, built as it is on notions of causing 'harassment, alarm or distress'. Smith et al. identify this as the 'criminalization of incivility'[53] and note that this approach,

> which amplifies perceptions of low-level deviance by tying it to disreputable classes, exaggerates its consequences through indexing to urban poverty and then looks down the social hierarchy to allocate blame [and] is hardly novel. As the literature on moral panics and moral crusades has long made clear, stories with innocents and victims often draw upon the tacit repertoires of class-based disorder.[54]

In the case of social media, one can see the easy application of such notions with respect to what might be regarded as anti-social. Indeed, there are claims that complaints to police about anti-social behaviour already represent a substantial part of all such complaints and that in time all such complaints will have an online element.[55] The problem for law, as always, is in determining which forms of behaviour fall over the threshold for police attention. As Travis quotes one officer, 'people throughout history have shouted abuse at each other and had disagreements and arguments and possibly said things that they regret later, and the police have never investigated every disagreement between everyone'. Crown Prosecution Guidelines for England also contain such dilemmas. They provide guidance in the case of communications that are grossly offensive, indecent, obscene or false (much of which is an offence under section 127 of the Communications Act); there is a high evidential threshold to be met, and 'in many cases a prosecution is unlikely to be required in the public interest'.[56] The guidelines quote the remarks of Lord Chief Justice, Lord Judge in *Chambers v DPP*,[57] where the appellant had tweeted about blowing up an airport as a joke following a flight delay caused by adverse weather conditions:[58]

> Satirical, or iconoclastic, or rude comment, the expression of unpopular or unfashionable opinion about serious or trivial matters, banter or humour, even if distasteful to some or painful to those subjected to it should and no doubt will continue at their customary level, quite undiminished by [section 127 of the Communications Act 2003].[59]

In *Chambers v DPP* the defendant was initially convicted of the offence though on appeal that conviction was overturned. While this might suggest that some form of justice was done, the initial police investigation had concluded that 'there is no evidence at this stage to suggest that there is anything other than a foolish comment posted on "Twitter" as a joke for only his close friends to see'. However, the Crown Prosecution Service decided to prosecute Chambers. Thus, while the appeal judges decided that the tweet was in effect a joke, the prosecution service and the Crown Court judge that convicted Chambers of the offence took a different view. These different views need to be explained in terms of the struggle the law has in defining what is in effect appropriate behaviour in these cases involving social media.

Part of this struggle is in determining how what might be defined as a tweet of a 'menacing character' under the relevant law might be so defined in a way that is consistent with freedom of speech and expression. Resorts to principles of statutory interpretation as to what is 'reasonable' or what is to be regarded as the 'ordinary meaning' of a word often do more to explain why different actors come to different conclusions than they explain or assist in the final determination of a word's meaning. In *Chambers v DPP* Lord Judge said:

> a message which cannot or is unlikely to be implemented may nevertheless create a sense of apprehension or fear in the person who receives or reads it. However unless it does so, it is difficult to see how it can sensibly be described as a message of a menacing character. So, if the person or persons who receive or read it, or may reasonably be expected to receive, or read it, would brush it aside as a silly joke, or a joke in bad taste, or empty bombastic or ridiculous banter, then it would be a

> contradiction in terms to describe it as a message of a menacing character. In short, a message which does not create fear or apprehension in those to whom it is communicated, or who may reasonably be expected to see it, falls outside this provision, for the very simple reason that the message lacks menace.[60]

In effect this is somewhat circular, as it ultimately relies on the notion that if a person receiving a communication is not menaced by it then it cannot be characterised as menacing. Such legal approaches are commonplace, of course, but quite unhelpful to politicians and others seeking to provide 'clarity' as to what is to be regarded as appropriate behaviour.

Likewise, in Nova Scotia, the Cyber-Safety Act 2013 (NS) was eventually struck down as too vague for protection under Canada's Charter of Rights and Freedoms. Section 3 of that Act defined cyber-bullying as

> any electronic communication through the use of technology including, without limiting the generality of the foregoing, computers, other electronic devices, social networks, text messaging, instant messaging, websites and electronic mail, typically repeated or with continuing effect, that is intended or ought reasonably be expected to cause fear, intimidation, humiliation, distress or other damage or harm to another person's health, emotional well-being, self-esteem or reputation, and includes assisting or encouraging such communication in any way.

The Act was challenged in *Crouch v Snell*.[61] In that case the relationship of two business partners had broken down, and one of them then engaged in a smear campaign against the other on social media where both were active. The court was asked to decide if the Act breached the Canadian Charter of Rights and Freedoms, s. 2(b), which protects 'freedom of thought, belief, opinion and expression, including freedom of the press and other media of communication'. The essence of the argument presented to the Nova Scotia Supreme Court was that the definition of cyber-bullying contained in the Act was too broad. The court accepted that the Act, in attempting to address cyber-bullying, did restrict free expression; however, it went beyond what was justified to achieve this, with the definition in particular being described as a 'colossal failure'.[62] Thus, while popular discourse can speak of appropriate and inappropriate behavior online as if there is a clear demarcation, the law must strike a difficult balance:

> The Cyber-Safety Act seeks to balance an individual's right to free speech against society's interests in providing greater access to justice to victims of cyberbullying. The question is whether the Act strikes the appropriate balance. While there is no question that protection against

cyberbullying is an important objective, there is a difference between a statute's objectives and its effects.[63]

The English Crown Prosecution Service guidelines also engage with this context. They point out that the hundreds of millions of communications each month on various forms of social media could lead to a potentially very large number of cases under the legislation that regulates malicious or offensive communications. The guidelines refer to the potential 'chilling effect on free speech' and ask prosecutors to 'exercise considerable caution' before bringing charges under the relevant legislation.[64] The guidelines then make explicit reference to article 10 of the European Convention on Human Rights and the need to interpret the legislation consistent with the article that provides for freedom of expression.[65] Reference is also made in the guidelines to the judgment of the European Court of Human Rights in *Sunday Times v UK (No 2)*,[66] citing the passage in the judgment that states that 'article 10 protects not only speech which is well-received and popular, but also speech which is offensive, shocking or disturbing'.[67] The guidelines then proceed to make the point that freedom of expression may be restricted when the response is necessary and proportionate.

It is the question of when a restriction on freedom of expression is necessary and proportionate that uncovers the final twist in the tale here. We may ask, given the various concerns and cautions expressed by the courts above and the CPS guidelines, who then tends to be prosecuted, blamed or scapegoated in cases where the use of social media is said to be 'inappropriate'? Are young people subject to some embedded constraints on their use of social media that makes them less likely to escape prosecution?

The CPS guidelines explain that the prosecution of cases involving a restriction on free expression in social media is unlikely to be necessary and proportionate where:

1 The suspect has expressed genuine remorse;
2 Swift and effective action has been taken by the suspect and/or others, for example, service providers, to remove the communication in question or otherwise block access to it;
3 The communication was not intended for a wide audience, nor was that the obvious consequence of sending the communication, particularly where the intended audience did not include the victim or target of the communication in question; or
4 The content of the communication did not obviously go beyond what could conceivably be tolerable or acceptable in an open and diverse society which upholds and respects freedom of expression.[68]

One can see in these pre-conditions to prosecution the catch-22 that some people may find themselves in. To express remorse assumes that one accepts that one had done something wrong to feel remorseful about. In effect, this requirement attaches to the fourth requirement as both beg the question, against whose values will the matter of what is deemed 'tolerable or acceptable in an open and diverse society' be judged? It might be expected that young people are more likely to challenge acceptable norms and that this will play out on social media. Particularly if childhood and youth are seen as a period of preparation for becoming in the future a responsible adult citizen, it is more likely that unacceptable views expressed in social media by young people will be constructed as inappropriate and potentially criminalised for not conforming to those expectations of young people. The dilemma for the law, and the problem with the guidelines, is if a person is choosing to exercise their right to freedom of expression – even if it is only to acknowledge that their view may be unfashionable or shocking – then what are they expressing remorse for if they choose to do so? It seems that can only be explained in terms of upholding certain expectations around manners rather than a legal response. If so, then is it the proper domain of the law to regulate good manners?

1.4 Social media, riots and the law: communication problem or underlying social discontent?

The import of the discussion so far is that the law, in seeking to balance so many different values and interests, appears unable to provide clear guidance about the required forms of behaviour online. Yet at the same time, one can see that what the law is attempting to do, in recognising that social media is at the end of the day a mere form of communication, is to ensure that the fundamental freedoms that have traditionally attached to other forms of media also attach to social media. The difficulty for those who hold power in society is that this means that if social media is a more immersive and participatory form of media then subversive and challenging ideas may be more easily spread by it. Gone are the days when a few press barons could set the political narrative and ensure that the status quo is broadly bolstered with token examples of 'diversity' of opinion thrown in on occasion. Social media in this sense has the capacity to disrupt the established power relationships in society.

For that reason, it should come as no surprise that traditional holders of power should seek to undermine the legitimacy of social media by casting it as part of the problem to do with changes in society that threaten the social order. Thus, social media is marked as a medium that divides communities, makes it easy to insult others, encourages uncivil behaviour and undermines, in the case of young people, parental authority. There may be 'good' aspects of social media, but the project must be to ensure that the 'bad' areas of social media do not contaminate the minds of the young. In effect, the moral crisis of social media is a smokescreen for the discrediting of a form of communication that threatens established power in society.

Much of this view of social media relies on the notion of a binary divide in social media and digital technology – that is, that there are 'good' features that need to be nurtured and there are 'bad' aspects that need to be outlawed. For example, the UK Conservative Party's manifesto for the 2017 general election outlined a regulatory regime for social media (as an aspect of digital regulation) that wants Britain to be the best place for digital business, while at the same time protecting the vulnerable, primarily children and young people, from harm online. In stressing the need for online to be the 'safest place', the manifesto asserts:

> Where technology can find a solution, we will pursue it. We will work with industry to introduce new protections for minors, from images of pornography, violence, and other age-inappropriate content not just on social media but in app stores and content sites as well. We will put a responsibility on industry not to direct users – even unintentionally – to hate speech, pornography, or other sources of harm. We will make clear the responsibility of platforms to enable the reporting of inappropriate, bullying, harmful or illegal content, with take-down on a comply-or-explain basis.
>
> We will continue to push the internet companies to deliver on their commitments to develop technical tools to identify and remove terrorist propaganda, to help smaller companies build their capabilities and to provide support for civil society organisations to promote alternative and counter-narratives. In addition, we do not believe that there should be a safe space for terrorists to be able to communicate online and will work to prevent them from having this capability.[69]

What such political party statements tacitly acknowledge is that to this point social media content has been subject to little regulation. However, they also fail to engage with the definitional dilemmas that courts must consider, and most importantly they construct children and young people as vulnerable and in need of protection from harm so as to presumably be allowed to focus on gaining the necessary skills to be able to function as productive adult digital citizens in the future. There is no narrative addressed here which accepts that social media provides to young people a *current* voice to participate in politics as current citizens, nor discussion about how the right to do so might be protected or even facilitated.

The riots that occurred across England in August 2011 are an example of the way in which social media has been demonised as the catalyst for criminal behaviour. The riots began in London and spread to other cities, including Birmingham, Coventry, Leicester, Manchester and Liverpool. The causes have been widely debated, and reasons given on one side include racial tension, class tension, unemployment and austerity policies of government,[70] while more conservative explanations focused on a breakdown of morality and on criminality and gang culture.[71] Social media was said to have allowed organisers to co-ordinate the riots as well as inflame tensions by their posts.[72] However, posts to social media also allowed police to identify perpetrators as well as prompted people to come together after the riots to clean up.[73] Parallels were drawn with the use of social media during the so-called 'Arab Spring' uprisings, which have led some to label the August 2011 riots the 'English Spring'.[74]

After the riots, some politicians, including the then-prime minister, called for greater restrictions on the use of social media during such times of civil disturbance. BlackBerry Messenger, due to its encoded system, made it impossible for law enforcement agencies to access what was happening on that system,[75] which then led to calls for it to be shut down during such events. The then-prime minister, David Cameron, said in Parliament of the riots:

> Everyone watching these horrific actions will be struck by how they were organised via social media. Free flow of information can be used for good, but it can also be used for ill, so we are working with the police, the intelligence services and industry to look at whether it would be right to stop people communicating via these websites and services when we know they are plotting violence, disorder and criminality.[76]

In response to a question from another member of Parliament responding to the prime minister's linking of gang culture and technology with the riots and in particular 'internet footage glorifying gangs and knives',[77] he suggested that social media companies 'should think about their responsibilities and about taking down those images. That is why the Home Secretary is going to have meetings with those organisations to see what more can be done'.[78] Other views of social media did claim that it also was used 'for positive activities such as organising clear-ups',[79] but this was not a challenge to the underpinning nature of the riots or what might have explained them in ways other than due to moral decay or family breakdown. This is simply the notion that there are 'good' and 'bad' aspects to social media, and that a strategy that targets the bad aspects will allow the state to have the upper hand. In reply to this other view of the role of social media, David Cameron said:

> The Hon. Gentleman makes a good point. It is why the Home Secretary is going to explore the issue with the social media companies and other services. The key thing is that the police were facing a new circumstance. Rioters were using the BlackBerry service – a closed network – so that they knew where they were going to loot next, and

> the police could not keep up with them. We have to examine that and work out how to get ahead.[80]

This then led to calls for tough sentences for those who 'misused' social media.[81] What is remarkable about the debates is how social media, constructed as having 'good' uses as well as 'bad' uses, is then portrayed as part of the reason for the riots. This even led to some arrests for 'inciting public disorder through social media',[82] leading to the prime minister responding that '[w]e have to make sure that people who use this new technology for evil purposes are properly prosecuted and convicted'.[83]

1.5 Competing narratives of social media: law, the fear of unregulated social media and the reassertion of old forms of legal control

These debates on the United Kingdom riots and social media tell us more about the limitations of the law than they do about the actual role that social media can play in creating social disturbance. With more recent terrorist incidents also being in part explained by 'online radicalisation', the calls for greater regulation of social media and the Internet continues now some 6 years after the riots. Clearly, attempts to shut down or prohibit such online activity are feeble given the nature of digital technology. Certainly, some community leaders and politicians speak to the need for changes in education, culture, opportunities and engagement with young people as a means of reducing resort to harmful acts. However, the concern here is with the manner in which social media is painted as central to this process as if it, captured by certain individuals, is allowed to 'do evil'.

What really seems to be occurring is a failure to accept that while social media may facilitate communication between groups of people seeking to take part in violent and other acts, it is nevertheless a medium of communication, and so the message that it sends still needs to resonate with the individuals who read, listen or watch it.[84] What then occurs is the characterisation of some uses of social media as 'evil' while accepting that other uses are 'appropriate'. In this debate, there is little consideration given to the worthiness of using social media to challenge orthodox views or policies. Terrorist acts make the narrative that social media should be used only for 'appropriate' purposes easier to argue, but they do not remove the need for the debate around how such judgments should occur.

But there is an inherent contradiction within the discussion about the need to regulate social media. The very essence and supposed strength of social media is that it is 'beyond jurisdiction', a space that governments cannot reach easily and thus allows for open participation by people previously outside access to mass media. Social media thus challenges the power of media oligarchies.[85] For those who have been empowered by such change, the need for regulation is no comfort, but instead represents the winding back of their recently acquired influence over political debate. While not exclusively so, it is particularly a new generation of tech-savvy young people that claim to have been so empowered and who have absorbed the different norms of a social media culture. This is an important point too, but this is not the same thing as saying that social media is without 'laws' or 'rules'; it is that those norms which govern it are created from within the community rather than imposed by states with diverse agendas. After all, part of the apparent ethos of social media is to ensure greater accountability of those that govern. That those same institutions should regulate social media will be viewed as threatening to that accountability. Social media as a tool of transgressive practice is regarded as its strength and the exalted reason for its existence. Transgression in this narrative is inherently good.

However, for those within the older generation who held power through their management and control of traditional mass media, social media is seen to be a lawless space without rules and itself wholly unaccountable. Dangers to children and young people are highlighted, and the manner in which social media infringes on such areas as privacy and reputation are constantly debated. This narrative of social media makes it ripe in the eyes of those who subscribe to it for extensive legal regulation and severe punishment for any transgressive use of the technology. Within this narrative, transgression is inherently bad as it associates social media with danger and harm. Every opportunity to portray social media as dangerous is seized upon as an opportunity to extend that regulation.

For many, the law's role will be presented as one that must mediate between these two narratives. This often leads to a further narrative that seeks to 'balance' and compromise between different approaches. However, this itself depends on a view of law as one that can strike a balance between fundamentally different ideas about social media. In many areas, where difference in approach is based on competing and opposed value judgments, to speak of 'balance' makes little sense. The role of social media must come down to a choice between ways of understanding its role that cannot always be effectively reconciled, if at all.

This is clearly seen in the debates around the positive aspects of social media in the aftermath of the London riots. Such applauding of social media did not challenge the view that social media in that instance and in the eyes of the established political order otherwise facilitated civil disorder. That use of social media represented transgression and was *ipso facto* inappropriate and often illegal was seen to be beyond question. The positive role of social media that was portrayed as the alternative was one which reduced it to a civic information device, a noticeboard for community clean-ups or where to find information about what to do in a 'practical' sense. In effect, the narrative of social media that underpins this understanding of its positive role would see social media's role in bringing the powerful to account neutered.

Old forms of legal control and traditional legal remedies that have evolved from the interests of the powerful are now challenged by what ordinary people say, including the young, on social media. Laws that defend privacy and loss of reputation are much more likely to be resorted to by those with power and influence and represent these older understandings of law's role. Such laws have always been seen to be in some tension with laws that protect free speech, but that was before so many were able to speak on a global scale. A truly participatory democracy demands laws that make the powerful accountable for the decisions they make that affect the non-rich and powerless. But they also demand new types of laws that assert more positive claims by people who have been left behind by what has gone before.

1.6 Re-making the law: social media, youth empowerment and law's anxieties

Richard Chalfen has argued that young people relate to digital technology and online interactions in ways that are quite different from adults.[86] Chalfen contends that 'young people live at the intersection of four different sub-cultures',[87] a 'media culture' that enables young people to be media makers as well as consumers, a 'techno-culture' that immerses young people in the means to engage with digital technology (for example, the ubiquity of smartphones), an 'intense visual culture' in which young people have adjusted to being in the gaze of others constantly and an 'adolescent culture' where the moment is the present.[88] Such approaches to understanding young people and social media rarely feature in policy debates and the relevance of the law's response for young people's lives. There is instead much more attention on the need for young people to grow up to become future adult citizens that adopt certain understandings of the place of social media in society. One example of this is the attempt to make young people fear what they place about themselves on the Internet in case it comes back to haunt them later in life. Chalfen might suggest this completely misses the mark about how young people relate to social media.

However, that is not to suggest that young people must suffer the consequences of their own immaturity in this space. Rather, it is necessary to consider the extent to which they are in fact 'digital pioneers' who are mapping new ways of using social media to enable and empower communities. If so, then that throws down a direct challenge to how the state and established corporate interests see the place of digital technology and social media. That place has, as Christian Fuchs observes, much to do with how corporations have co-opted the technology for their profit-making purposes.[89] He explains how digital technology has remade the nature of work and allowed corporations to become 'prosumers',[90] where technology actually now does some of the work previously done by employees. The obvious example of this is self-service checkouts at supermarkets, but one can see how social media can create 'fan bases' that encourage consumers to advertise and encourage others to purchase goods or services from the organisers of, say, a Facebook fan page.[91] In this way, corporations have a vested interest in social media being populated by users that understand their relationship with the media in terms of its importance to the capitalist marketplace.

Within this construction of social media, the binary of good and bad uses is necessary to direct people towards that use which is consistent with corporate and state interests that preserve their power and influence. While that is not to say that regulation is always detrimental to the broader population, the boundaries of that regulation are rarely investigated carefully other than within traditional notions of balancing rights and seeking to preserve orthodox legal concerns with privacy, free speech and data surveillance. However, this is not to suggest that the technology does not create often-contradictory positions around these issues due to the nature of that very technology.

What we need to imagine is how young people wish to relate to social media and how this may create new norms and expectations. To some extent, some of these norms evolve from the form of the technology, alongside the ethos out of which it springs. An example of this is the Twitter terms of service, which on first glance offer a counter-narrative to the need to regulate and proscribe harmful or dangerous activity in social media. Those terms of service include the following warning about exposure to harmful material and what users should expect of the service if they are exposed:

> Any use or reliance on any Content or materials posted via the Services or obtained by you through the Services is at your own risk. We do not endorse, support, represent or guarantee the completeness, truthfulness, accuracy, or reliability of any Content or communications posted via the Services or endorse any opinions expressed via the Services. You understand that by using the Services, you may be exposed to Content that might be offensive, harmful, inaccurate or otherwise inappropriate, or in some cases, postings that have been mislabeled or are otherwise deceptive. All Content is the sole responsibility of the person who originated such Content. We may not monitor or control the Content posted via the Services and, we cannot take responsibility for such Content.[92]

They then proceed to articulate in effect new forms of responsibility:

> You are responsible for your use of the Services and for any Content you provide, including compliance with applicable laws, rules, and

> regulations. You should only provide Content that you are comfortable sharing with others.[93]

What these terms of service create is a wholly different set of norms around how harmful material should be handled. Some of these emanate from a notion of unregulated and free media. But other aspects contradict any notion that this is a simple equation. There is a simple form of individualism at work here – you will have responsibility for what you see and how you handle it. But the anxiety of the law is that is has been criticised through history for not always protecting everyone equally. To stifle what is posted on social media may be done in the name of reputation protection, but at what cost to free speech, which is now also valued in our legal system? Facebook also stresses that what you post on Facebook is owned by you and that the privacy of that information and who may see it can be controlled by you in the privacy and application settings.[94] The challenge to the state in times of anxiety about terrorism and online harassment is that to grant such control to individuals empowers them to both allow themselves to be gazed upon by others and to remove themselves from the same gaze. Law's anxiety is to mediate between the surveillance that social media facilitates on the one hand and to permit the freedoms once perhaps claimed in name only but now more in reality to take place. This also highlights how law is a 'messy institution' that has its own internal battles over the function, purpose and meaning of law, as well as over what its political objectives should be. Many people will speak of children's and young people's rights, the participation of children and young people or the need to protect the child or young person online in the context of social media, but law will question each of these terms and likely come up with different answers. Law is often concerned with the detail of what to other disciplines are broad, aspirational goals. Law's purpose is often as practical as it is ideological, and our purpose is to make sense of it all.

Notes

1 Helen Pidd 'Victim's Brother: Stop Using Manchester Attack to Denounce Immigration' *The Guardian* 31 May, 2017: www.theguardian.com/uk-news/2017/may/31/manchester-attack-victim-martyn-hett-brother-dan-stop-using-politicise-immigration, accessed 1 June, 2017.

2 See e.g. Anna North 'Donald Trump's Twitter Comedy' *New York Times* 31 May, 2017: www.nytimes.com/2017/05/31/opinion/donald-trumps-twitter-comedy.html, accessed 1 June, 2017.

3 Astra Taylor *The People's Platform: Taking Back Power and Culture in the Digital Age* (London, Fourth Estate, 2014), p. 3.

4 Ibid.

5 The decline of the state is of course also part of this, and the increased power of corporate interests in determining law social policy.

6 Stanley Cohen *Folk Devils and Moral Panics: The Creation of the Mods and Rockers* (London, MacGibbon and Kee, 1972).
7 Ibid., pp. 44–45.
8 Ibid., p. 204.
9 For this critique see e.g. Anthony Synott 'Little Angels, Little Devils: A Sociology of Children' (1983) 20 *Canadian Review of Sociology and Anthropology* 79–95.
10 See e.g. David Archard *Children; Rights and Childhood 2nd edn* (London, Routledge, 1993), Michael D.A Freeman *The Rights and Wrongs of Children* (London, F. Pinter, 1983), David Oswell *The Agency of Children: From Family to Global Human Rights* (Cambridge, Cambridge University Press, 2013).
11 Children's Commissioner for England *Growing Up Digital: A Report of the Growing Up Digital Taskforce* (London, January, 2017).
12 Ibid., p. 16.
13 Ibid., p. 3
14 Ibid., p. 5.
15 Ibid., p. 3.
16 Ibid.
17 Ibid., p. 4.
18 Ibid., p. 4. Reference is also made here to the LSE *EU Kids Online* (2012), which had similar findings, including parental concern with the amount of time their children spend online.
19 Alison James and Alan Prout 'Re-presenting Childhood: Time and Transition in the Study of Childhood' in Alison James and Alan Prout (eds.) *Constructing and Reconstructing Childhood: Contemporary Issues in the Sociological Study of Childhood* (Classic Edition, Routledge, Oxford, 2015), pp. 202–219.
20 *Growing Up Digital: A Report of the Growing Up Digital Taskforce*, op.cit., p. 3.
21 Ibid., p. 212, citing John C. Holt *Escape from Childhood: The Needs and Rights of Children* (Harmondsworth, Penguin, 1975), p. 22.
22 Ibid.
23 Louis Reynolds and Ralph Scott *Digital Citizens: Countering Extremism Online* (London, Demos, 2016), p. 9.
24 Ibid.
25 Commonwealth of Australia *Report of the Royal Commission on Television* (Canberra, Government Printing Office, 1954), p. 83.
26 Brian Simpson *Children and Television* (London and New York, Continuum, 2004), p. 19 citing Newton N. Minow and Craig L. LaMay *Abandoned in the Wasteland: Children, Television and the First Amendment* (New York, Hill and Wang, 1995), p. 20.
27 Simpson, op.cit., p. 22.
28 However, with recent terrorist incidents, calls by politicians for more regulation of the Internet demonstrate both these recurring issues as well as the difficulties with social media. See e.g. [Guardian article June]
29 See e.g. Dinah Shelton, ed. *Commitment and Compliance: The Role of Non-binding Norms in the International Legal System* (Oxford, Oxford University Press, 2000); Kenneth Abbott and Duncan Snidal 'Hard and Soft Law in International Governance' (2000) 54 *International Organization* 421–456.
30 See e.g. Jan Klabbers 'The Redundancy of Soft Law' (1996) 65(2) *Nordisk Journal of International Law* 167–182.
31 The Report of the Nova Scotia Task Force on Bullying and Cyberbullying (A. Wayne MacKay, Chair) *Respectful and Responsible Relationships: There's No App for That* 29 February, 2012.
32 Ibid., p. 4.

33 See Wendy Gillis "Rehtaeh Parsons: A Family's Tragedy and a Town's Shame" *thestar.com*, 12 April, 2013, accessed 12 June, 2017; 'Rehtaeh Parsons, Canadian Girl, Dies After Suicide Attempt; Parents Allege She Was Raped by 4 Boys' *www.huffingtonpost.com.au* 12 April, 2013, accessed 12 June, 2017.
34 The Report of the Nova Scotia Task Force on Bullying and Cyberbullying, op.cit., p. 6.
35 Ibid.
36 Ibid.
37 See e.g. Lucas Graves 'Everyone's a Reporter' *Wired.com* 9 January, 2005, accessed 12 June, 2017; Asina Pornwasin 'With Social Media, Everyone's a Reporter!' *The Nation* 29 November, 2015, www.nationmultimedia.com, accessed 12 June, 2017.
38 The Report of the Nova Scotia Task Force on Bullying and Cyberbullying, op.cit., p. 7.
39 Ibid.
40 Ibid., p. 10.
41 Ibid., p. 7.
42 Ibid., pp. 13–14.
43 Ibid., p. 16.
44 Phillip Smith, Timothy L. Phillips and Ryan D. King *Incivility: The Rude Stranger in Everyday Life* (Cambridge, Cambridge University Press, 2010), p. 1.
45 Ibid., pp. 1–2.
46 Ibid., p. 2.
47 Ibid.
48 Ibid.
49 Crime and Disorder Act 1998 (UK), s.1(a).
50 Ibid., ss.34–42.
51 Ibid., ss.59–75.
52 Anti-social Behaviour, Crime and Policing Act 2014, s.22
53 Phillip Smith et al., op.cit., p. 2, citing Nick Cohen 'Turning Right to Wrong' *The Observer* 1 August, 2004.
54 Ibid., p. 3.
55 Alan Travis 'Online Antisocial Behaviour Complaints "Becoming a Real Problem for Police"' *The Guardian* 24 June, 2014, guardian.com, accessed 12 June, 2017.
56 Crown Prosecution Service *Guidelines on Prosecuting Cases Involving Communications Sent via Social Media*, www.cps.gov.uk, accessed 12 June, 2017.
57 [2012] EWHC 2157.
58 'The Actual Tweet Was: Crap! Robin Hood Airport Is Closed "You've Got a Week and a Bit to Get Your Shit Together Otherwise I'm Blowing the Airport Sky High!!"' https://en.wikipedia.org/wiki/Twitter_Joke_Trial, accessed 12 June, 2017 citing Paul Chambers, 11 May, 2010. '"My Tweet Was Silly, but the Police Reaction Was Absurd"' – The Guardian' *Guardian London*, accessed 17 September, 2010.
59 Crown Prosecution Service, op.cit.
60 [2012] EWHC 2157.
61 [2015] NSSC 340.
62 Ibid.
63 Ibid.
64 Crown Prosecution Service, op.cit.
65 Ibid.
66 [1992] 14 EHRR 229.
67 Crown Prosecution Service, op.cit.

68 Ibid.
69 The Conservative and Unionist Party Manifesto *Forward Together: Our Plan for a Stronger Britain and a Prosperous Future,* (2017), p. 79.
70 See e.g. The Guardian and London School of Economics and Political Science *Reading the Riots: Investigating England's Summer of Disorder,* (2011)
71 Ibid.
72 See e.g. Josh Halliday 'UK Riots "Made Worse" by Rolling News, BBM, Twitter and Facebook' 28 March, 2012, www.guardian.com, accessed 30 July, 2017; Iain McKenzie 'Is Technology to Blame for the London Riots?' *BBC News* 8 August, 2011, www.bbc.com, accessed 30 July, 2017.
73 Colin Sullivan and Mike Lyons 'Social Networks in the 2011 London Riots' Civic Media' 11 December, 2014, www.medium.com, accessed 30 July, 2017.
74 Gwynne Dyer 'Class at root of rioting in London' *Toronto Sun,* 10 August, 2011, www.toronto.sun, accessed 30 July, 2017.
75 James Ball and Symeon Brown 'Why BlackBerry Messenger was Rioters' Communication Method of Choice' *The Guardian* 8 December, 2011, www.theguardian.com, accessed 30 July, 2017.
76 Prime Minister David Cameron, *Daily Hansard,* 11 August, 2011, Col. 1053.
77 Heidi Alexander MP, *Daily Hansard,* 11 August, 2011, Col. 1067.
78 Prime Minister David Cameron, *Daily Hansard,* 11 August, 2011, Col. 1067.
79 Dr Julian Huppert MP, *Daily Hansard,* 11 August, 2011, Col. 1078.
80 Prime Minister David Cameron, *Daily Hansard,* 11 August, 2011, Col. 1078.
81 James Clappison MP, *Daily Hansard,* 11 August, 2011, Col. 1081.
82 Robin Walker MP, *Daily Hansard,* 11 August, 2011, Col. 1092.
83 Prime Minister David Cameron, *Daily Hansard,* 11 August, 2011, Col. 1092.
84 'Fighting the cyber-jihadists' *The Economist,* 10 June, 2017, p. 52.
85 See e.g. *Guardian* reference to why the right-wing tabloids got the recent UK election result so wrong.
86 Richard Chalfen '"It's Only a Picture": Sexting, "Smutty" Snapshots and Felony Charges' (2009) 24(3) *Visual Studies* 258–268.
87 Ibid., p. 260.
88 Ibid.
89 Christian Fuchs *Culture and Economy in the Age of Social Media* (New York and London, Routledge, 2015).
90 As Fuchs notes this is a concept coined by Toffler: Alvin Toffler *The Third Wave* (New York, Bantam, 1980) cited in Fuchs, op.cit., p. 118.
91 One supermarket chain is said to be very good at doing this, and has been able to construct a narrative of themselves as a maverick that takes on large supermarket operators even though they themselves are a multi-national corporation.
92 Twitter Terms of Service, https://twitter.com/en/tos.
93 Ibid.
94 *Facebook Terms of Service,* https://m.facebook.com/terms/, accessed 18 June, 2017.

Chapter 2

Recreating families in social media

In the previous chapter, we have seen how much of the anxiety directed towards young people's use of social media now revolves around its perceived connection with moral decay, civil disorder, sexualised behaviour and, in more recent years, terrorist acts. The argument has been advanced that much of this anxiety is not created by these matters per se, but rather that a moral panic has been created to both distract attention from the deeper inequalities in society and to construct a narrative that portrays social media as something that can be a force for 'good' that transcends these other concerns. In terms of this narrative, 'good' use often means usage that is consistent with the needs of the state and corporations to advance their interests. The role of law as perceived by these interests is to advance this objective.

One problem that the state has, however, is that the relative autonomy of the law means that it cannot always be relied upon to regulate social media on these terms. While protection of corporate objectives is a clear aim of the law, so too is upholding free speech and privacy, for example. The law then is a 'messy' institution to achieve these objectives, and this is one reason why attacks on the judiciary by conservative politicians have become more and more commonplace in many Western democracies. 'Activist' judges are seen to be 'ideological', and the implicit statement within that criticism is that 'law' is a neutral force that should be applied without regard to any broader context. The use of the fear of terrorism to stoke this criticism of the judiciary assists in constructing this narrative because at a general level the need to address such acts is seen to be unarguable. Social media does not create these narratives, but it does intensify the debates.

The problem with law as a 'messy' institution is that its internal logic demands scrutiny of detail, and the demand that the law regulate social media, whether to combat acts of terrorism, address the posting of sexualised images or cyber-bullying, will always lead to the legal question of how one is to define such acts. State and corporate interests are often served by not descending into such detailed examination of the phenomenon seen to be antagonistic towards their interests. It is for this reason that in relation to the law's relationship with social media, and how it further connects to young people's use of it, there is often a lack of deep discussion. Fuchs observes that social media 'has intensified the historical trend that boundaries play between play and labour, work time and leisure time, production and consumption, the factory and the household', causing 'public and private life to blur'.[1] Thus, while debates about the law's role in regulating social media occurs in the context of civil disorder and moral decay, it is less often analysed as a legal problem in terms of other relationships and areas of life that it affects. The purpose of this chapter is to engage with some of those areas, and to begin this analysis with the re-making of family life and law in and through social media.

2.1 Social media and family life

The relationship between new communication technologies and family life further demonstrates many of the various tensions identified in the first chapter. The need to protect children online is a clear extension of a more general obligation on parents to care for their children. Of course, the obligation to care for children is on another level imposed on the whole community, through such examples as the United Nations Convention on the Rights of the Child (UNCROC), which imposes an obligation on nation states to look after all children. This connection and disconnection between the broader community's responsibility to care for children and the role of parents is a tension in family law and one which is rarely, if ever, connected to our understanding of the relationship between young people and social media. In many ways, it is impossible to understand the place of social media in family life without also understanding the legal contradictions present in allowing both the state and parents to be regarded as the carers of children.

It is possible to identify this in the articles within UNCROC itself. For non-lawyers, the Convention appears to guarantee a host of rights for children. The reason I stress the perspective of non-lawyers is that this has become a document often cited in discussions about children beyond the discipline of law, especially in areas where lawyers often do not enter. Outside the discipline of law, such documents can appear to have greater clarity than lawyers may accord them. For example, the over-arching principle in the UNCROC, as in all areas affecting children, is that the best interests of the child shall be the primary consideration.[2] On the surface, this expectation appears uncontroversial. To suggest that to deal with children in ways other than in their best interests would be clearly objectionable. However, while such a phrase has the function of setting a standard that all in society will subscribe to, a closer examination shows it to be as much smokescreen as standard. In the implementation of such a standard, which appears in many areas of family and child law, courts have struggled to reach any consensus as to its precise meaning. At best, it is taken to be a reference to values, norms or common sense about how children should be treated and raised. It is only in the detailed reading of such cases that one grasps both the almost 'meaningless' worth of the best interests principle and at the same time, due to its centrality in matters to do with children, its significant meaning in terms of its real-world implications for decision-making. If all decisions must be made in the best interests of children, then – even though it may be used to justify any outcome – it will still operate as the reference point.

How does a principle or standard have meaning and no meaning at the same time? Brennan, in the High Court of Australia's decision in Marion's Case,[3] identified the inherent problem with the best interests principle. He said that 'the best interests approach does no more than identify the person whose interests are in question: it does not assist in identifying the factors which are relevant to the best interests of the child'.[4] In effect this involves a value judgment about what lies in the best interests of a child, which then means that the principle becomes a 'contest' between different views about that matter. In the end, that matter will come down to who holds the power to decide:

> it must be remembered that, in the absence of legal rules or a hierarchy of values, the best interests approach depends upon the value system of the decision-maker. Absent any rule or guideline, that approach simply creates an unexaminable discretion in the repository of the power.[5]

In the case of most children it is to the parents or family that one turns to find those who will act as their protector. The UNCROC acknowledges the central role of parents and family in looking after children:

> States Parties shall respect the responsibilities, rights and duties of parents or, where applicable, the members of the extended family or community as provided for by local custom, legal guardians or other persons legally responsible for the child, to provide, in a manner consistent with the evolving capacities of the child, appropriate direction and guidance in the exercise by the child of the rights recognized in the present Convention.[6]

The notion that parents and other guardians of a child will provide guidance and direction is then qualified by the words 'in a manner consistent with the evolving capacities of the child'. This idea that a child's need for protection and direction is subject to their evolution from childhood to adulthood is at the root of many anxieties about children. It underpins the reasons of the majority in the case of *Gillick*,[7] which lays down what is regarded as the legal test for a child's capacity to make their own decisions about matters that affect them.[8] Lord Scarman said in that case that the basic principle was that 'parental right yields to the child's right to make his own decisions when he reaches a sufficient understanding and intelligence to be capable of making up his own mind on the matter requiring decision'.[9] This notion of the 'maturing minor' both embedded in one action the basis of children's rights to autonomy and the ongoing role of parents and guardians in overseeing their children's development. It is a tension that underscores the messy nature of law in clarifying the position of children. As Lord Scarman himself pointed out:

> Certainty is always an advantage in the law, and in some branches of the law it is a necessity. But it brings with it an inflexibility and a rigidity which in some branches of the law can obstruct justice, impede the law's development, and stamp upon the law the mark of obsolescence where what is needed is the capacity for development. The law relating to parent and child is concerned with the problems of the growth and maturity of the human personality. If the law should impose upon the process of "growing up" fixed limits where nature knows only a continuous process, the price would be artificiality and a lack of realism in an area where the law must be sensitive to human development and social change.[10]

This approach, however, creates frustrations for those who seek clarity around not only how to raise and guide children but also about what constitutes good and bad parenting. As the state has withdrawn from regulation of the marketplace, it has increased its intervention in family life consistent with the manufacture of the moral crises discussed in the first chapter. For parents, this creates anxiety around their parenting, for to be considered a 'bad' parent has social and legal consequences in increasing areas of parenting.[11] Social media brings many of these strands together, as its public nature puts families under the spotlight. Thus, while the law claims flexibility in child rearing as a matter of practicality, many parents seek certainty in knowing how to parent. Lord Scarman perhaps rather unfortunately suggested that this could be better done by legislators:

> If certainty be thought desirable, it is better that the rigid demarcations necessary to achieve it should be laid down by legislation after a full consideration of all the relevant factors than by the courts confined as they are by the forensic process to the evidence adduced by the parties and to whatever may properly fall within the judicial notice of judges. Unless and until Parliament should think fit to intervene, the courts should establish a principle flexible enough to enable justice to be achieved by its application to the particular circumstances proved by the evidence placed before them.[12]

I say 'unfortunately' because the above comments of Lord Scarman suggest that the process of how to guide a child through their use of social media can be done by legislative fiat. However, what has occurred instead of legislation is a plethora of documents and guidance statements that purport to reduce to writing the parenting process in relation to young people's social media use, many of which are produced by the corporations that provide the social media platforms, or organisations that present themselves as concerned about child welfare. In attempting to present the choices for parents as clear and manageable, they give the appearance of removing many of the uncertainties surrounding young people's use of social media. Of course, what they actually do is deny to children and young people the benefit of the 'messiness' of the law's construction of their rights. In response to *Gillick*, John Eekelaar wrote that the decision gave children 'that most dangerous but most precious of rights: the right to make their own mistakes'.[13] This is an entirely uncomfortable proposition for many parents, as it requires them to relinquish power and control over their children. After *Gillick* many courts were said to have stepped back from this consequence of its reasoning. In many ways, social media has become the new battleground between adults and young people over this right to make mistakes.

2.2 Good parents, bad parents: from family and child surveillance to re-writing the rules of internal family functions

Law's messiness – that is, the manner in which it must balance many competing concerns in relation to how people seek to live their lives – does create a supposed barrier for those who crave certainty in the regulation of family life. There is also the broad cultural concern that family life is private and intimate and not the proper place for law to intervene, even though there is a strong narrative that sits against that view of law's role.[14] In effect this opens the family to the possibilities of other forms of regulation that undermine the aim of law to ensure the inclusion of competing views of family life. By that I mean that if law is not allowed to regulate family life, there is the greater likelihood that the norms of the most powerful members of the family will prevail, or from outside the family, the concerns of the interests most able to have their norms internalised within the family will have influence. In addition, much of family law is expressed in general terms, for example, that we should always act in the child's 'best interests'. This is so vaguely expressed that a more specific articulation of what this means could be seen as the state overreaching into private life. The consequence of all of these factors is that guidance and advice that is written by corporate interests in social media (sometimes in collaboration with the state) fills the vacuum of understanding about how good parents and young people should act in relation to social media. These 'rules' in effect become a de facto ‘family law’ in the area and begin to recreate family life in the context of new technology.

One organisation, Connectsafely.org, has written a guide which begins by attempting to put parents’ minds at ease and to claim space for children to use social media:

> Though there’s nothing inherently dangerous about Instagram, the main things parents worry about are typical of all social media: mean behavior among peers and inappropriate photos or videos that can hurt a child’s reputation or attract the wrong kind of attention. Parents are also concerned that people their kids don’t know can reach out to them directly. Kids can learn to manage these risks, which is why we wrote this guide.[15]

Connectsafely.org is a non-profit organization that includes amongst its supporters Facebook, Google, LinkedIn, Kik, Yahoo and Twitter. The thrust of this guide is to in effect educate parents about Instagram, reassuring them that it ‘is just an extension of their [children’s] “real world” social lives, giving them new chances to hang out with their friends during in-between moments’,[16] before going on to cite ‘research’ that teens still mainly socialise face-to-face and so parents ‘could talk with [their] kids about the wisdom of keeping their Instagram experience anchored in their offline life and friendships’.[17] In response to thoughts about prohibiting their children from Instagram, it is pointed out that even if that was to occur, other children may post your child’s photos online; thus, ‘your kids can be on Instagram even if they’re not on Instagram’.[18] Beyond that it is also pointed out to parents that ‘there’s a risk of social marginalization for kids who are not allowed to socialize in this way that’s now so embedded in their social lives. Wise use tends to be better than no use’.[19] Thus, finally, it is claimed that parents need to keep talking with their children ‘to figure out what’s appropriate for them, in terms of safety, privacy, reputation and time management’.[20] It then concludes with the remark:

> It generally just works better to talk with our kids about their favorite tools – with genuine interest, not fear – because they’re more likely to come to you if they ever need help.[21]

Whether any of this is good advice or not, the fact that it now exists indicates subtle but important shifts in parenting relationships with children. One could say that this guide might be viewed as reflecting corporate interests and those of their fellow travellers by advancing the ‘inevitability’ of the acceptance of their new technology and forms of communication. Instagram, after all, is at the end of the day a profit-generating enterprise.[22] But there are other levels on which this guide operates. While parents have always sought advice about how to act in their children's best interests, the advent of social media presents as an overwhelming force that parents can be baffled by. The Instagram guide proceeds from that premise so that parents talking to their children is not just about their place in guiding their children, but is also to allow parents to be in effect educated by their children about how the technology operates. In this way, the guidance may be to talk with your children, but one may ask who in effect is controlling the conversation, or thought to be doing so, by the new media corporations.

United States Federal Trade Commission advice to parents on social networking claims that '[p]arents sometimes can feel outpaced by their technologically savvy kids'.[23] This document also urges parents to talk to their children about social media, stressing the need for information privacy, what privacy settings to use, posting only information that parents and children are comfortable for others to see, protection from online bullying, and the avoidance of sex talk.[24] In other words much of this guide is peppered with references to fear and danger. It begins with the question, 'It's 10 p.m. Do you know where your children are?'[25] It references the similar childhood experience of those who are now parents, but now with the added 'twist' – 'and who they're chatting with online'.[26] The guide also suggests that parents sign up for the same sites as their children, keep computers in an open place within the home, review the child's online friends list and consider parental control functions.[27] While much of these suggestions seem based on the need to protect the vulnerable child, the guide also advises parents to tell their children to 'trust their gut if they have suspicions'.[28]

This latter advice may seem to acknowledge some capacity in the child or young person to make their own judgments, but it probably comes more from a resigned acceptance that young people's use of social media is in fact very hard to control. Even the notion that computers should be kept in public spaces within the family home is already surpassed by the fast take-up of mobile technology. The days of the desktop computer being used in the living room while parents oversee the young person's use of it are already in the past for most families. Nevertheless, there is in the guide a tone that the underlying culture is one of placing young people under surveillance. If the Internet is the 'wild west', strong notions of children and young people being 'little devils' that must be kept in check in such spaces continue.

This is manifest in other documents that seek to educate parents about their children's online activities. A guide provided by the computer security company McAfee says that one risk in the use of social media is children and young people's provision of 'too much information' of a personal nature that can lead to cyber-bullying, predators pursuing them, invasion of privacy and identity theft.[29] The example used in this section of the guide is about a young person who was rejected admission to a college after having talked about it in positive terms during the visit, and who later 'trashed' the college online.[30] This idea that young people will suffer the consequences of their immaturity, naivety or essential 'wildness' is also a recurring theme in discussions of online control of young people. In relation to cyber-bullying, for example, this leads to claims that it is easy for children to become victims due to the amount of personal information they feel inclined to share. But it also leads to concerns that children and young people will also become cyber-bullies themselves. The McAfee guide advises parents of the signs to look out for to tell whether their child is a perpetrator:

- Switching screens or closing programs when you walk by
- Using the computer late at night
- Getting upset if he/she cannot use the computer
- Using multiple online accounts or an account that belongs to someone else

> If you detect any of these signs, talk to your kids about the issues around cyberbullying as both a victim and a perpetrator. Encourage them to not condone or support others who are cyberbullying. Ask them questions based on the 'warning signs' and then sit back and listen.[31]

The sense of this being about the interrogation of young people is apparent. Indeed, the guide later suggests that parents police their children's online behaviour. This includes searching their children's names online to see whether others are impersonating them, looking at their children's friend list, considering letting them only friend people they know offline and creating their own profile and becoming part of their children's online life.[32] The guide also suggests that parents use technology to monitor and protect their children through privacy settings, have up-to-date security software and use parental monitoring software.[33] This latter guidance then leads to a final 'security software checklist' for parents to ascertain what they need to look for to protect their children online. This includes the blocking of inappropriate content on the web and any programs the parents wish to block, a social networking feature that 'records postings of inappropriate or personal information and conversations to help determine if cyberbullying activity is taking place', email blocking, time limits for computer use online, monitoring and recording of instant messaging to ascertain if children are engaging in inappropriate dialogue, usage reports 'which you can use as conversation starters to educate your children', email notifications 'when your children attempt to access objectionable material' and blocking of objectionable YouTube videos.[34] It may not surprise that the guide then points out that McAfee Family Protection software has all these features and 'empowers you to say "yes" to your kids so they can make the most of their digital lives'.[35]

A critique of such a document does need to note that the construction of the vulnerable, naïve or even wild child is important here to ultimately create a market for family protection software. However, there are more profound shifts taking place within families and their regulation that are also occurring in this narrative. First, there is the role of corporate players in family life. Their market is the adults in this space, and they, in seeking to act in their children's best interests, are themselves vulnerable to the portrayal of the Internet as a dangerous space for children that requires parents to become both educator and monitor of their children. In doing this, the corporate interests co-opt not only the language of child protection but also of children's rights. A properly educated child is also an 'empowered' child, according to this guide, who can proceed to enjoy their digital life. Finally, this digital life is no doubt based on being a productive member of society who passively consumes the products to be marketed to them. In suggesting that what is needed is the filtering of 'inappropriate' or 'objectionable' content, such guides play to stereotyped and conservative notions of what children should be seeing and participating in online. If such guides were truly about empowering anyone, then why would they not open for discussion the normative issues of what is 'good' and 'bad' on the Internet? They also imply that children and young people are consumers of online material. That they may also create their own online content is barely mentioned, other than with reference to the child or young person as cyber-bully. Yet if they can create such malicious content, what other content may they also generate of a positive nature?

The tone of many forms of guidance, whether from government or corporate bodies, is that the Internet is a dangerous place for children and young people and that the role of parents is to monitor, control and protect their children online. Even the Australian office responsible for this area is named the Office of the Children's e-Safety Commissioner. Consistent with the above guidance documents, this office also advises parental behaviour which includes the encouragement and modelling of 'good behaviours with your kids around their use of connected devices', including 'not bringing devices to the dinner table'.[36] This office also advises parents to keep to the same boundaries they set for their children with respect to where in the house computers and devices are used, and to also 'establish and maintain trust' due to the difficulty of monitoring a child's online activity at all times.[37] The apparent contradiction between establishing family rules around online activity that run to such detail as to whether devices should be used at the dinner table on the one hand, and then an acceptance that the practical use of mobile technology requires parents to also build trust does not appear to prevent such guidance documents promoting both approaches. One doubts that in relation to adult relationships it would be possible to promote trust through also placing the other party under effective surveillance. Yet this goes unremarked on in debates about young people's use of social media, so powerful are the concerns and fears about their online activities. Also unremarked upon is the acceptance that state agencies, or corporate entities, have a role in prescribing conduct within the family home. Of course, while information provided in those guides to parents is about how to address contemporary areas of concern, the law must also consider whether a child's unrestrained use of social media would indicate parental neglect, or conversely that a parent who bans a child from social media use is perceived as a hyper-responsible parent and too controlling. In all of this, however, there is little mention of the child or young person's right to access such media.

Popular discourse tends towards absolutist responses, so when celebrities decide to ban their children from using social media, the narrative becomes one of them trying to be responsible instead of questions being asked about their ability to make judgments. In 2013 celebrity chef Jamie Oliver announced that he was banning his eldest daughter, then aged 11, from using a mobile phone or social media.[38] His reported concerns were the potential for his children to be bullied on social media.[39] Other parents in the same report also reacted to the way the Internet was painted as a dangerous place. But the fear was not just of the online world; there was fear also of the greater freedom mobile technology gave children to construct their own virtual world, one parent commenting, 'smartphones mean that all of us are in our own private worlds, having private relationships with the internet and social media'.[40] Other parents saw good and bad in social media and undertook the various monitoring and guidance practices discussed above. But it is clear that the concern with protecting their children from the 'bad' aspects was also tempered by the fear that their children could be the ones behaving inappropriately online: 'They don't comprehend the repercussions or foresee the issues that might develop. I think every parent also worries that their child might be the one bullying or not being nice to others online'.[41]

2.3 Making parents accountable

An important way in which social media, as a part of new digital technology, is re-writing family responsibilities is with respect to who is given responsibility for the form of regulation that occurs with respect to this space. The UNCROC may regard parents as having ongoing responsibility for the welfare and protection of children, as does family law, whether in the UK, Australia or other jurisdictions. However, the nature of this technology has created a narrative that in effect disempowers adults by requiring the inclusion of children and young people as part of the solution (often 'empowering' them, it is said) before re-imposing new responsibilities – some of which are discussed above – back on parents. In effect, this is a new form of state control of family life.

An Australian Parliamentary Committee reported in this area in 2011.[42] It was particularly focused on issues relating to cyber-bullying and other risks to children online and presented the problem in terms of the 'knowing' child or young person as against the 'ignorant' parent:

> Parents/carers have the ultimate responsibility for educating and protecting their children, including in the online environment. Adults and young people use technology in different ways, and new communications technologies are becoming increasingly foreign to many parents/carers, thus 'reducing their ability to protect their children'. More often than not, children know more about the Internet and mobile phones, etc., than adults. Rapidly emerging new technologies are increasingly leaving many adults behind.[43]

The Committee also remarked that '[p]arents, carers and teachers can . . . have such limited understanding and awareness of the issues that they are 'very reluctant' to deliver, and totally lack confidence in delivering, such curriculum material or information about cyber safety as is available in Australia'.[44] Given the legal obligation on parents to protect their children, such narratives create definite anxieties about the responsibilities of parenting, especially when the focus is on child protection from bullying, sexual predators or sexualisation. At the same time, to the extent that the empowerment of children and young people's right to access new media also becomes part of this narrative, the 'messiness' of such terms and claims makes the role of parents even more problematic.[45] This also creates conditions where parents are both fearful of their role and fearful of the new power that young people have in a practical sense based on their perceived greater knowledge of the technology. This, however, does not absolve parents from responsibility to control their children online, and as the Australian Parliamentary Committee stressed above, parents have the ultimate responsibility to protect their children online. However, what may be easy to overlook here is that the Committee constructed this part of the discussion around the response of 'adults' to cyber-safety issues, and as the above passage indicates, parents, in this context, are expected to deliver a certain message – or more specifically a curriculum – to ensure their children are both protected and behave online. This is to be done, overall, because as the Committee also noted, 'some young people are "fearless but naïve" and dismissive of these risks and fears. They can be more concerned about slow Internet connections and viruses on their computers'.[46] Parents and other responsible adults, it seems, are to ensure that such children learn to act more appropriately.

The above narrative is now so strongly embedded in discussions about online activity and social media that the need for state-sponsored – and parent/teacher-delivered – cyber-safety curriculum and guidance is regarded as self-evident. The created office of an e-Safety Commissioner in Australia in 2015 further embeds this in the legal regime that regulates this space. The Enacting Online Safety for Children Act 2015 (Cth) provides that the functions of the Commissioner include 'to support, encourage, conduct, accredit and evaluate educational, promotional and community awareness programs that are relevant to online safety for children'[47] and 'to formulate, in writing, guidelines or statements that . . . recommend best practices for persons and bodies involved in online safety for children' and 'are directed towards facilitating the timely and appropriate resolution of incidents involving cyber-bullying material targeted at an Australian child'.[48] The process of making complaints to the e-Safety Commissioner about cyber-bullying also provides that as well as the child, a 'responsible person', which includes a parent or guardian of the child, may also make a complaint to the Commissioner.[49] Of concern, however, is that while this process is on the face providing a process for concerned parents, amongst others, to initiate a complaint to protect their child, it also raises the question as to how the state may respond to parents who do not make such complaints.

The response to cyber-bullying on social media by the Australian Parliament represents the soft forms of social control identified by Stan Cohen.[50] The clear message of the Australian scheme is that all adults – parents, teachers, and relevant state agencies – have to work together to address 'inappropriate' online activity. This also means that parents must accept their current incapacity and lack of knowledge with respect to online communications. And again, the need for parents to 'talk' to their children is often stressed, as one senator remarked during debate on legislation addressing children's online safety:

> We also need parents to learn how to talk to their children about cyber-bullying, how they can cope with it, and the importance of their child talking to someone they trust about it when it happens. I recall during the inquiry that a lot of young people would tell us that they would not actually tell their parents they were being bullied because they thought their parents' response would be just to take away the iPhone, the iPad or the computer or whatever instrument was being used. It was quite interesting that a lot of parents thought that if you did that or somehow stopped them using it that the bullying would automatically stop, but it does not. What often happens is that even if the young person is not even able to physically view the bullying at a precise moment, up to thousands of other people certainly can if the perpetrator has a wide network.[51]

The same senator also referred to the need for parents to work in partnership with schools, and that the committee report referred to above observed the importance of parental involvement 'in all aspects of cyber safety education . . . particularly as it helps to reinforce the messages provided by schools and government'.[52]

What is concerning here is that there is in this discussion no consideration of the 'messiness' of the key concepts in the debate. What constitutes cyber-bullying is rarely, if ever, discussed and so the need to protect children from this 'bad' aspect of online activity is logged without dissent or debate. And while 'empowering' children and 'including' children in responses to such behaviour is often lauded as a sign that the child's right to participate in the regulation of the behaviour meets their human right to participate in the process, this does require an implicit acceptance of the underlying definitions of both what is considered to be 'inappropriate' as well as what constitutes 'participation'.

Of particular note here is that the e-Safety Commissioner is to have regard to the United Nations Convention on the Rights of the Child when performing that office's functions under the Act.[53] But that Convention, as we know, has a mix of both protection rights as well as autonomy rights for children. There is nothing in the legislation to explain *how* the Commissioner should take that Convention into account. To paraphrase Brennan, in Marion's Case, against what hierarchy of values is that Convention to be read by the e-Safety Commissioner? The UNCROC contains so many disparate statements about the roles of parents and guardians of children that one might reasonably conclude that its aim is to ensure the preservation of diversity in terms of raising children across the globe. Where in that purpose is the place for parents to ensure that they reinforce the messages provided by schools and government? Perhaps of greater importance as a legal question is what are the consequences for parents who fail to do so?

Michael King and Christine Piper have remarked that the relative autonomy of law means that child welfare law as a part of law can choose how or if it considers the evidence of child welfare science when deciding the best interests of children.[54] In seeking to formulate guidelines about how to address children's online activity, there often seems to be a selective approach to evidence that supports the guidance created. The normative basis of what might be regarded as 'inappropriate' online activity is too 'messy' for lawmakers to engage with, preferring instead to adopt the certainty that comes from co-opting terms such as 'empowerment' of young people, including parents in the team that works with schools and government so that they 'talk' with their children, and 'educat[ing]' those parents in the risks of online activity and the set of strategies to avoid them. The science in the debates in this area tends toward the citing of statistics that focus primarily on the incidence of social media use by young people and then somehow connecting, or assuming a connection, between those figures and mental-health problems experienced by young people. As one

Australian senator remarked on the debates on the bill establishing the e-Safety Commissioner:

> A 2014 study from the Social Policy Research Centre at the University of New South Wales estimated that 20 per cent of young Australians aged between eight and 17 have been victims of cyberbullying during one year, with 463,000 children estimated to have been affected. We know that increasing numbers of children and young people have access to the internet, particularly now on smartphones, and that in 2011 the Australian Communication and Media Authority identified social media as the primary form of digital communication between children over 13 years of age. If we take those statistics into account and then consider the sobering statistics we face in relation to the general mental health of young people in Australia, we realise what a complex picture we have to consider.[55]

There is of course no discussion in such debates about the methodology of such research or the definitions employed. This is not to suggest that cyberbullying does not damage people, but are the best legal and policy responses based on loose relationships and no discussion of meanings given to terms? In addition, how should all of these considerations be balanced with young people's free speech rights and parents' choices about how their children should be allowed to develop? Such matters go to the heart of what is considered to be in the best interests of the child – the key legal standard that applies in this context. It is a standard rooted in values, yet this point is rarely taken up by policymakers, other than to assume that good values are represented by not using social media to annoy others. Do parents have the right or obligation to encourage their children to use social media to annoy others? And what might 'annoy' mean in this discussion?

Peter Nikken and Marjon Schols do speak to other implications for parents when they say it is expected that the parental role is to send certain messages to their children about social media use. Their analysis of the literature on parents as mediators and monitors of children's use of social media found that the capacity of parents to perform that role varied according to their level of education and income level, as well as gender and age.[56] What this means is that parental approaches to the mediation of their children's social media use vary considerably.[57] They also noted that parents who were more concerned about the risks and harms of new media use did more to protect their children by monitoring, restricting or supervising usage and critically talking to their children about the media, while parents who considered that new media offered many educational or entertainment options co-used the media or actively talked about it with their children.[58] Such conclusions fundamentally qualify the guidance in the documents referred to above that parents should 'talk' with their children about their use of social media. Clearly, *how* parents will talk with their children about social media must be influenced by their own views, yet such documents, as with the political debates, fail to engage with that rather obvious point. Perhaps such vagueness represents some deference to diversity by default, or perhaps it comes from an assumption that such talking will focus on harm minimisation rather than discussion of the limitless potential of social media for free expression.

However, a more troubling aspect of the Nikken and Schols research is its reference to the different consequences for children's social media use arising from different parental approaches and parents' perceptions of their child's capacity to use the media.[59] Apart from the parent's views on the value of the media referred to above, they also found that the parent's view of the child's skillset also influenced how they mediated its use. Where they regarded the child as having low skills, they were less actively involved in supervising the child's use or imposing restrictions on usage.[60] They concluded that higher-educated parents and those with higher incomes structured their children's media use by using newer forms of technology compared with lower-income parents, who had less capacity to buy the latest technology.[61] They refer to the work of Paus-Hasebrink et al.[62] on older children that parents from socially disadvantaged backgrounds have fewer skills to mediate their children's use of media and that '[t]his uncertainty and inconsistency may lead children from low-income households to exploit their parents' lack of consistency and use any kind of media whenever and wherever they want'.[63] This has the sense of a concern with the 'wild child' or 'little devil' unrestrained and out of control, and aligned with the activities of poorer parents may have the chilling effect of labelling those parents as more likely to be 'bad' parents in relation to the social media use of their children.

Nikken and Schols conclude with reference to parents as role models and also on the need for tailoring guidelines for different types of parents as well as for different types of children. While such diversity of approach may be well-meaning, for lawmakers one can see in this work the potential for targeting guidance to those parents who fail to intervene in their children's social media usage, particularly once the connection between social disadvantage and rebellion, hostility to the current order or even indifference is assumed. In a word, poorer parents may be set up to fail if this research is read in a particular way. Paus-Hasebrink et al. concluded in their overview of approaches across a range of countries:

> In general, children from higher educated parents use the internet more competently and have more competent parents to help them and to mediate their internet use. This results in higher opportunities for these children, but can also backfire because they are also subject to more risks online. Children from lower educated and lower SES

> parents, on the other hand, generally use the internet less, thus experiencing fewer opportunities and risks. However, if they experience a risk, they are also less competent in dealing with the risk and developing resilience.[64]

The risk for parents (and children) is that such conclusions may become some justification for state intervention in all families, but more so those where the children appear to be more 'out of control'. In effect, this construction of families raises the likelihood that some will be seen to be more worthy of control than others.

2.4 Making children accountable

While parental role models and the state's co-option of parents into patterns of control over their children through the manipulation of meanings within parental duty laws is one aspect of making families accountable in the age of social media, another and more direct way of controlling children online is of course to legislate and establish rules for children's behaviour directly. Although as we have seen there can be references to children's rights and creating empowered and resilient children in that space, it is suggested that much of this is obfuscation. Legal definitions have to be interpreted, as do children's rights conventions, and in the reading of them there are often gaps through which those rights appear to sink at times. However, this is not always the case, and so the notion that the law is a 'messy' institution to achieve any policy objectives is always present in the discussion.

We may start here with the example of the definition of cyber-bullying in the Australian cyber-safety law mentioned above. While this legislation is not specifically directed at the behaviour of young people online, although the victim must be a child, it has been noted in many of the debates on cyber-bullying that children and young people are often victims and perpetrators of this behaviour. Section 5 of the Enhancing Online Safety for Children Act 2015 (Cth) provides that when material is provided on a social media or other relevant electronic service and which an 'ordinary reasonable person' would conclude was intended to have an effect on a particular Australian child and which 'would be likely to have the effect on the Australian child of seriously threatening, seriously intimidating, seriously harassing or seriously humiliating the Australian child', then the material is to be regarded as cyber-bullying material.[65] Resort to such concepts as the 'ordinary reasonable person' are another example of the 'messiness' of law, as it is designed to both impose a standard on the judgment that must be made about what is inappropriate behaviour while at the same time not restricting free expression. But who is the ordinary reasonable person? Are they even children or young people? Such terms may seem to inject into the process a sense of 'reason', but the vagueness of the term also creates a fair degree of uncertainty as to what the final outcome will be.

In Australian law, the 'ordinary reasonable person' is borrowed from defamation law. The question is whether the ordinary reasonable person referred to here is a reference to 'mainstream' opinion or whether it embraces minority views about relevant material.[66] Baker explains that in defamation law the legal issue is not about whether a person has suffered, 'but whether there has been a breach in the rules of civility that may have led to the dignity of the plaintiff or defendant being compromised'.[67] Baker refers to the case of *Hepburn v TCN Channel Nine*[68] which put the test in terms of whether an appreciable or substantial group held the viewpoint of the material.[69] In the case of assessing social media posts, one can see that viewing this question from within the techno-culture of young people may be viewed quite differently to how an older and less tech-savvy generation member may see the matter.

The relevant New Zealand legislation takes a slightly different approach to the Australian Act. Section 22 of the Harmful Digital Communications Act 2015 (NZ) creates an offence of 'causing harm by posting digital communication'. To commit the offence, the digital communication must be posted with the intention to cause harm to a victim, 'posting the communication would cause harm to an ordinary reasonable person in the position of the victim', and the post does cause harm.[70] Thus, while this law uses the concept of the 'ordinary reasonable person', it is qualified by being such a person 'in the position of the victim'. This might suggest that the fictional person against whom the standard is determined has at least some of the characteristics of the victim. However, it might also be argued that depending on the victim, the constructed person may be far from ordinary and reasonable! The New Zealand law does also qualify the process of deciding how to categorise the communication further. To determine whether the digital communication would cause harm, a court may take into account any matter it 'considers relevant', including 'the extremity of the language used', 'the age and characteristics of the victim', 'whether the digital communication was anonymous', 'whether the digital communication was repeated', 'the extent of circulation of the digital communication', 'whether the digital communication is true or false' and 'the context in which the digital communication appeared'.[71] Whether the court may or would consider the age and characteristics of the accused person might depend on how the court – and the community at large – considers the extent to which the use of social media by young people is understood. Certainly the emphasis within the section is on the needs and effects on the victim, even considering that the New Zealand legislation does expand the range of considerations and open up the possibility of delving into the socio-cultural context of social media use.

However, in seeking to control the online child from the dangers they are seen to face online from the vantage point of those who are less immersed in new technologies, there is more at stake than disputes over who is an ordinary reasonable person to judge online activity. As discussed in the previous chapter, the role of the law is often framed in relation to young people and social media use as being about established legal concepts such as privacy, data protection and sexual harassment. The social media world that many young people move in may raise some of those concerns but has constructed new ways of forming identity, group attachment and appearance. The often-used example of warning young people that what they post online may be there for a thousand years is often less of a fear for them than it is in an invitation for ongoing celebrity status. To that extent the law may treat young people's use of social media as creating a set of serious problems, but that same law struggles with the way in which young people treat such use as a 'game' that often challenges established norms. How does law regulate transgressive play online? Where are the traditional legal concepts that embrace that social construction of social media?

2.5 Online and offline: different worlds or reconstructing the new?

Young people are said to move between online and offline worlds seamlessly at times. Yet the full meaning of this is seldom explored. There may be a sense that this has something to do with how they spend time – and in some adult eyes 'waste' it – yet the merging of worlds can mean much more. It was argued above that social media is changing the internal functions of families and that traditional legal concepts are limited in how they can address such change. For example, there is often mention of the child's right to privacy as if this was a simple and clear notion that the worst parts of social media undermine. But how does this claimed right sit with the child's pursuit of their identity – which is also a right of the child[72] – where privacy rights might get in the way of such identity formation?

Piermarco Aroldi and Nicoletta Vittadini discuss this in the context of adopted children and the role of social media.[73] As they note, adoptees can now access information about their birth parents (and vice versa) and follow those people anonymously via social media whereas previously they would have to use the family courts to access that information.[74] Thus, there has been a shift away from court-based decisions that seek to balance the right to know one's birth parents with the best interests of the child towards a circumvention of the law altogether.[75] In this sense, social media could be regarded as converting a legal problem involving privacy and identity rights to something which goes beyond law and into a form of transgressive practice. Of course, this exposes both adopted children and the birth relatives they find in potentially risky situations as they may have romanticised the families or parents they are looking for, and the reality may be from disappointing to even dangerous.[76] Aroldi and Vittadini suggest that the rights of adopted children 'are in conflict in the digital and networked world'.[77] They are concerned that social media facilitates avoiding the legal protections that exist for such children and argue for more social-media-savvy practitioners in this area.[78]

In this example, we can see that social media enables the adopted child to move beyond the law and recast how their identity may be reclaimed. This is not to deny that there are pitfalls in taking this course, but it cannot be asserted that the former law has always worked towards a positive outcome for children seeking to establish their identity in this area, as the history of adoption law would suggest. Digital communications and the new media in a practical sense have provided a range of different options to such children. My concern, though, is also with the way in which this practice challenges law. The legal discourse provides notions of conflicting rights that can at the least offer some juristic basis for either utilising social media to go around the old law or alternatively providing legitimacy to laws that might restrict its use. In either case it also underlines the messiness of the law once again, for in seeking to provide children and young people with some rights here, there is an almost immediate claim that these must be balanced against the privacy rights of the birth parents, for example. In seeking to empower the young person, there is in the same rationale the basis for disempowerment. This should not surprise us, of course, for ultimately what social media represents is the potential for transgression, and until that transgressive practice is accommodated by the law it remains outside the law and a threat to its order. The real question, then, is whether social media as transgression can be embraced by the law or whether there is an inevitable and irresolvable tension between them.

Notes

1 Fuchs, op.cit., p. 118.
2 UNCROC, art. 3(1).
3 *Secretary of the Department of Health and Community Services v JWB and SMB* (1992) 175 *CLR* 218.
4 Ibid., per Brennan, J.
5 Ibid., per Brennan, J.
6 UNCROC, art. 5.
7 *Gillick v West Norfolk and Wisbech AHA* [1985] UKHL 7.
8 The case involved consent to medical treatment, but it is contended that the principles are of more general application with respect to a child's capacity to make their own decisions.
9 *Gillick v West Norfolk and Wisbech AHA*, per Lord Scarman.
10 Ibid.
11 One small example of this is the increased use of punishment of parents for non-school attendance to take advantage of cheap travel deals. Another example is

where parents who fail to send their children to school are denied certain welfare payments.

12 *Gillick v West Norfolk and Wisbech AHA*, per Lord Scarman.
13 John Eekelaar 'The Emergence of Children's Rights' (1986) 6 *Oxford Journal of Legal Studies* 161.
14 See e.g. Frances E. Olsen 'The Myth of State Intervention in the Family' (1985) 18 *University of Michigan Journal of Law Reform* 835–864.
15 Connectsafely.org a *Parent's Guide to Instagram* (2014)
16 Ibid.
17 Ibid.
18 Ibid.
19 Ibid.
20 Ibid.
21 Ibid.
22 Saqib Shah 'Instagram Is Set to Turn a Huge Profit for Facebook This Year' 16 April, 2016, www.digitaltrends.com, accessed 26 June, 2017.
23 Federal Trade Commission *FTC Facts for Consumers: Social Networking Sites: A Parent's Guide* (September, 2007).
24 Ibid.
25 Ibid.
26 Ibid.
27 Ibid.
28 Ibid.
29 McAfee *A Parent's Guide to Social Networking Sites* (2009)
30 Ibid., p. 9.
31 Ibid., p. 16.
32 Ibid., p. 21.
33 Ibid., p. 22.
34 Ibid., p. 26.
35 Ibid.
36 Office of the e-Safety Children's Commissioner *Parent's Guide to Online Safety* (Australian Government, undated), p. 16.
37 Ibid.
38 Viv Groskop 'Children and the Internet: A Parent's Guide' *The Guardian* 3 November, 2013, www.theguardian.com/technology2013/nov/03/internet-children-parents-safety, accessed 20 June, 2017.
39 Ibid.
40 Ibid.
41 Ibid.
42 Parliament of the Commonwealth of Australia *High-Wire Act: Cyber-Safety and the Young: Interim Report: Joint Select Committee on Cyber-Safety* (Commonwealth of Australia, June, 2011).
43 Ibid., para.1.48.
44 Ibid., para.149.
45 Yet this is a much smaller part of the discussion usually, given the focus on risks to children rather than their autonomous participation.
46 *High-Wire Act: Cyber-Safety and the Young*, para.1.51.
47 *Enacting Online Safety for Children Act 2015* (Cth), s.15(1)(f).
48 Ibid., s.15(1)(p).
49 Ibid., s.18(2)(a).
50 Stan Cohen *Visions of Social Control* (Cambridge, Polity Press, 1985)
51 Senator Bilyk *Second Reading Speech Enhancing Online Safety for Children Bill 2014, Enhancing Online Safety for Children (Consequential Amendments) Bill 2014 Hansard* (Australian Senate) 3 March, 2015, p. 1037.

52 Ibid.
53 *Enacting Online Safety for Children Act 2015* (Cth), s.12.
54 Michael King and Christine Piper *How the Law Thinks About Children 2nd edn* (Aldershot, Ashgate, 1995).
55 Senator Wright *Second Reading Speech Enhancing Online Safety for Children Bill 2014, Enhancing Online Safety for Children (Consequential Amendments) Bill 2014 Hansard* (Australian Senate) 3 March, 2015, p. 1042.
56 Peter Nikken and Marjon Schols 'How and Why Parents Guide the Media Use of Young Children' (2015) 24 *Journal of Child and Family Studies* 3423–3435.
57 Ibid.
58 Ibid., p. 3425.
59 It is important to note that Nikken and Schols did study a sample of young children from 0 to 7 years; however, the broader implications for children in general may still be valid, and indeed they did acknowledge that their findings were consistent with research on older children, citing Patti Valkenburg, Marina Krcmar, Allerd Peters and Nies Marseille 'Developing a Scale to Asses Three Styles of Television Mediation: "Instructive Mediation", "Restrictive Mediation" and "Social Coviewing"' (1999) 43 *Journal of Broadcasting and Electronic Media* 52–66.
60 Nikken and Schols, op.cit., p. 3433.
61 Ibid.
62 Ingrid Paus-Hasebrink, Philip Sinner and Fabian Prochazka *Children's Online Experiences in Socially Disadvantaged Families: European Evidence and Policy Implications* (London, EU Kids Online/EU Kids III/ Reports/Disadvantaged_children.pdf)
63 Nikken and Schols, op.cit., p. 3433 citing Paus-Hasebrink, op.cit., p. 11.
64 Paus-Hasebrink et al., op.cit., pp. 8–9.
65 *Enhancing Online Safety for Children Act 2015* (Cth), s.5.
66 Roy Baker 'The "Ordinary Reasonable Person" in Defamation Law' (2003) 22(4) *Communications Law Bulleting* 20–23.
67 Ibid., p. 21
68 [1983] 2 NSWLR 682.
69 Baker, op.cit., p. 23.
70 *Harmful Digital Communications Act 2015* (NZ), s.22(1).
71 Ibid., s.22(2).
72 UNCROC, art. 8.
73 Piermarco Aroldi and Nicoletta Vittadini 'Children's Rights and Social Media: Issues and Prospects for Adoptive Families in Italy' (2017) 19(5) *New Media and Society* 741–749.
74 Ibid., p. 744.
75 Ibid.
76 Ibid., pp. 745–746.
77 Ibid., p. 746.
78 Ibid., p. 747.

Chapter 3

Social media, young people and transgression

3.1 A new family law in the age of social media

The previous chapter argued that the effect of social media has been to re-make the rules of family life. In effect, it has enabled young people to challenge many of the norms by which they have been parented, but at the same time this has led to a fear of the 'wild child' that leads the state and many adults to seek to hold children to account for their online behaviour. Part of the response on the part of the state through various regulatory agencies has been to co-opt parents in the surveillance and control of their children online. This creates a paradox in that while social media is often depicted as a means of individual expression and direct engagement, much of the state's (and as a consequence the law's) response has been about how to instil order and control in its processes. Much of this is motivated by fear *of* children and young people, though this is also often disguised as fear *for* children and young people.

The problem in all of this, however, is the 'messiness' of law for creating law and order. By this I mean that while the law can be seen as an agent of order and control, it also contains within it notions that commit to free speech, rights to participate and to be included, for example. In the context of children and young people such documents as UNCROC are grounded in this messiness – as it includes articles that would justify parental guidance and control as well as other articles that emphasise the autonomy rights of young people with no easy way of reconciling the two. There is no simple definition of 'children's rights' in this space. Autonomy for young people will often be viewed as transgression and challenge to parental and state authority. The best interests of the child have likewise often been used to deny children a voice, inclusion in matters that affect them and participation in the processes that impact their immediate and future lives on paternalistic grounds. However, this is not a matter of progression from a past time of denial of children's rights to an enlightened present. We continue to seek to decide matters for children in their best interests, and certain forms of transgression cannot be justified simply because it gives children a voice. The difficulty, it is often said, is to determine when it may be justified.

Another context for this discussion and one which flows from the positioning of debates about social media and young people within discussions about a new family law is that discussion about the nature of childhood and the rights of children is not new to the law. As is often observed in family law practice, the decisions of family courts must be highly pragmatic; otherwise, they will usually fail for not meeting the realities of the lives of the people, adults and children, involved. As the *Gillick* decision discussed in the previous chapter demonstrates, the courts have had to address the capacity of children to make their own decisions about their needs for decades, if not more. But as Michael Freeman has noted, also many decades ago, there is a tension between the protection rights of children and the autonomy rights of children that such discussion gives rise to.[1] This creates 'messy law', law often informed by ideology, values, prejudice, evidence or ignorance about child development as much as by any actual child welfare science. In many ways, this is the nature of law as a relatively autonomous institution that can decide 'the law' with or without reference to the scientific literature in an area.[2] Of course, we can aim to improve this decision-making by arguing for more informed choices, but even then, as Brennan in Marion's Case indicates, in the case of children and their best interests, at the end of the day the matter is often one of values.

For scholars in some disciplines, the matter appears to be, in part at least, the extent to which advocating for children's rights within digital environments can create a set of aspirations to meet the interests of children.[3] The concern from such perspectives is that the child is often referenced in debates about such online worlds in relation to their rights as they are affected by the loss of innocence, privacy, freedom and vulnerability[4], but less so in relation to their participation rights.[5] As stated above, this is not a new tension for the law, as cases such as *Gillick* demonstrate. And while the UNCROC may be regarded as aspirational for many in society, the reality for lawyers is that its increasing incorporation into decision-making about children gives it a practical, if no less problematic, effect. The dilemma for the law and lawyers is that the problems with such documents do not arise in relation to how many people are aware of them, or how well drafted they are in themselves as to what they mention or do not mention. Instead, for lawyers the problem with documents such as UNCROC is rather with respect to the underlying tensions about the place of children in society vis-à-vis adults and the power relationships that underpin the discussion of how they are to be interpreted. The questions for lawyers in this area are not simply about whether children have their rights (of all kinds) formally recognised in the law, but also involve asking who will interpret and define those rights to give them practical effect. The 'best interests' of the child may justify action to protect the child from harm, but this has also acted as a smokescreen to legitimate actions later regarded as against the interests of children.[6] 'Children's rights' as a concept carries similar problems in definition. The law, viewed from this vantage point, is not viewed as some neutral instrument but is produced by a system that oppresses certain groups. As Carol Smart asks in relation to the efficacy of domestic violence laws, why would one place faith in a legal system that is produced by a patriarchal society to solve the patriarchal relationships which produce violence against women?[7] In relation to the treatment of children, then, why should we expect the law that is produced by the same society that sees advantages in the marginalisation and control of children to offer the liberation of children from such treatment?

Of course, as even Smart recognises in relation to her example, this does not mean one should not support law reform in these areas for the small gains that can be made.[8] The messiness of the law means that there are often inconsistencies in how law oppresses people, including children. However, this way of looking at law does place many cautions in the path of those who believe that it might offer some way through the maze. Thus, while I would agree that children's transgression in how they use social media may change how we think about the norms in this space,[9] I am not convinced that the law can or should even accommodate this for two reasons. The first is that a children's bill of Internet rights must be interpreted, and this will depend on who conducts this process. There are no guarantees that this will produce better results for children's autonomy rights. The second reason is that once transgressive practices are accommodated within the law, they are no longer transgressive, and thus the capacity for thinking beyond the boundaries may be lost. In the following part of this chapter, then, I will begin to explore the extent to which the practice of social media and the law can embrace various forms of transgression as legitimate on the part of young people, and how that might impact on accountability mechanisms within society with the proviso that the role of law in this regard must be heavily qualified.

3.2 Challenging concepts of childhood through online behaviour

We can no longer say that the law fails to take into account the autonomy rights of children and young people when deciding upon matters that affect them. However, as we have seen there is little consistency of purpose or focus in this regard. Clearly, social media and digital communications are changing the basis upon which we assess the relationships of adults and children, but this remains a work in progress. The point has been made that family courts by necessity have had to engage with the way in which social media is altering intra-family relations. For example, in the Australian case of *Niu and Maple*[10] the family court had to decide parenting arrangements for a twelve-year-old child. Under Australian family law there are various matters that the court must consider when deciding such cases. These include 'any views expressed by the child' (giving the views such weight as the child's maturity and understanding, for example, might indicate)[11] and the capacity of each of the child's parents to provide for the needs of the child.[12] In this case, each parent wished to have sole parental responsibility for the child and for the child to live with them. This requires a rebuttal of the presumption in Australian family law that it is in the best interests of the child that the parents have equal, shared parental responsibility for the child.[13] Thus, the court had to assess whether it was in the child's best interests for only one parent to have parental responsibility.

To determine this question, the court in *Niu and Maple* had to assess each parent against the considerations in the Act. In assessing the father's relationship with the child, the judge Cleary, J, commented on the father's oversight of the child's social media postings:

> The fact that the father has installed tracking software on his daughter's telephone to identify messages sent and social media postings, indicates that he does not have the easy trusting relationship that he suggests. I have no doubt that the father loves his daughter and wants to do whatever he can for her to make her life enjoyable and successful. I am not entirely satisfied that he has the capacity to meet her needs in terms of supporting her relationship with her mother, allowing her to be completely candid with him and enforcing reasonable age appropriate rules.[14]

Later in the judgment he also commented on this again:

> The father is clearly anxious about the coming years of the child's adolescence. He has installed spyware on the child's telephone and has described her behaviour as 'sneaky, secretive and deceptive'. He is critical of her for 'not using her own brain'. He considers she is overinfluenced by the mother. However it is the mother's ability to talk to her daughter and to allow emotions, including anger and defiance, to be expressed and then addressed; that is more likely to assist the child through the coming years.[15]

The child had also expressed a view that she wanted to live with one parent only instead of having an equal time arrangement and that she did not fear losing contact with the other parent as she could always ring them when she wanted to.[16] In determining this was the view of the child, Cleary commented:

> I accept that this would be the child's genuine view. She has her own mobile telephone and is a confident user of that phone and of social

> media. Further, approaching 12 years, her attachments are solid with each of her parents and she has no fear and there is no reason for her to have a fear; that either parent would withdraw from her life, quite the contrary.[17]

In the result, the court decided that the child would live with the mother solely, but it is of interest for present purposes as to how the case was influenced by the online and digital communication behaviour of both the father and the daughter. With respect to the father, his use of tracking and monitoring software made him look suspicious and less trusting of his daughter at a time in her life when her developmental needs might be best served, it could be said, by the development of trust. On the daughter's side, her 'digital confidence' appears to have reassured the judge about her capacity for both independent thought and a capacity to sustain contact with the non-resident parent. It should also be emphasised that this case involved a twelve-year-old young person.

What is immediately apparent in this case is a conflict between the narrative of control and monitoring of a child's online activity as good parenting discussed in the previous chapter and a legal construction here that makes such surveillance appear to be that of a suspicious and less worthy parent. It also says something about how the use of technology can permit children and young people to claim agency and for 'digital confidence' to arm them with the assurance characteristics of a mature person. Digital communication behaviour thus may shift the boundaries of how legal judgments are to be made about children and young people's decision-making capacity.

However, this does not reduce the messiness of the law but merely adds to it. For a start, the conflict identified above with this aspect of family law and the earlier control of children online through legislation, rules and guidance suggests different parts of law can have different constructs of the child. Within family law, there is also no simple consensus on the decision-making capacity of children. In the High Court appeal in the decision of *RCB*[18] in which the court had to consider whether four sisters aged from 9 to 15 should have been provided with separate legal representation in a *Hague Convention on International Child Abduction* case, one High Court judge, commenting on the argument of the children's aunt that the children should have been able to instruct a lawyer to in effect put their views to the court, said:

> This contention assumes that each child can be equated with a capable adult. It assumes that each child was capable of giving instructions to the ends described in the contention. . . .
>
> These assumptions are factually false in respect of many children. And they are legally incoherent in respect of most children. Contrary to the assumptions, unlike most capable adults, a child is almost invariably

> under the control of other people who owe the child legal duties. Inevitably, that child is vulnerable to their influence.[19]

It is difficult to reconcile this view of the child with what was said in the earlier decision that focused on the digital confidence of the child. But it does underscore how competing conceptions of the child continue to operate in the same area of law and ultimately can perhaps only be explained by the different values, knowledge and understanding of children held by the key actors in such decision-making, which are often subject to challenge and re-assessment. This leads to the important role of transgression in online activity in establishing new norms and ultimately changing, qualifying or even bypassing the law in order for competing narratives of children and young people to be heard.

3.3 Transgression, digital third spaces and the re-making of law

What is of interest in these case examples is how the practices of new media begin to shape and inform our judgments about the child's best interests, participation rights and childhood. This is not to say that this development is linear and progressive. As the last case example indicates, older views of childhood live on through older generations. They also illustrate the potential for change in this area through the pushing of boundaries and challenges to older conceptions of the child or young person and define what is to be meant by a child's right to be included and involved in matters that affect them. However, the law is not the only discipline that has had to address this area.

The re-shaping of urban environments by young people's transgressive and often-illegal acts has a long history in urban planning and design literature. Skateboarding is one example of an activity that young people engage in and in doing so occupy urban spaces in ways that challenge established norms about the use of space and which by the nature of those activities often 'annoy' others. Iain Borden has written of such young people as in effect 'urban warriors' who are 'rethinking the city through their actions'.[20] To achieve this, 'by highlighting conflicts (especially private property and social use, rational efficiencies and social space), skaters use their position of weakness (youth) to irritate authority and convention, thereby making comments about the whole nature of the city'.[21] There are clear parallels between youth using urban space to disrupt and critique the conventions of the city and young people's use of social media that re-thinks cyberspace as more than a new form of marketing for established corporate and other powerful interests. In fact, young people's use of social media to disrupt in this manner even flows into how the city is read. Tom Mordue says of cities:

> in a quest to stimulate private consumption, modern urban development and spatial management have eroded participatory

> public spaces in cities by encouraging economic individualism at the expense of social intermingling and spontaneous contact between strangers.[22]

Written before social media 'took off', this passage is chillingly prophetic in terms of foretelling the challenge that social media presents to the privatisation of public space and, one might also say, the privatisation of public discourse. Social media, seen as an instrument of challenge and transgression of boundaries, may threaten many powerful interests that control the norms within the media and certain other spaces. The real contest then may well not be between 'good' and 'bad' uses of social media, but between those who view it as a means to bring strangers together and those who wish it to be a simple marketing tool. Robin Stevens et al. also connect young people's use of social media with urban studies literature that values the role of bringing people together in order to deal with social exclusion and marginalisation.[23] Drawing on the work of Ray Oldenburg[24] and his notion of 'third places' (that is, those places in cities that provide support and comfort after home and work), Stevens et al. see social media sites as a third place for disadvantaged youth.[25] These digital third spaces

> provide both personal and social good, contributing to individual connectedness and a sense of refuge while promoting civic responsibility, community maintenance, and revitalization . . . These spaces are still clearly located within an existing geographic community and are easily accessible. Ideally, these online spaces are welcoming and allow participants to feel immersed in such a way that the computer-mediated environment feels secondary.[26]

Stevens et al. then pose the question, what are the benefits obtained and threats posed by such spaces?[27] Their conclusion is that 'social media has the potential to help youth overcome social disconnection that can result from neighborhood disorder'.[28] They found that social media sites were connected to the local area of the youth surveyed and so merged the offline and online worlds. This did create problems in that threats in the local area could then play out on social media. This drama – on Facebook in particular – could then spill over into violence in their real world.[29] Young women were also sexually exposed and bullied online, which created more disadvantage for them, but withdrawing from Facebook meant the loss of other benefits from remaining on the site.[30] The benefits of social media included 'that it serves an accessible communications channel to transfer information and could be used to reduce communication inequalities', even if the information being shared was often negative.[31] But overall, Stevens et al. saw social media as having more potential benefits than actual benefits for disadvantaged youth:

> Although there is potential to view social media as a digital third space, the evidence from this community of youth does not resonate with previous research that suggested social capital could be created through online community integration. Rather, Facebook primarily operates as a digital community where social problems are magnified. While the amplification of social problems occurs in other communities, in disadvantaged neighborhoods, the stakes can be higher with violent consequences. As such, providing disadvantaged communities greater access to social media alone is not a sufficient strategy to ensure equal access to the benefits of being networked.[32]

Their final remarks are for the need to better understand the differences in the way social media is used and what it includes across different groups of young people.[33] Disadvantaged youth, reflecting their lives online, may increase their marginalisation and create despair instead of building resilience. This has a particular resonance for those calling for digital rights for young people online and their connection with creating resilient youth. The actual use of social media by diverse groups of young people means that we need to have a more nuanced understanding of social media than the 'good' versus 'bad' narrative we currently create around it.

Zizi Papacharissi explains this in terms of how we tend to understand new technology around 'the discursive polarities of utopia and dystopia'.[34] However, in a somewhat contrary vein to the conclusions of Stevens et al. that more evidence-based understanding of young people's use of social media is necessary, Papacharissi also points out that the myths of new technology also have great value in that 'the power of the myth lies not in its ability to reflect reality, but rather in the promise it holds for escaping or reinventing it'.[35] She argues that while we need to 'ground our expectations of technology in reality, it is equally necessary to acknowledge the myths that drive our proclivity to use it'.[36]

The relevance of Papacharissi's observations for the law is profound. Law, as we have seen, is a messy institution that does not simply and directly respond to social realities or scientific findings. It is heavily influenced by these myths – of what we believe to be the 'reality' as far as social media is concerned in this instance. The answer to changing the law often has as much to do with changing the narrative as it has to do with making more 'informed' policy decisions that result in 'better' regulatory frameworks. It is probably as important that we understand the myths that surround new technologies and their connections to young people as it is that we understand how young people are using social media. Much research on social media appears to count the numbers of hours spent by young people on social media sites, or the number of pictures, sexual or otherwise, they are exposed to, and so on. But this has as much relevance for understanding young people and social media as knowing the number of football matches that are played each weekend tells us how people feel about the sport. What we need to know is how the fears, fantasies and future hopes of young people are fuelled by that use, which is of course impossible to simply count. For the law to properly respond to young people and social media, we need to rethink what this media *means* to young people. If it promises the centrality of transgression and challenge – even if not always achieved – then how should we understand that practice in shaping the law's response?

3.4 Social media and spontaneity: political and legal transgression as a way of creating an identity

Article 8 of the United Nations Convention on the Rights of the Child articulates the right of a child to have the preservation of their identity respected, 'including nationality, name and family relations as recognized by law without unlawful interference'. Article 29(1)(c) provides that the education of a child will be directed towards '[t]he development of respect for the child's parents, his or her own cultural identity, language and values, for the national values of the country in which the child is living, the country from which he or she may originate, and for civilizations different from his or her own'. The use of the term 'identity' in these articles appears to be much narrower than the way 'identity' is often expressed in society. Often, identity refers to the way we feel about ourselves, or in relation to aspects of our inner self such as our gender, sexuality or passions. The law tends to struggle with these more intimate aspects of self, and often identity in law focuses more on outward manifestations of identity such as name, ethnic origin or family status, such as the UNCROC articles above tend to focus on. For present purposes, we might understand the law's approach to identity as a more 'traditional' form whereas much of the extra-legal literature on identity and digital technology refers to a post-modern form of identity that is 'fluid, non-stable and nomadic'.[37] While other disciplines discuss young people engaging in 'identity tourism', exploring alternative identities in a way that liberates and empowers them,[38] more conservative adult interests see these 'explorations' as making those young people vulnerable to the agendas of corporate interests that control media imagery and advertising.[39] Such interests often attempt to co-opt the law to enforce child protection regimes against such identity activity.

It is to other articles of UNCROC that we have to look to see how the rights expressed in them affect the development of the child's identity in the more expansive and non-traditional way. Thus, ensuring children have a right to have their own views and to express them;[40] the right to freedom of expression;[41] the right to freedom of thought, conscience and religion;[42] the right to freedom of association and assembly;[43] and protection of privacy, family, home or correspondence and from attacks on honour and reputation,[44] and in recognition of the centrality of mass media in society and assurance that children have 'access to information and material from a diversity of national and international sources, especially those aimed at the promotion of his or her social, spiritual and moral well-being and physical and mental health',[45] UNCROC holds that all these have implications for a young person's identity. The clear import of the rights and protections contained in these articles is that they feed the child's sense of who they are, allowing them to develop their identity and define their being.

The need to facilitate the development of the child's sense of identity does also exist in specific laws in some places. In the state of Victoria, Australia, the Child Wellbeing and Safety Act 2005 contains provisions that require the providers of services to children to 'acknowledge and be respectful of the child's individual identity, circumstances and cultural identity and be responsive to the particular needs of the child'.[46] This Act does not create any legal rights for anyone,[47] but this provision does indicate the possibility of asserting the child's identity rights in a broader sense within the law.

The point of this discussion is that children's identity is formed in various ways that often require the child to have access to spaces to explore their hopes and needs that define who they are or who they want to be. danah boyd notes the manner in which many spaces within which children have traditionally engaged such exploration of themselves in relation to others have become privatised, subject to greater parental and legal control or placed under increased surveillance.[48] Some of these changes have occurred because of the perceived risks posed to young people by strangers, some have occurred because of the fear of young people loitering in public spaces and some are due to the increased emphasis on young people's time being structured so as not to waste time and ensure their future.[49] As boyd notes, this leaves little opportunity for 'casual sociality'[50] and causes young people to turn to social media for this purpose.[51]

In effect, the use of the law to exclude young people from public (physical) spaces has pushed them towards social media. Child curfew laws,[52] child safety orders,[53] and other forms of anti-social behaviour orders frequently have a spatial element to them that prohibits the young person from being in certain spaces at certain times, or at all. In Victoria, proposed reforms to deal with a concern in the increase of youth crime include a youth control order that will provide the court with the option of restricting the places the young person can be in or at what times, as well as directing 'that the child not use specified social media if this is required for the protection of the community'.[54] While there has been some support for the orders, which are characterised as intensive supervision, others are less sure of their need.[55] Regardless of their efficacy for criminal justice purposes, it is the manner in which the increased legal regulation of young people in space, including cyberspace, creates anxieties for those young people with respect to their access to their own spaces that is of concern. It may be a fair point to consider how young people act online towards others, but the legal criteria for determining what is appropriate or what is 'required for the protection of the community' is vague, and a failure to assert some right on behalf of young people to such spaces as a part of their identity formation may lead many young people to abandon the spaces altogether for fear of being criminalised or labelled as deviant and so affecting their future well-being.

One question is whether young people are capable of self-regulation of such spaces online as a means of having legitimacy in claiming a right to such spaces.[56] The problem is that how adults view their social media activities will often tend to be that of seeing young people transgress boundaries of what is appropriate, whereas young people, often aware of the risks, regard their online behaviour as necessary participation in public life.[57] In other words, they are giving effect to their right to participate in matters that they consider affect them. Rights in this sense are powerful and valuable commodities as they require the powerful to act. They challenge the established order and empower the powerless to claim space.[58] Much of the current debates on children's rights in digital environments misunderstand this sense of a right. The promotion of 'digital resilience' in children,[59] for example, while important for children, is more about making them 'strong' to stand up to what others do to them online. A right to participate and express oneself online must also include the capacity to be annoying, even 'really annoying' at times, and to claim this is a right. Rights asserted against powerful interests will never be defined as 'appropriate' by those interests, and it is highly likely that at times it will be deemed necessary to prohibit such behaviour 'to protect the community'. Sometimes there is no 'balance' between the right to do something and the responsibility to others in how it is done. Instead, there are difficult and uneasy choices. Transgression is often an important part of the legal process because it establishes the boundaries before change occurs. This is apparent in some recent examples of young people's use of social media where it became part of acts of transgression which called into question the established order.

3.5 Social media and protest: the Arab Spring, occupy and digital rights

In this section, I am going to develop the argument that current calls for a digital charter of rights for children may make little sense. Instead I am going to argue that if we are serious about empowering young people online, we need to better articulate and understand their rights under such documents as the UNCROC.

What do I mean by this? Demands to articulate the digital rights of children and young people carry the likelihood that children and young people simply being active online becomes the achievement rather than any assessment of the content of what they are doing in terms of social outcomes. As the tendency to see the online world in terms of 'good' content and 'bad' content has shown, much of the law's purpose (amongst other institutions) seems directed towards steering children away from the bad and towards the good. However, this does not interrogate the nature of that content and any contested meanings about it. It is more likely that what is termed 'good' in this context is that which reinforces certain romantic notions of childhood, supports the ongoing power of adults to determine what is in a child's best interests and, as we begin to see in more recent years, does not worry governments with challenges to their moral authority. There are parallels here with children's participation in urban planning. For many practitioners and scholars in this field, the test of advancing children's rights in planning is whether they are 'really listened' to or 'really included' in decision-making. It is often not considered what this actually means in many disciplines. To be really included in urban planning and design requires children and young people to be informed about urban planning and design so they can actively participate.[60] Instead of considering the various ways in which children can 'participate', it is too often assumed that if children are talking they have something to say.

Papacharissi discusses how new technologies have allowed us to feel a part of events, such as during the Occupy Movement or the Arab Spring. Her argument is that social media allows the participants to tell a story and draw us into their experience. However, this creates a feeling about such events but does not necessarily mean those who are drawn in to it fully understand or are informed about the meaning of what is occurring. It is an affective connection, as Papacharissi describes it, that has to be carefully analysed to understand how and whether at all it leads to social change.[61] However, for her the research questions are not to do with 'whether these are indeed social media revolutions, and whether tweeting the revolutions can in fact make or break a revolution in the making', which is where popular debate is stuck.[62] For her, the more interesting area for enquiry relates to the content of social media. Her work indicates that 'the internet pluralizes but does not inherently democratize spheres of social, cultural, political, or economic activity'.[63] In other words, while social media may facilitate radical social movements, it is other factors that create such movements, or as Papacharissi puts it, 'the historically singular interplay of the various sociocultural, economic, and political conditions' create the impact of what media facilitates.[64] She utilises the concept of 'affect' to explain the characteristics and nature of new media. That is, social media creates a feeling about a narrative, a feeling of engagement with, say, a political movement.[65] She adds,

> online activity, however, cannot be confused with impact. Yet, depending on context, online activity may introduce primary disruptions to the stability of powerful hierarchies that grant a movement momentum, which may accumulate over time. On a secondary level, online activity may energize disorganized crowds and/or facilitate the formation of networked publics around communities, actual and imagined . . . These publics are activated and sustained by feelings of belonging and solidarity, however fleeting or permanent those feelings may be . . . This is perhaps why the influence of social media in uprisings that take place in autocratic regimes frequently persists despite attempts to shut down the networked infrastructure that supports them.[66]

Her work engages with a sense that the use of social media is not the end in itself but that it instead generates a 'feeling of community' that is part of a wider process of engagement but does not necessarily lead to real change or community unless other social factors are at work. For political movements such as Occupy or the Arab Spring, creating a narrative through social media and gaining many 'likes' does not necessarily translate into a real revolution or change in society. Thus, while 'affect' is somewhat emotional, this is not to trivialise its importance as it is recognised that such feelings are part of the process of how people understand information.[67] But it is also important to realise that 'affects typically do not connect to behaviors in a linearly causal way'.[68] The challenge for the law in this analysis of social media is how to understand the way in which social media impacts on society. If we are seeking to regulate social media through law, then what exactly are we regulating? Papacharissi describes affect – which characterises social media – as something that is of a 'fluid and visceral nature', which makes it difficult to understand but at the same time is a useful concept that 'may be a useful component in interpreting forces that drive co-occurrences moving in patterns defined by network complexity'.[69] As she says, it assists in understanding 'non-linear linear relationships and processes through which intensity augments communicative patterns in a manner that is not linearly causal, but non-linearly substantial'.[70]

It is in this understanding of social media that we see the fundamental mistake and problem in characterising social media as having 'good' and 'bad' aspects such that the aim of the state, with respect to young people's use of it, must be to steer them towards the positive features. If young people are to have digital rights to use social media, then that right must be one that acknowledges that 'use' of social media is not the end in itself. Access to it is a right because of the conditions it creates for a range of other activity that may, or may not, flourish and from which young people may enhance, or harm, their lives. The law, to date, worries about the regulation of online 'activities' as if it can identify the harmful acts to target and eliminate. But social media is more a 'space' within which events take place, and no one can say for certain how or whether at all those events will lead to positive or negative outcomes. It would be like banning playgrounds because a child fell off the swing. This can happen, but there are a host of other activities that do not involve such harm. And of course, even the act of falling off a swing can teach a child many things about the consequences of one's actions.

What this leads to is a claim that children and young people must have a right to access social media to engage in challenging, transgressive or annoying behaviour, however described. It is only in those spaces that – risky as they are – social change may take place. But as Papacharissi demonstrates, this does not mean that such change must or will occur for social media to be deemed worthy of such access for children and young people. This will depend on a host of other social factors. However, unless children have the right to enter this space to see what happens next, then as an avenue of potential change in their lives it will be cut off to them. Papacharissi also refers to the seminal work of Mary Douglas, *Purity and Danger*.[71] Douglas, according to Papacharissi, 'contrasted the concepts of pollution, dirt, and contagion with the sacred, clean, and taboo to show how hierarchies of order are structured upon rituals devised to recognize the potency of disorder'.[72] She continues:

> Disruptions, caused by disorderly expressions that do not align with established rituals, attain power through contagion. Power takes form in the shape of contagion by polluting the established order through disruptions, which are ephemeral until they become ritualized and thus normalized into the ritualized order.[73]

This process of change indicates how disorder creates new forms of order. It is within the boundary spaces that change emerges:[74]

> Douglas suggests that margins are dangerous because that is where the structure of ideas, bodies, or thought is most vulnerable and less formed. Affective contagion is marginal because its not yet formed shape affords it potential for subversion. Once framed, contagion becomes categorized, formed, and embedded within a system of rituals. Unformed, it derives power from its potential, which is where affect lies.[75]

The value of these perspectives is that it suggests that social media does not create social change but facilitates it. The direction in which social media will develop communities is at the outset unknown, which is highly problematic for law. It is easier to say that various risks will come from posting your naked image online and to assert the taboos of shame and disgust to support this than to consider that while such behaviour may have harmful consequences for the individual, it might also create the circumstances where a person in posting their image online discovers their sexual power or confidence. Thus, the Arab Spring was not a creation of social media, but the postings about it did weave a narrative that led to a deeper questioning about various political regimes.

This returns us to Donnison's view of the value of rights. If the reason for possessing a right is to challenge those with power, then notions that children's rights in the digital world are to provide them with 'resilience' is a right that seems rooted in the view that bad things can happen *to* young people online and so they must be empowered to deal with what is targeted at them. But if providing children and young people with digital rights is about ensuring they can, through digital spaces, pursue their right to an identity, or free expression, or free assembly, then we do have to become smarter at understanding exactly what those rights are purporting to guarantee. The idea that the empowerment of young people online is directed towards ensuring they pursue 'good' and virtuous activities that do not jeopardise their future employment prospects – the often-said 'watch what you post on Facebook; it may be seen by potential employers' refrain – may have merit, but how do we place the claim that young people in pursuit of their right to free expression have the right to go online and express their individual or group identity, visually or otherwise, even if that makes other people uncomfortable? If the right to identity is important, then why does that not qualify what others can do with those posts in protection of those rights?

3.6 Imagining disorder: young people and the right to be 'really annoying' online

There is no question that much activity on social media is simply 'annoying'. The point has already been made that much of the law's focus on social media is to address the perception that harm to privacy, reputation and self-esteem can occur in this space, and so it must be consequently regulated as not to do so would be breaching the victims' rights in various ways. Much of this aspect of online behaviour can be linked with the view that social media has the potential to encourage incivility. Two questions arise here. The first is whether it should be a concern of the law to regulate for good manners if the actual focus in this area is the problem of incivility. The second question is whether the right to free expression and to be 'yourself' online should qualify any form of legal intervention into this domain.

The history of legal regulation in this manner has some of its history tied up in the activity of 'hacking'. Until 1990, in England there was no general offence making hacking into a computer unlawful. The Computer Misuse Act 1990 created the offence of unauthorised access to computer material;[76] in effect, this criminalised merely looking at data stored on another person's computer without permission. The Act followed from a report by the English Law Commission that considered the need for such an offence. A working paper produced by the Commission gave a number of arguments for and against such an offence. In favour of the offence, the Law Commission said that one argument in favour

> acknowledges the importance of computers for society as a whole and suggests that those who use and rely on computers may be inhibited from making full use of them, if they fear that others might obtain unauthorised access to information held on them. For this reason, it is in the public interest that society must try to deter hacking either generally, or at the very least in respect of computers holding certain kinds of information.[77]

Another reason advanced in favour of creating an offence was that the hacker could inadvertently damage the computer or the data being looked at. On the other side were the arguments that, there being no general right of privacy in English law, without some aggravating aspect to the act it was not the sort of behaviour usually subject to a criminal sanction.[78] The Commission noted that '[i]nformation is not property in English law . . . and it is no offence, as such, to read someone else's correspondence or files'.[79] The other argument against creating the offence related to the difficulty of enforcement, and although the Commission noted that in cases where the harm was great then such difficulty may not be a good reason for not creating an offence, however, where the harm was not so great then creating a criminal offence may be less justified. The working paper then noted that '[i]t is arguable that mere hacking falls into the latter category'.[80]

The description 'mere hacking' is illuminating as it is consistent with another comment in the working paper that the Law Commission

> [shared] the view of the Scottish Law Commission that at present there is insufficient evidence of the scale and consequences of computer misuse to conclude that it 'would of itself suggest an impending crisis of a kind that demanded prompt legislative action'.[81]

However, by the time the New Zealand Law Commission looked at the same need for a criminal offence in this area in 1999,[82] the view was that unauthorised access to computers was 'a serious problem'.[83] The New Zealand Law Commission then went on to articulate a number of reasons for creating a criminal offence for unauthorised access that resonate with justifications given today for regulating social media. The New Zealand Law Commission identified the public interest in the use of computers and the concern that unless penalised, 'reprehensible conduct' would inhibit the use of computers.[84] The Commission also identified the harm that unauthorised access could do, even though as we have seen the laws being proposed at this time did not carry with them any requirement for harm in addition to unauthorised access for an offence to be committed. What informed debates at this time was the particular vulnerability of powerful interests storing their information in ways that could be accessed without any breaches of physical security. Simply looking at data during such access was not the concern; it was the potential to commit harm that was being punished under the proposals (and subsequent laws) at the time. The New Zealand Commission identified these interests clearly:

> It is necessary to protect commercial information which may be of immense value. For many businesses operating in this environment, the information which is stored on their computer system will be its most valuable commodity. It is important to recognise and protect the intellectual capital of information stored on a computer. The importance of information as a business asset in the knowledge economy may justify redefinition of information as a property right for both civil and criminal law purposes. In essence, it is both the information and the systems which we are proposing to protect in our recommendations in this report.[85]

The NZ Commission also discussed the main argument against the creation of a criminal offence of unauthorised access: such information, viewed in other ways – for example, simply reading it over the shoulder of another person – would not be an offence.[86] However, although it would be an anomaly to create an offence for one form of viewing but not another, it was felt that 'the public interest in encouraging the use of computers and in protecting the community from the misuse of computers outweighs the concern about this anomaly'.[87] However, the actual justification for a new offence at the time was more to do with what a hacker *might* do once they had gained access rather than what they *did* do. The narrative around unauthorised access thus became one about potential harm rather than actual harm:

> The consequences of unauthorised access, in the digital age, go far beyond what is possible with paper-based or manual systems. Unlike access achieved by other means, where access is achieved by unauthorised computer access, the person who achieves access may use the computer to amend or otherwise use the information. The possible consequences of amending information stored on a computer are wide-ranging and serious. Such conduct could affect the country's

> economy and the lives of many people. Also, a person who gains unauthorised access to information stored in a computer may be tempted to go on and commit more serious activities such as theft or destruction of data.[88]

Of course, the creation of a simple offence of unauthorised access also would mean that there would be no need to prove actual theft or destruction of data to prove the offence. Given the powerful interests that relied on such forms of data storage, this would make their lives a lot easier if their cyber-security was breached. Once the breach occurs, an offence has been committed. But what is also noteworthy is that in these narratives of around 30 years ago, discussion of accountability and scrutiny are missing. So too is any concern – as the NZ Commission accepts – in creating inconsistencies in the law. The moral panic about what *could* happen online dramatically pushed aside hundreds of years of legal principle. In other words, there was a danger – not discussed or noted at the time – that people accused of such a crime would be punished not for what they did, but for what they could have done.

The reform of this area of the law was remarkably similar in the United States and has confirmed many of the fears associated with the manner in which the laws have been drafted. The impetus to reform in that country has been stated to be the 1983 movie *WarGames*.[89] The storyline in that movie involved a teenage hacker accessing NORAD's computer system and almost starting World War III.[90] This ignited a moral panic about hackers and what harm they could cause, leading a House of Representatives committee to describe the movie as a 'realistic representation of the automatic dialing and access capabilities of the personal computer'.[91] This led to the passing of the Computer Fraud and Abuse Act 1984 which initially only applied to bank- and defense-related computer systems,[92] but over the following years it was extended to eventually include all computers and increased penalties, including long prison sentences. Stephanie Schulte argues that the criminalisation occurred at a time when 'Cold War fears of Soviet power and technological supremacy converged with anxieties about teenaged rebellion'.[93] In particular, she notes that the referencing of *WarGames* in the debate 'engaged a "teenaged technology" discourse, which cast both internet technology itself and its users as rebellious teenagers in need of parental control'.[94] This discourse, according to Schulte, enabled government to cast the regulation of the Internet in terms of parental guidance rather than the 'suppression of democracy and innovation'.[95] In time, this narrative evolved further into a discourse that regarded computers and the Internet as part of a productive economy, provided they were controlled by responsible adults.[96] As she writes, 'what was conceptualized – in popular culture, news media and policy images in particular – as an out-of-control technology jockeyed by rebellious teenagers was re-imagined as a "user-friendly" tool controlled by productive adult "users" '.[97]

We continue to play out these same themes in the age of social networking and social media. Schulte writes somewhat[98] optimistically about the way in which social media might play a role in social change. In the context of discussions of the Arab Spring and what is sometimes referred to as the 'Facebook Revolution', she acknowledges that there was even at the beginning of that period criticism about how deep such change would be in relying on social networking, in that this could encourage in effect armchair revolutionaries and rely on 'weak ties'. However, she also notes that there was a successful narrative constructed that portrayed social media as democratic and participatory:

> As blogs gave way to microblogging and other social media, companies like Twitter capitalized on these visions of blogging and mapped visions of political legitimacy and authenticity onto a new (but related) technological practice. Ultimately, all of these shifts together worked to reconfigure new media political participation as idealized and revitalized democratic civic engagement and was part of a larger policy shift toward governmental 'transparency'.[99]

Her conclusion is that in that sense, describing events as the 'Facebook Revolution' made sense.[100] Whether or not the narrative that was constructed about the role of social media in the Arab Spring (or the Occupy Movement) was completely accurate with respect to its influence, the narrative nevertheless gained some currency. While this gives rise to some hope that progressive social change might be furthered by social media communities, the lesson from the history of hacking is also important to remember. It is not contested that the Arab Spring and social media nexus were driven by a younger generation, and that their aim was to contest the power of certain elites in their countries. In this, they were seen as modern-day hackers, young people rebelling against those with power and prepared to do harm online to achieve that change. Instead of turning the new technology to productive use in the service of the state and global capitalism, they were using it for 'ill'. They were in effect being 'really annoying'.

3.7 Social media, the law and challenging order

There are a number of lessons for understanding law's relationship with social media in this discussion. The law's 'messiness' in addressing the various strands that inform narratives of social media arises because those same narratives are also messy. Indeed, Schulte says of her project that it is 'to illuminate the messy processes of culture and history as they occur, or as ideas, policies, cultural actors, agents, and artifacts operate in tandem, in opposition, and by indirection'.[101] The simple fact is that aspects of social media can be seen as democratic and participatory, while powerful economic interests would much rather see its primary function as a marketing tool. The law cannot easily mediate between the two of them as they are often in opposition and 'balance' is not always possible. What the law can do, however, is ensure that while the protection of economic interests may be a legitimate part of its function, so too is the guarantee of free expression, dissent and assembly (or networking).

The history of the regulation of hacking shows how a moral panic about a perceived teenage rebellion along with other social anxieties of the time can combine to create laws that favour some interests exclusively and create vague and unclear offences that over time simply broaden to catch more and more perceived threats to the prevailing social order. The challenge for society in the age of social media is whether history will repeat, and social media will be constructed again as a youth rebellion that justifies increased parental guidance to ensure that those young people use new technologies 'appropriately' and 'productively'. Or will the law intervene to ensure at least that alternative narratives are created and at the very least people will be empowered sufficiently to have some choice as to how they define 'appropriate' in this context? In other words, will the law narrow the focus or embrace and defend a more diverse understanding of the uses to which social media can be put?

Notes

1 Michael D.A Freeman *The Rights and Wrongs of Children* (London, F. Pinter, 1983).
2 King and Piper, op.cit.
3 See e.g. Sonia Livingstone and Amanda Third 'Children and Young People's Rights in the Digital Age: An Emerging Agenda' (2017) 19(5) *New Media and Society* 657–670.
4 Ibid., p. 660.
5 Ibid. passim.
6 See e.g. *Re Gault* 387 U.S. 1 (1967), United States Supreme Court.
7 Carol Smart *Feminism and the Power of Law* (New York, Routledge, 1989).
8 Ibid.
9 Livingstone and Third, op. cit.
10 [2014] FamCA 421.
11 Family Law Act 1975 (Cth.), s.60CC(3)(a).
12 Ibid., s.60CC(3)(f).
13 Ibid., s.61DA.
14 *Niu and Maple* [2014] FamCA 421 at para.100.
15 Ibid., para.145.
16 Ibid., paras. 136, 138.
17 Ibid., para.139.
18 *RCB as Litigation Guardian of EKV, CEV, CIV and LRV v The Honourable Justice Colin James Forrest* [2012] HCA 47.

19 Ibid., paras. 51, 52, per Heydon, J.
20 Iain Borden *Skateboarding, Space and the City: Architecture and the Body* (Oxford and New York, Berg, 2001), p. 228.
21 Ibid., p. 246.
22 Tom Mordue 'Tourism, Urban Governance and Public Space' (2007) 26(4) *Leisure Studies* 447–462.
23 Robin Stevens, Stacia Gilliard-Matthews, Jamie Dunaev, Marcus K. Woods and Bridgette M. Brawner 'The Digital Hood: Social Media Use Among Youth in Disadvantaged Neighborhoods' (2017) 19(6) *New Media and Society* 950–967.
24 Ray Oldenburg *The Great Good Place: Cafes, Coffee Shops, Bookstores, Bars, Hair Salons and Other Hangouts at the Heart of a Community 2nd edn* (New York, Marlowe, 1999).
25 Stevens et al., p. 951.
26 Ibid.
27 Ibid.
28 Ibid., p. 962.
29 Ibid.
30 Ibid., p. 963.
31 Ibid.
32 Ibid., p. 964 (references omitted).
33 Ibid.
34 Zizi A. Papacharissi *A Private Sphere: Democracy in a Digital Age* (Cambridge, Polity Press, 2010), p. 7.
35 Ibid., p. 8.
36 Ibid.
37 Kristina Abiala and Patrock Hernwall 'Tweens Negotiating Identity Online – Swedish Girls' and Boys' Reflections on Online Experiences' (2013) 16(8) *Journal of Youth Studies* 951–969, citing: Sherry Turkle, *Life on the Screen: Identity in the Age of the Internet* (London, Weidenfeld and Nicolson, 1995); Rosi Braidotti *Nomadic Subjects: Embodiment and Sexual Difference in Contemporary Feminist Theory* (New York, Columbia University Press, 1994); Helen Kennedy 'Beyond Anonymity, or Future Directions for Internet Identity Research'(2006) 8(6) *New Media Society* 859–876; Gil Valentine 'Theorizing and Researching Intersectionality: A Challenge for Feminist Geography' (2007) 59(1) *The Professional Geographer* 10–21; Donna Haraway, *Simians, Cyborgs, and Women: The Reinvention of Nature* (London, Routledge, 1991); B. Holm Sørensen ''Chat – identitet, krop og kultur' [Chat – Identity, Body and Culture] in B. Holm Sørensen (ed.) *Chat: Leg, identitet, socialitet og læring* [Chat: Play, Identity, Sociality, and Learning] (Ko¨penhamn, Gads forlag, 2001), pp. 15–36.
38 Abiala and Hernwall, op.cit., p. 955.
39 Ibid.
40 UNCROC, art. 12.
41 Ibid., art. 13.
42 Ibid., art. 14.
43 Ibid., art. 15.
44 Ibid., art. 16.
45 Ibid., art. 17.
46 *Child Wellbeing and Safety Act 2005* (Vic), s.5(3)(b).
47 Ibid., s.4.
48 danah boyd *It's Complicated: The Social Lives of Networked Teens* (Yale University Press, Kindle Edition, 2014) (Kindle Locations 1448–1449).

49 boyd and others about structured time for young people. (Alison James and Prout)
50 boyd, op.cit., location 1489.
51 Ibid., location1496.
52 Such laws exist or have existed in various jurisdictions and at various levels (e.g. at a local level or State/national level) e.g. Crime and Disorder Act 1998 (UK), ss.14 (now repealed). They can also exist at an informal level, e.g. as a condition of entry to a shopping centre by in effect prohibiting children's presence after a certain time unless accompanied by an adult/guardian.
53 Crime and Disorder Act 1998 (UK), s.11.
54 *Children and Justice Legislation Amendment (Youth Justice Reform) Bill 2017*, cl.13, proposed new *Children, Youth and Families Act 2005*, s.409F.
55 See e.g. Melissa Davey '"What Is the Evidence?" Commissioner Questions Victoria's Youth Justice Crackdown' *The Guardian (Australia)* 4 July, 2017 www.guardian.com, accessed 4 July, 2017.
56 See boyd, op.cit., location 3266.
57 Ibid., location 3304.
58 David Donnison 'Rethinking Rights Talk' in Lionel Orchard and Robert Dare (eds.) *Markets, Morals and Public Policy* (Sydney, The Federation Press, 1999), p. 226.
59 See e.g. Children's Commissioner for England *Growing Up Digital: A Report of the Growing Up Digital Taskforce* (London, January, 2017), p. 4, (Children's Commissioner for England).
60 Rae Bridgman 'Criteria for Best Practices in Building Child-Friendly Cities: Involving Young People in Urban Planning and Design' (2004) 13(2) *Canadian Journal of Urban Research* 337–346.
61 Zizi A. Papacharissi *Affective Publics: Sentiment, Technology, and Politics* (Oxford Studies in Digital Politics, 2015) (OUP, USA), p. 31.
62 Ibid., pp. 7–8.
63 Ibid., p. 8.
64 Ibid.
65 Ibid., pp. 8–9.
66 Papacharissi, Zizi A. *Affective Publics: Sentiment, Technology, and Politics* (Oxford Studies in Digital Politics), pp. 8–9 (Oxford University Press, Kindle Edition).
67 Ibid., p. 12.
68 Ibid.
69 Ibid., p. 17.
70 Ibid.
71 Mary Douglas *Purity and Danger* (first published 1966)
72 Ibid., p. 18.
73 Papacharissi, A. Zizi *Affective Publics: Sentiment, Technology, and Politics* (Oxford Studies in Digital Politics), p. 18 (Oxford University Press, Kindle Edition).
74 Ibid., p. 19.
75 Ibid.
76 Computer Misuse Act 1990, s.1.
77 The Law Commission *Computer Misuse* (Working Paper No. 110) (London, HMSO, 1988), p. 77.
78 Ibid., p. 81.
79 Ibid.
80 Ibid., p. 82.
81 Ibid., p. 84.

82 New Zealand Law Commission *Computer Misuse* (Report no. 54) (Wellington, 1999).
83 Ibid., p. 12.
84 Ibid., p. 13.
85 Ibid., pp. 13–14.
86 Ibid., p. 14.
87 Ibid., p. 15.
88 Ibid.
89 Declan McCullagh 'From "WarGames" to Swartz: How U.S. Anti-hacking Law Went Astray' *CNET news* 13 March, 2013, https:www.cnet.com/au/news/from-wargames-to-aaron-swartz-how-u-s-anti-hacking-law-went-astray, accessed 7 July, 2017.
90 Ibid.
91 Ibid.
92 Ibid.
93 Stephanie Ricker Schulte *Cached: Decoding the Internet in Global Popular Culture* (Critical Cultural Communication) (New York University Press, Kindle Edition, 2013), p. 24.
94 Ibid., p. 16.
95 Ibid.
96 Ibid., pp. 55ff.
97 Ibid., p. 56.
98 Ibid., p. 140 citing Malcolm Gladwell 'Small Change: The Revolution Will Not Be Tweeted' *The New Yorker* (October 4, 2010).
99 Ibid., p. 141.
100 Ibid.
101 Ibid., p. 9.

Part II

Narratives of social media future

Chapter 4

Social media and controlling young people's identity in a networked age

The Internet is often presented as a place where one can explore alternative identities. The sense that it is a virtual space, with relative anonymity, has furthered the notion that one can choose to be someone or something different online than who one is offline. Of course, law enforcement agencies and scammers already exploit that feature by posing as children to catch sexual predators in the former case or to cheat people of their money in the latter. However, others may explore their sexual identity in chat rooms or pretend to be someone else simply as a game. As with any space in society, people will enter it to possibly discover something about themselves or for a myriad of other reasons.

As mentioned in the previous chapter, the child's right to an identity tends to be drafted narrowly in children's rights conventions and charters. The *Growing Up Digital Taskforce Report*[1] referred to in Chapter 1 only mentions 'identity' once, in this narrow sense, that is, in relation to the child's right to a name, nationality or family life specifically. This appears in that report in the included Children's Rights Alliance Digital Convention, which is an attempt to connect the UNCROC with the digital world.[2] This document only seeks to add to the relevant UNCROC protection of identity that '[e]very child's digital identity should be protected from being hacked'.[3] As discussed in the previous chapter, it is to many of the other rights mentioned in UNCROC that we have to turn to understand which rights seek to guarantee the development of a child or young person's identity.

The problem for the law, then, is how to articulate and understand identity in the context of social media. We may accept that social media creates communities, but are all online communities acceptable? What should be the legal narrative around the child's identity in the context of social media? Can such a narrative embrace a set of diverse understandings of identity, particularly as it applies to young people?

4.1 Creating identities online: from role models to subversives

The definitions of acceptable behaviour are so fixed in terms of the dominant understandings of what is appropriate or acceptable that any challenge to these views are often summarily dismissed. We can return to the example of computer hacking here as it has been shown to have commenced a moral panic about new technology and the harm that rebellious youth might cause with it. It also illustrates both the messiness of the notion of identity and the dilemma this creates for the law in how to embrace or control it. It can be argued that hacking has created a sub-culture or an identity for many, usually young people. The name 'hacker' itself is a label that lends a certain status to those to whom it is applied. In terms of the implications of all this for the law, it is important to explore this sub-culture for a moment.

The starting point is the culture of consumption in which society is immersed. Christopher Stanley describes this as 'a culture that literally 'plays at life' and where transgression (in the sense of 'doing wrong') can become a leisure activity in itself'.[4] He refers to the congregation of young people in shopping malls, the site of so much of this culture of consumption, but where youth act as 'space invaders': 'young people, cut off from the power to consume but still subject to the representation of the banal violence of consumption, have the power to invade this space of consumption.'[5] Thus, simply being there, not to consume but to simply occupy the space, becomes an act of transgression, 'inappropriate' in the eyes of those who own and control those urban spaces. A 'customer notice', for example, in the Headrow Shopping Centre in Leeds in 2004 proclaimed, 'For the Benefit of the Majority of Our Customers, Groups of Youths Congregating In This Shopping Centre, Will Be Asked to Vacate The Premises'.[6] The transgression is to be there; the fear is what they *could* do, not what they have done. But this is the analysis often provided from a critique that focuses on how the powerful define the circumstances. For such youth, the sub-culture that it gives rise to and the identity it provides to them arises from the 'delight of being deviant'.[7] To be in the shopping mall allows them to subvert the normal use of the space; to be 'asked to vacate' affirms what they have become.

The connection with hacking is apparent and obvious. As Stanley explains:

> For the computer hacker the technological apparatus which has now become ubiquitous can be utilised not simply for playing games which are sold by the multinational computing companies but for playing games which engage with the production of objectivised meaning and reality. The hacker (as expert and therefore as legislator) can experience the thrill of deep penetration and disruption of the 'reality' of unauthorised and classified computing networks. The hacker appropriates these networks and inverts them in a statement that 'I was here, it was easy, wise up'. In planting a virus or bug which can be pre-timed the

> hacker not only exerts his or her (assumed) identity but can also demonstrate a symbolic violence in the ordered world of the 'safe' network. There is the excitement of the risk and the chase but it is only through the distanced corridors of cyberspace.[8]

Thus, unlike many of the laws that proscribe unauthorised access to computer systems around the world, the main danger posed by hackers is not to the data as much as it is to the idea that the computer system and its data are secure. To be in the space is the main objective of the hacker, and criminalisation only confirms the marginalised identity of the hacker rather than deterring him or her.[9] The aim of the hacker is to invert the dominant narratives that surround such spaces, to engage 'in the shaping of desires, fantasies, pleasures and identities within established boundaries of meaning but inverting and appropriating these boundaries'.[10] For Stanley, the lure of excitement is central to this process. He notes that '[t]he struggle to construct an identity which does not involve hyper-conformity or sublimation engages in the idea of excitement in transgression'.[11]

In effect, hackers create a counter-narrative about technology and its place in modern society. This represents a major threat to powerful interests. If one returns to the justification for the need for criminal offences for unauthorised access to computer systems, the rationale was that this was important to protect state and commercial entities who stored valuable data on those systems. The notion that such systems might be a 'playground' confronts this idea as well as the official purpose of new technology, as does the notion that youth should be doing anything other than preparing themselves for using such technology in the service of those same state and corporate interests. Hackers represent alternative narratives of governance and surveillance; as Stanley suggests, 'the hacker can enter a secret world of an alternative governmentality, the external order of regulation through surveillance by information'.[12] Hackers, then, do not represent disorder, but alternative notions of order. This is not to pretend that hackers represent a simple progressive critique of the state or society. Many hackers have a perspective of the state which may at times be described as anti-authoritarian, anti-state and anti-government.[13] However, as Kevin Steinmetz's work shows, hackers are not against government; they often want to make it work better and be more accountable.[14]

All this suggests that hacker culture can be about re-making space in ways which are considered more just and in the public's best interests. It is about recasting the narrative and not destroying it. As Stanley says of hackers (and other transgressive examples of joyriding and raving), they 'demonstrate a transition in the nature of right and wrong, good and bad, order and disorder'.[15] Importantly, this leads to a transformation in the shape and meaning of the law. It is subversive because it claims the law for others and does not accept that it exists to serve the interests of one particular group. Activities such as hacking

> are transgressive since they 'carry law away' in the sense of appropriating either directly or indirectly, elements of the dominant regulatory forms of the contemporary – the satiation of desire through consumption – and inverting technologies of power into technologies of counter-power. In this process they do not claim 'other space' but rather move within established space, reinventing the tame zone as the wild zone in the establishment of particular manifestation of desire.[16]

Thus, hackers are able to form a culture and a narrative from 'within' the dominant meanings given to spaces. This represents a highly threatening and disruptive process that can undermine the legitimacy of established order by advancing an alternative form of organisation and order that uses much of the same internal logic of the current order. In other words, if the law purports to value freedom of speech and expression and the importance of transparency and accountability, then hacking culture takes the law at its word and propels this logic through its activities. If the messiness of law creates ambiguity and vagueness that can be manipulated by powerful interests to turn the law to their use, hacking turns that ambiguity and vagueness in the law back against itself to re-define legal meanings and the role of law. Hacking culture can carry law into places powerful interests have tried not to take it and in doing so can recast the role and function of law.

The relevance of this discussion of hacking for young people and social media is that it provides the backdrop against which this new communication technology arrived and which on its face promises to enable almost anyone to write alternative narratives about power in society as well as about the role of law. As we have seen in relation to new technologies, there is a tendency to portray their arrival and effects in terms of either utopian or dystopian narratives. In relation to social media, the moral panic surrounding young people and their online activity has been documented above, and this continues to play out today. This dystopian narrative is placed against the utopian view that with proper parental guidance, education about 'responsible' and 'appropriate' online behaviour and a 'balanced' approach to its use, social media can be a force for 'good' in society. While it cannot be contested that young people experiment with their identity through social media, the key to the utopian vision is that they are provided with 'positive' role models[17] in that space rather than those who espouse subversive values and who disrupt the very definitions of what is 'good' and 'positive' online.

4.2 Young people and autonomy rights online: who controls the child or young person's identity in social media?

Articulating a view that asserts the autonomy rights of children or young people is to those people who see children as 'innocent and vulnerable', as danah boyd observes, 'often activist in nature, even if heretical to some'.[18] This makes it very difficult to be other than subversive if one advances the notion of childhood as other than an age of innocence in the eyes of those same people. However, as the history of hacking and new technologies have highlighted, the reality of new technology is that children and young people have been able to claim in a practical sense a high degree of autonomy with respect to their use of social media, especially after the advent of mobile technology. The point is that for those who contest this autonomous view of the child, there will be a continuous push for greater state or parental control over young people online in the desire to steer those young people to the 'good' parts of the online world. It is this latter impulse that continues to muddy the discussion about the 'real' dangers online and the capacity of the child to make their own decisions in cyberspace. However, we can nevertheless investigate the legal discourse that does surround young people's practice of social media to see if the law at least provides the space for young people to claim or control their own identity online.

If we turn to Instagram's terms of use we find some interesting and embedded assumptions about children's capacity within those terms. The first is that one has to be at least 13 years old to be able to use the service at all.[19] This age relates to the United States' Children's Online Privacy Protection Act 1998,[20] which prevents an operator of a website or online service from collecting information from anyone under 13 without parental consent.[21] Under that Act a child is defined as an individual under 13.[22] In effect, it places the privacy of personal information about children under 13 in the control of their parents. The reason given on the Federal Trade Commission's (FTC) website as to why the Act only applies to children under 13 is that the United States Congress recognised 'that younger children are particularly vulnerable to overreaching by marketers and may not understand the safety and privacy issues created by the online collection of personal information'.[23] However, in relation to older children or teenagers, the FTC website notes that it 'is concerned about teen privacy and does believe that strong, more flexible, protections may be appropriate for this age group'.[24] In effect, this is the same notion as appears in the House of Lords decision in *Gillick* (discussed above in Chapter 1) and that of the 'maturing minor' and all the uncertainty that creates in terms of how much autonomy to grant a child or young person.

The debate over which age range should be protected under this legislation is a continuing one in discussions about online risks and harm. In one

FTC report[25] the views of a 'diverse coalition of consumer advocates and others' were said to support more protections for teens between the ages of 13 and seventeen.[26] In particular they were said to not understand 'the long-term consequences of sharing their personal data'.[27] Against more protections for this group 'industry representatives and privacy advocates' claimed that having different rules for teens would create practical problems with age verification and could lead to the barring of teen audiences altogether.[28] One preferred approach suggested was 'to explore educational efforts to address issues that are unique to teens'.[29] The Commission concluded that there should be some 'soft' protections for teens through the use of 'privacy-protective default settings' that would 'function as an effective "speed bump" for this audience and, at the same time, provide an opportunity to better educate teens about the consequences of sharing their personal information'.[30] This relied on social-networking sites acting in accordance with these principles rather than being legislatively required to do so.

In the report, the FTC also referred to a need to give teenagers more information about whether and how their data has been shared 'because of their particular vulnerability to ubiquitous marketing messages and heavy use of social media and mobile devices'.[31] Reference was also made to the 'right to be forgotten', derived from the French Data Protection Authority and a principle advocated for all to remove information that one has posted online about oneself.[32] This was said to be particularly relevant for youth 'who might not appreciate the long-term consequences of their data sharing' and who 'tend to be more impulsive than adults and, as a result, may voluntarily disclose more information online than they should, leaving them vulnerable to identity theft or adversely affecting potential employment or college admissions opportunities'.[33] In these remarks in this report we see once again the view of the young person as vulnerable and unable to make 'good' decisions about their actions. They reinforce the idea of childhood and youth being a time of preparation for the future where long-term consequences have to be considered and for which most young people are thought to be usually unprepared. Whether or not young people are best advised to protect their online privacy most of the time, it is the view of the child as 'impulsive' and 'vulnerable' underpinning this discussion that makes it very difficult for young people to claim autonomy rights in digital spaces.

The narrative of young people as vulnerable that is woven through the FTC report can be contrasted with the terms of use of various social media sites. Instagram, for example, has a clause in its terms of use that addresses the issue of how users of the application interact with other users. That clause says:

> You are solely responsible for your interaction with other users of the Service, whether online or offline. You agree that Instagram is not

> responsible or liable for the conduct of any user. Instagram reserves the right, but has no obligation, to monitor or become involved in disputes between you and other users. Exercise common sense and your best judgment when interacting with others, including when you submit or post Content or any personal or other information.[34]

While reliance on users exercising 'common sense' and their 'best judgment' in this area may be regarded as a derogation of responsibility on the part of Instagram by some, it can also be constructed as an attempt on their part to treat their users as having some degree of maturity.[35] What must also be recognised here is that, formally, this guidance is directed to all users, being those 13 years old and over. Whether by design or default, Instagram treats its thirteen-year-old users as having the capacity for making some judgments at least, and while this does not necessarily assume they will be as wise as someone much older, it is more of a reflection of the reasoning in cases such as *Gillick* than the FTC report can claim to be.

Given the difficulty of monitoring all activity in a social networking site, it is no surprise that the providers seek to limit their liability by, apart from more formal limitation of liability clauses, asking their users to exercise common sense. Of course, what constitutes common sense in any given situation is often unclear, and so it is a 'messy' solution to unwise use. However, as with any narrative, part of its effect is not just the substantive content of the guidance, but how it makes people feel. In this instance, there is in effect a sense that the user is to be trusted to make some judgments. Another example of this is contained in most social networking sites' terms of use where reference is made to respect for the rights of others. In the Facebook terms of service, there is a clause headed 'Protecting Other People's Rights', which begins, 'We respect other people's rights, and expect you to do the same'. It then proceeds to list various expectations around the treatment of copyrighted material, the collection of information about others, not posting identification documents and sensitive financial information of other people and privacy rights of others.[36] It is notable that these expectations are not stated in terms of guidance or rules but instead are written using notions of rights.

In using the language of rights, it is likely that the Facebook terms of service speak more directly to youth than do the FTC report's concerns about their impulsive behaviour. This does not mean that the Facebook terms begin and end the debate on how to conceptualise young people in digital spaces. However, what this does do is begin a process where the language of rights or 'rights speak' becomes more central to the discussion and can be further evolved. For example, dana boyd has asked:

> What can and should networked rights look like? Who has the right to my relationships on Facebook? Me? The other people? Facebook?

> The global nature of this only makes it more difficult to untangle the boundaries, both culturally and with respect to jurisdiction. Whose rights to a particular piece of content matter? What happens when content flows across boundaries? The policy issues around participatory culture are going to get more complicated, not less.[37]

This discussion is much more complicated than simple assertions of children's digital rights, and it requires a lot of thought about the content of those rights. This is further emphasised by the implications of the General Data Protection Regulation (GDPR) of the European Union (EU), which is to take effect on 25 May 2018. Its broad aim is to increase data protection for all persons within the EU, but it also contains special provisions with respect to children. In stating its underlying principles, the GDPR accepts that view of the child which generally sees them as vulnerable:

> Children merit specific protection with regard to their personal data, as they may be less aware of the risks, consequences and safeguards concerned and their rights in relation to the processing of personal data. Such specific protection should, in particular, apply to the use of personal data of children for the purposes of marketing or creating personality or user profiles and the collection of personal data with regard to children when using services offered directly to a child. The consent of the holder of parental responsibility should not be necessary in the context of preventive or counselling services offered directly to a child.[38]

The regulation also notes that in general, information about data collection online should be provided in clear and understandable ways, and in the case of children who 'merit specific protection, any information and communication, where processing is addressed to a child, should be in such a clear and plain language that the child can easily understand'.[39] To this point the view of the child is of one that is vulnerable and in need of protection. A later part of the preamble that deals with the right to remove personal data and a 'right to be forgotten' is said to have particular relevance 'where the data subject has given his or her consent as a child and is not fully aware of the risks involved by the processing, and later wants to remove such personal data, especially on the internet'.[40] While this at first accepts that a child may have consented on their own behalf, it is then heavily qualified with reference to that child not being 'fully aware' of the risks involved. Of course, this is the terminology of 'messy law', as it creates a standard beyond being simply 'aware' to a notional point that many adults may not even reach. In doing so, it potentially confines children to a vulnerable or immature status while retaining the chimera of an attainable legal standard.

The part of the GDPR that has become the most controversial is that part of the regulation which in effect raises the requirement of parental consent for data collection in relation to a child from 13 to 16 years old.[41] However, the age at which parental consent is required may be lowered by a member state, but this cannot be lower than 13 years.[42] The Belgian Children's Rights Commissioner has already asked the Belgian government to lower the age to 13.[43] The arguments of the Belgian Commissioner included that placing the responsibility on the parents to determine if their children are to have access to social media removes responsibility on the part of social media providers to make their sites appropriate for children in terms of having child-friendly terms of use and accessible complaints mechanisms.[44] The children's rights perspective being advanced in this instance was one that placed children's rights to access social media and participate in it as having an importance on the same level as their right to be protected from harm. But it also recognised the responsibility of social media providers to affirm those rights by their actions. It suggests that a parental guidance approach without this occurring may in fact leave children and young people with very little formal application of their rights, and by 'formal' I am referring to the reality of children accessing social media sites below the relevant age because of the practical difficulties in creating a parental consent verification system that is foolproof.[45] This latter point raises the whole issue of how cyberspace allows individuals to be other than who they 'really' are, including with respect to their age.

4.3 Social media and the reconstruction of the law of childhood

While recasting one's age seems to be the obvious example of a child reconstructing themselves as an older child or young person, there are other examples of the way in which social media enables children to change their roles. One example is what has come be to be known as 'sharenting', that is, where parents post photographs of their children online. An interesting by-product of the online-privacy debate has been the raising of the issue of whether parents have the right to post or share photographs of their children online. Stacey Steinberg puts it in terms of '[p]arents, acting in the best interests of their children, can act as shepherds of their children's online privacy until the children assume ownership over their digital identities'.[46]

Clearly, much of the concern about sharing children's images online relates to the perceived risks of doing so, especially in relation to sexual predators and paedophiles using the images for their sexual titillation or to locate children. Steinberg cites a statement from the Australian e-Safety Commissioner 'that almost half of all images found on the paedophile image sharing site she reviewed were originally posted with a parent's innocent intent on social media and family blogs' and suggests that parents should be cautious about posting images of their children in any state of undress, although as she noted in relation to the Australian reference that many of the images of children were not of them in that state but at the beach or undertaking sporting activities.[47] Other concerns in relation to the sharing of children's images relate to 'digital kidnapping' in which other adults take the image and present it as their own child,[48] children being bullied because of embarrassing images being shared,[49] or more generally being made the subject of amusement because of the nature of the images.[50] Steinberg does acknowledge that there are benefits of parental sharing of a child's images:

> Sharenting gives children a positive social media presence to help counteract some of the negative behaviors they might themselves engage in as teenagers. Additionally, by sharing on social media, parents offer their children positive networks by inviting supportive family members and friends into their daily lives. But these positive benefits must be carefully weighed against the dangers of sharing a child's personal information in such a public space. By understanding this complex taxonomy, scholars can better discuss children's rights online.[51]

However, on closer analysis it becomes apparent that much of this concern with children's digital rights is not actually a concern with their rights in childhood, but with their future rights and reputation as an adult. Steinberg cautions parents to consider how sharing images of their children can affect 'their child's current and future sense of self and well-being'.[52] This begins with the concern that 'parents must consider that one day their children will likely come face-to-face with their parents' past online disclosures'.[53] While this is not exclusively an issue for the child in later life, it does relate to future experiences and in that sense at least would include their adult lives. The other concern in this regard identified by Steinberg is the effect that parents' sharing has in terms of the role model it sets for their children. Essentially, it normalises sharing of images and so leads children to also engage in that behaviour. The problem here then becomes one of 'oversharing' and so 'can create issues for the child's reputation on into the future'.[54]

While the debate is cast in terms of an emerging law of children's privacy rights online, I would suggest that this is not in fact what is occurring. The concern is much more about the consequences for the child's life into the future as an adult, which really seems to be about recasting how the legal standard of acting in the child's best interests is to be defined and understood. Steinberg states that her concern is with the example of parents posting online the images of children who, unlike adults and teenagers, are not aware of the consequences of having their images shared.[55] This suggests a focus on children being unable to speak for themselves, as would be the case of infants and very young children. Yet prior to expressing this as the focus, Steinberg states the problem:

> A parent's own decision to share a child's personal information online is a potential source of harm that has gone largely unaddressed. Children not only have interests in protecting negative information about themselves on their parent's newsfeed, but also may not agree with a parent's decision to share any personal information – negative or positive – about them in the online world. There is no 'opt-out' link for children and split-second decisions made by their parents will result in indelible digital footprints. While adults have the ability to set their own parameters when sharing their personal information in the virtual world, children are not afforded such control over their digital footprint unless there are limits on parents.[56]

The notion that the child is unable to understand the consequences of having their images shared on one hand but then is capable of being able to 'not agree' with their parent's decision can only be understood in terms of a temporal shift. It is the fear that in adulthood children will confront their parents with the question, 'Why did you do that to me?' Faced with the imprecision of the best-interests standard, which rarely works to understand actions with the benefit of hindsight, parents might be forgiven for seeking a different current standard for determining how to behave in relation to their children in the hope of avoiding that uncomfortable question later in life. It is the same dilemma currently faced by parents who have children born with the genitalia of both sexes and are asked to make a decision as to which sex they wish their children to be raised as, often with the implication that 'corrective' surgery will then also be performed on the child. There is now a discourse that suggests that the child has been denied their choice in the matter when parents make this decision at their birth, and that as adults they may later condemn their parent's decision. This is presented in that discourse as the child's right to make a decision in the matter, and it contends that any decision should be delayed until the child is mature enough to make their own decision.[57] The flaw in this reasoning is that this has little to do with the autonomous rights of the *present* child. It may have something to do with the rights of adults to voice concern about their treatment as a child, but in relation to debates about how to treat a child *today*, this is no more than using such rights discourse to justify a certain view of the child's best interests.

This idea that the child may subsequently complain about the decisions made by their parents when they were young also requires a high degree of imagination about the future child as an adult. It adopts a romantic notion of the child growing into an adult who rejects stereotypes and gender roles imposed by society. This could be the case, but why do such arguments against parents who make decisions at birth not also consider, as uncomfortable as it may be, that the adult child may be happy they did not have to be the trailblazer who challenged gendered orthodoxies? In other words, if parents decided to wait until the child became old enough to make their own decisions, then may not the child also potentially ask the parents why they did not decide for them? The analogy with what happens on social media is apt, because parental caution about what a child posts now, or is posted about a child, is more about the future adult the child will grow up to be than it is about the present child. In this case it cannot simply be about *children's rights*; it is driven more by a fear of a future adult asserting their right to question and perhaps even sue parents who acted or did not act in ways that are agreeable to the grown-up child, now an adult. As Steinberg notes:

> Information shared on the Internet has the potential to exist long after the value of the disclosure remains, and therefore disclosures made during childhood have the potential to last a lifetime. This issue is ripe for a child-centered, solution-focused discussion to ensure the protection of the best interests of children that is responsive to the age and developmental stages of children as they mature. While today's young people will be the first to settle into adulthood under this new landscape, future generations will follow in their path.[58]

Recourse to 'child-centred' notions often disguise mere shifts in thinking about what is in a child's best interests. The parent who shares images online of their child for relatives and friends to see is, after all, simply following a view that it is in the child's best interests that absent grandparents or good friends share in their child's development through those posts and so have some connection with the child. As is common when matters such as this are debated, there are some brief reasons given as to why image sharing presents risks to a child, but little detailed discussion as to the child's interests in having this connection embedded in their lives. Steinberg seems to see the sharing of a child's image in social media and the 'likes' this generates as 'validating feedback' that leads to the parent 'feeling supported in their decision to share information about their lives and the lives of their children', which then leads to more sharing without considering the breach of the child's privacy rights that occurs.[59]

The difficulty with this approach is that it assumes a neatness in the law about the relevant and prevailing rights that should determine this issue. One media report on the phenomenon of 'sharenting' put it in the following terms:

> Parents may not realise it, but by posting photos and videos of their children online, they are creating an identity for their children that

might not be welcomed, according to psychologist Dr. Arthur Cassidy, who specialises in social media.

'One of the major arguments is, do parents have the right to assume control over their child's identity?' he said. 'They believe, this is our child, we own their identity. But children believe they can change and control their identity online'.[60]

The same reports also create a similarly confusing picture of children's capacity by claiming that the issue arises because children 'too young to have any choice in the matter' are having their lives recorded on social media by doting parents, but when the child reaches 12 or 13 they feel embarrassed, ask the parents to remove the material and then claim that '[i]f I had been asked [at the time], do you want these photos out there for all to see, I would've probably said no'.[61] The rather obvious point to make here, and which is not made in such reports, is that if the child had been asked 'at the time' of the posting, they would not have been able to exercise a choice due to their lack of capacity. Certainly, by 12 or 13 a child is becoming a young person with increasing levels of maturity (as the case of *Gillick* notes), but in their earlier years their meaningful participation in such decisions will be small to non-existent. The child that would have 'probably said no' is the child imagined as an adult or more mature child or young person who may indeed could have said 'yes'. But, in fact, this is not even the correct test or formulation of what might happen. The mature adult would arguably say, 'I realise that I was too young to decide; you are my parents, and in the absence of my ability to decide for myself you had to exercise your judgment. The appropriate legal standard to do this is to make such a decision according to my best interests. This requires a judgment on your part which is value laden, but nevertheless has to still be done to the best of your ability'.

The vagaries of the best-interests standard and the 'messiness' of its application are well known. For those who crave certainty in the law, as we have seen in Lord Scarman's judgment in *Gillick*, there is little comfort to be had. However, the matter of parental sharing of images has subtly shifted the discussion of such matters away from the exercise of parental judgment in the best interests of the child and towards some fictional construction of the adult child who may later in life decide the matter and somehow absolve the parent from having to act in the present. It is really an absurdity, but one which seems to have traction because it seems to have some appeal to a certain notion of 'children's' autonomy rights that might be more properly regarded as residing in the adult the child will become.

Even a cursory glance at the UN Convention on the Rights of the Child will show that the role of parents in making judgments on behalf of their children is embedded in the main document that embodies children's rights in international law. The narrow reference to the child's right to identity in the Convention places this in the context of the child's right to nationality, name and family relations.[62] Article 7 provides that children have 'the right to know and be cared for by his or her parents'.[63] Article 5 recognises the responsibilities, rights and duties of parents 'to provide, in a manner consistent with the evolving capacities of the child, appropriate direction and guidance in the exercise by the child of the rights recognized [by the Convention]'.[64] And article 18 is central to this discussion, providing that there is

> recognition of the principle that both parents have common responsibilities for the upbringing and development of the child. Parents or, as the case may be, legal guardians, have the primary responsibility for the upbringing and development of the child. The best interests of the child will be their basic concern.[65]

Of course, other articles speak to the autonomy rights of the child, but the same document also contains the above articles which refer to the role of parents in the upbringing of their children. Consistent with those articles, it is clear that parents do, and should, shape their child's identity; how could they properly parent the child without doing so? What we need to ask in relation to the issues presented by the perceived problem of parental sharing of children's lives online is how it has come to be constructed as a problem that has caused a shift in the construction of the law of childhood.

Part of the answer may lie in the fear that there may be legal liability imposed on parents later in life for breaching their child's privacy rights as a child. There is a strong contemporary narrative that involves adults being held accountable for historical abuse of children. However, there are also other causes at work that explain the critique of parental control of children's online lives. The fear of future loss of reputation feeds directly into certain notions of the purpose of the Internet and social media. The notion that children are to be imagined as adults when understanding them today also resonates with ideas about the value of children, where their future value or worth informs how we treat them in the present.[66] There is a culture of childhood that often wants us to see in our children traits and capacities that are simply not yet evolved.

However, the culture of privacy that now embraces children's rights may have even deeper roots that further explain concern with such practices as parental sharing of children's images and other data. These lie more deeply within the nature of social media. As Fuchs observes, the discussion of privacy rights and social media occurs within the context of what one may see as the public sphere and 'transformative power' of this new communication technology.[67] He cites authors such as Yochai Benkler,[68] Zizi Papacharissi,[69] Manuel Castells[70] and Jean Burgess and Joshua Green,[71] who all argue that social media has created a new public sphere of participation that allows for democratic debate and dissent and new ways of being heard.[72] Fuchs disputes this 'public sphere idealism' and says that these approaches do not ask who owns Internet platforms and who owns social media.[73] He describes social media as a 'buzzword and marketing ideology' to attract users and investment to various platforms that are corporations aiming to make profits from advertising.[74] Fuchs points out the ways in which social media contains within it various contradictions and tensions. Drawing on Habermas, he analyses the economic and social context within which social media operates and how this in turn affects how truly 'social' social media is, and the extent to which the public sphere is a truly participatory place. He also connects this discussion with contradictions within notions of privacy protection.

Fuchs notes that the modern idea of privacy arises from the division of labour which leads to the separation of spheres – workplace/household, paid/unpaid, urban/rural, wage/reproductive labour, men/women and so on.[75] From this, another division of private/public also arises, and modern society associates the family as the private realm and the economy as the public realm.[76] This then connects with the idea of privacy, which is about 'the question of what dimensions of human life should be made visible to the public or should remain invisible'.[77] But this question is not a neutral one, and nor is the answer self-evident. Fuchs notes that privacy's connection with private property is apparent in the example of countries that operate as tax havens providing anonymity for wealthy people's bank accounts, which ultimately may protect tax evasion and also conceal wealth inequalities.[78] He also notes the criticism that privacy of family life has confined women to the household and hidden domestic violence, although bodily privacy acts to protect domestic violence victims from offenders.[79] Fuchs concludes that '[p]rivacy is a social, contextual, and relational moral value'.[80]

Fuchs also observes that social media has occurred as part of a broader trend in the 'liquefaction of boundaries'.[81] That is, we live in times where there has been a blurring of boundaries between work and leisure time, consumption and production, and private and public life, for example.[82] One way in which social media connects with this blurring of boundaries is the manner in which it integrates a person's various social roles – friend, citizen, worker, consumer, etc. – into one profile on social media such as Facebook.[83] It is true that social media allows users to control privacy settings so that some data is kept private (for friends), other data semi-public (for a group) and yet other data public (for anyone). But given the aim of social media companies to make money from their platforms, their 'capital accumulation model is to turn private, semi-public, and public user data into a commodity that is sold to advertising clients that present targeted advertisements to users'.[84] Fuchs demonstrates how social media privacy policies actually enable the social media provider to use the data provided for this purpose.[85] In other words, even if the data is kept private from most other users, it is not kept private from the social media provider. As Fuchs writes, social media companies 'are not just communication companies, but also large advertising agencies'.[86] Fuchs notes social media providers' interests are not consistent with the privacy rights of users:

> Schmidt [Google CEO] and Zuckerberg [Facebook CEO] argue for massive data sharing on social media. They do not mention, however, that this sharing is not primarily a sharing of data with friends and the public, but a sharing with Google and Facebook that are the largest data processors and data commodifiers in the world, which explains not just the recent rise of the term 'big data' but also social media companies' interest in hiding their commercial interests ideologically behind the ideas of sharing and openness.[87]

On the other hand, those same social media companies claim privacy over their own corporate structures, financial operations and tax arrangements.[88] Fuchs sees connections here with the contradiction over privacy, given on one hand the desire of governments to monitor all of a citizen's data online in the interests of national security, but then those same governments seeking to prosecute anyone that discloses information about them.[89] This leads Fuchs to ask why political activists would trust social media companies with their information when it can then possibly be controlled by corporate and state interests.[90] Fuchs concludes:

> Civil society is facing an antagonism between networked protest communication that creates political public spheres online and offline and the particularistic corporate and state control of social media that limits, feudalises, and colonises these public spheres.[91]

Fuchs does not discuss children and young people in the context of social media. However, his approach does have possible implications for their position and for the role of the law in regulating their relationship with social media. The assertion of a child's right to privacy online and to control what their parent is permitted to post about them without the child's consent may have to be considered as having little to do with the autonomous rights of the child and more to do with the interests of the corporate owners of social media platforms. When we take into account their purpose as a profit generator based on the commodification of personal data posted by social media users, those corporations have a clear interest in first ensuring that parents 'manage' their child's social media usage rather than prevent it. Within that framework of such management, they also have an interest in ensuring that information is as much as possible a true reflection of what the child wishes, desires and aspires to be. In effect, under the guise of the child's privacy rights, the parent is being removed as a controlling or guiding influence, other than to guide the child in the use of social media 'appropriately', which in this context means to be honest and truthful and to see social media as an important way to share information with others. Privacy rights become a smokescreen to justify social media companies dealing directly with the child and avoiding romanticised parental versions of the child's life. The value of the child's data commodity is in being able to directly engage with the child and so obtain more useful data rather than through the intermediary of the parent who may well filter the data, romanticise it or limit its scope.

Related to this way of understanding young people and social media is also the way in which 'empowering' the child by suggesting he or she should control what parents post operates to deny the parent any role in acting in the best interests of the child. Discussion which condemns 'sharenting' operates to create a broader culture within which parents are denied legitimacy in the lives of their children as far as protecting their interests are concerned. Google and Facebook become the 'parents' of such children and young people, as they appear to assert the child's right to privacy more effectively and sensitively in connecting it with the child's need for autonomy. However, all of this operates to the exclusion of any proper discussion of where the child's interests lie. While the best-interests standard is a messy aspect of law which often appears to be vague and ambiguous, it is nevertheless an important part of the legal process which can ensure some careful consideration of the child's well-being and welfare. Of course, it is this very messiness that allows corporate interests to invoke the best-interests standard, along with the co-opting of particular notions of children's privacy rights, to their own advantage. However, this does not negate the role of online transgression as a part of the way in which children and young people explore their identities, for the right to explore identity is a proper part of the child's interests. It is not the whole story, as Fuchs reminds us, but the legal construction of childhood is much more nuanced than the profit motives of social media companies would wish it to be and which we need to further explore.

4.4 The right of children to play with their identity

It might be thought that much of the discussion around identity formation online by young people is around their capacity to transgress boundaries in reshaping new identities for themselves. However, what we find in this space are contests not just between different ideas about identity but also over who should be shaping the child or young person's identity. We never see in draft statements about children's digital rights, the assertion of their right to play with their identity; indeed, the right to play (online) is rarely mentioned. Much of this is do with the increasing emphasis on children's digital skills being harnessed for their future, and such things as digital play are seen to be a less worthy, if not wasteful, way of spending their time. Indeed, do children even have a right to waste their time?

Alison James and Alan Prout comment on how childhood is constructed in a way that denies to children a 'present'. They remark that in sociological analysis

> children are not 'present' in their own right and that as a corollary, the 'present' of childhood is systematically down-played in favour of theoretical frames of reference which place the importance of childhood in either the past or the future.[92]

They also note adults' preoccupation with age in relation to children, in effect denying them their present age (and capacity) and instead focussing, for example, on what they intend to do when 'grown up'.[93] The relevance of this discussion about the focus on the 'future child' instead of their current reality for social media and law bears directly on questions of capacity to decide such matters as what to post online and whether their consent is needed before a parent does so. The fixation on age and assumptions about where a child sits in the journey towards adulthood as well as references to what a child 'will be' instead of where they are at the moment in terms of maturity makes it more likely that they will be treated either as not yet ready to fully participate in decisions that affect their lives or conversely, and perhaps counterintuitively, assumed to have that capacity well before it can be exercised in any meaningful way. James and Prout make the point in relation to teenagers that they suffer from '[t]he uncertain position of teenagers in western, industrialized societies, neither children nor adults, with a multiplicity of different cut off points' that avoid more careful scrutiny of where the individual sits socially.[94] Teenagers are 'messy' individuals who challenge authority at times and question orthodoxy as they test the world in which they are growing into. Their maturity is often questioned because of this behaviour, and parental guidance and control is often called for. However, younger children are more likely to seem 'angelic', the perfect child that adults wish their children to become in the future, and so their capacity to make 'good' decisions is, at times, less questioned. In this context, it should not surprise that the discourse around parents sharing images of very young children online gives rise to questions being asked whether the very young child should consent to their parents doing this. The manner in which this discussion leads to a reference to what the child might say as an adult looking back (and then saying they would not have consented) is nonsense unless we understand this as imputing to the young child the capacity to consent because of their purity.

What I mean by all this is that the practice of social media is requiring us to confront fundamental notions about the concept of childhood itself. We speak about the need for the child to consent in this space as if the legal meaning of consent is, and always has been, clear and unambiguous. But as Holly Brewer has shown, this is far from the case. She traces the manner in which the status of children altered as the nature of society transitioned from an authoritarian system of government to a democratic one through the seventeenth and eighteenth centuries. Prior to that change, children's capacity to consent was attached to their status; thus, children born into the aristocracy, for example, could enter into various legal relationships based on this status.[95] In effect, their status gave them the 'purity' to consent to those relationships, bearing in mind that the notion of 'consent' was different than the way it is used today. However, as society moved to democratic systems of government, consent's meaning shifted to and required a level of understanding in order, in the first instance, to agree to be governed. As Brewer explains, the changing status of children during this historical period reflected broader changes in society:

> 'Consent' has not had an unchanging meaning. The new principle that consent must be 'informed' and reasonable, which led to the exclusion of children, was part of what made democratic political ideology viable, acceptable, and above all, legitimate. It became the marrow of the law. The principle that responsibility was necessary for both criminal matters and voting became established as consent became more important to the law, at the same time as birth and perpetual status became less important.[96]

In the middle part of the eighteenth century, Brewer explains, 'some began to characterize teenagers, in particular, as ruled by passion, whereas adults were guided by reason'.[97] While much of Brewer's focus is on children's consent within family and work relationships, her book paints a broader picture about how consent has operated in law over time to reflect and create changes in how we construct childhood and indeed is itself part of broader shifts in social thinking about childhood. She remarks that these changes in childhood 'occurred within our ideas of justice but also within identity itself, within how we think about ourselves'.[98] But she also acknowledges that 'within culture and highly formalized systems of justice, broad variations can exist in how both identity and justice are constructed'.[99] She then concludes on this point:

> The shift within principles of justice described here both put much more emphasis on reaching and passing an age of reason and defined childhood as characterized most significantly by an almost complete inability to exercise judgment. In doing so, it elevated reason beyond all other human attributes. It put perhaps too much weight on this sudden transformation, on the difference between a child and an adult.[100]

At the point at which Brewer wrote this, she states that this remains fundamental to our law.[101] However, what we now have to consider is whether we are at a pivotal point in the history of childhood where the meaning of a child's capacity and the foundational principles on which that is understood are once again shifting. Brewer's work also illustrates that notions of childhood have not always been based on reason, and even in the age of reason, as she notes in the quote above, there is the possibility of taking the principle too far. Yet there is a striking relevance in Brewer's work for what we are experiencing today in the realm of social media. There is a strange convergence of corporate interests (with related shifts in emphasising individualism) with the state's interest in pursuing surveillance of individuals online (often in the name of national security) in a world of increasing inequalities that lays the foundation for a questioning of parental and family autonomy. While social media may have elements of a public sphere, as Fuchs highlights, the boundaries of that sphere are often limited and may well create false notions of participation. Instead, we may be experiencing an online world that is in battle between the need to control (especially the young) and the claimed right of people to assert their identity. Within that battle it may seem that children are asserting new rights, but it may be that what is also occurring is the removal of proper consideration of their best interests by the adults that may be most likely to defend them at least some of the time – their parents – and their replacement with the convergence of state and corporate interests, with their own agenda of monitoring the activities of citizens online.

Notes

1 Children's Commissioner for England *Growing Up Digital: A Report of the Growing Up Digital Taskforce* (London, Children's Commissioner for England, January, 2017).
2 Ibid., p. 17.
3 Ibid.
4 Christopher Stanley *Urban Excess and the Law: Capital, Culture and Desire* (London, Cavendish, 1996), p. 163.
5 Ibid.
6 Personal observation of the author (photographed) Leeds, 2004.
7 Stanley, op.cit., p. 163 citing Mike Presdee 'British Sociological Association Conference' *Unpublished paper*, 6–9 April, 1992.
8 Stanley, op.cit., pp. 163–164.
9 Ibid., p. 165.
10 Ibid.
11 Ibid.
12 Ibid., p. 166.
13 Kevin F. Steinmetz *Hacked: A Radical Approach to Hacker Culture and Crime* (New York, New York University Press, 2016), (Kindle Locations 2148–2446).
14 Ibid., Kindle Locations 2455–2456.
15 Stanley, op.cit., p. 167.

16 Ibid.
17 See e.g. Lyndsey Jenkins, Ruoyun Lin and Debora Jeske 'Influences and Benefits of Role Models on Social Media' in Yogesh Dwivedi et al. (eds.) *Social Media: The Good, the Bad, and the Ugly* (I3E 2016, Lecture Notes in Computer Science, vol. 9844. Springer, Cham, 2016), pp. 673–684.
18 danah boyd comment in *Henry Jenkins Participatory Culture in a Networked Era: A Conversation on Youth, Learning, Commerce, and Politics* (Cambridge, Wiley, 2016, Kindle Edition), p. 35.
19 Instagram, Terms of Use, clause 1.
20 15 U.S. Code Chapter 91.
21 Ibid., s.6502(1).
22 Ibid., s.6501(1).
23 Federal Trade Commission *Complying with COPPA: Frequently Asked Questions*, www.ftc.gov, accessed 10 July, 2017).
24 Ibid.
25 Federal Trade Commission *Protecting Consumer Privacy in an Era of Rapid Change: Recommendations for Businesses and Policymakers* (FTC Report, March, 2012).
26 Ibid., p. 59.
27 Ibid.
28 Ibid.
29 Ibid.
30 Ibid., p. 60.
31 Ibid., p. 70.
32 Ibid.
33 Ibid.
34 *Instagram Terms of Use, clause 7*, https://help.instagram.com/478745558852511, accessed 10 July, 2017.
35 Snapchat also includes a clause that reminds users to use common sense with respect to account security: Snap Inc. *Terms of Service, clause 9*, www.snap.com/en-US/terms/, accessed 10 July, 2017.
36 *Facebook Terms of Service, clause 5*, https://m.facebook.com/terms/, accessed 11 July, 2017.
37 Henry Jenkins, Mizuko Ito and danah boyd *Participatory Culture in a Networked Era: A Conversation on Youth, Learning, Commerce, and Politics* (Wiley, 2016, Kindle Edition) pp. 150–151.
38 *General Data Protection Regulation*, Regulation (EU) 2016/679, Preamble, cl. 38.
39 Ibid., Preamble, cl. 58.
40 Ibid., Preamble, cl. 65.
41 GDPR, article 8(1).
42 Ibid.
43 Valerie Verdoodt 'Children's Access to Social Media and the GDPR – "Please Mom, Can I Go on Facebook?"' *KU Leuven Centre for IT & IP Law*, www.law.kuleuven.be/citip/blog, accessed 19 June, 2017.
44 Ibid.
45 Ibid.
46 Stacey Steinberg 'Sharenting: Children's Privacy in the Age of Social Media' (2017) 66 *Emory Law Journal* 839 at pp. 882–883.
47 Ibid., p. 881.
48 Ibid., p. 854.
49 Ibid., pp. 854–855.
50 Ibid., p. 855.
51 Ibid.

52 Ibid., p. 882.
53 Ibid.
54 Ibid.
55 Ibid., p. 846.
56 Ibid., p. 844.
57 See e.g. Charlotte Greenfield 'Should We "Fix" Intersex Children?' *The Atlantic*, 8 July, 2014, www.theatlantic.com, accessed 30 July, 2017; Dana Ovadia 'The Birth of an Intersex Infant: Exploring the Options and Ethics Behind Decision-Making' (2013) 6(1) *Journal of Student Nursing Research* 17–20.
58 Steinberg, op.cit., p. 846.
59 Ibid., p. 846.
60 Kaye Wiggins 'Should Children Ban Their Parents from Social Media?' *BBC News* 2 November, 2016, www.bbc.com/news/business-37834856, accessed 19 June, 2017.
61 Ibid.
62 UNCROC, art. 8(1).
63 Ibid., art. 7(1).
64 Ibid., art. 5.
65 Ibid., art. 18.
66 See e.g. Viviana A. Zelizer *Pricing the Priceless Child: The Changing Social Value of Children* (New York, Basic Books, 1985).
67 Fuchs, op.cit., p. 317.
68 Yochai Benkler *The Wealth of Networks* (New Haven, Yale University Press, 2006)
69 Zizi Papacharissi 'The Virtual Sphere 2.0: "The Internet, the Public Sphere, and Beyond"' in Andrew Cahdwick and Philip N. Howard (eds.) *Routledge Handbook of Internet Politics* (New York, Routledge, 2009), pp. 230–245.
70 Manuel Castells *Communication Power* (Oxford, Oxford University Press, 2009).
71 Jean Burgess and Joshua Green *You Tube* (Cambridge, Polity Press, 2009).
72 Fuchs, op.cit., p. 315.
73 Ibid., p. 316.
74 Ibid., pp. 316, 343.
75 Ibid., p. 337.
76 Ibid., p. 338.
77 Ibid.
78 Ibid., p. 339.
79 Ibid., pp. 339–340.
80 Ibid., p. 340.
81 Ibid.
82 Ibid.
83 Ibid., p. 342.
84 Ibid., p. 344.
85 Ibid., p. 345.
86 Ibid., p. 346.
87 Ibid., p. 348.
88 Ibid.
89 Ibid., p. 353.
90 Ibid., p. 357.
91 Ibid.
92 Alison James and Alan Prout *Constructing and Reconstructing Childhood: Contemporary Issues in the Sociological Study of Childhood* (Oxford, Routledge Education Classic Edition, Taylor and Francis, Kindle Edition, 2015), p. 205.
93 Ibid., p. 206.

94 Ibid., p. 207.
95 Holly Brewer *By Birth or Consent: Children, Law and the Anglo-American Revolution in Authority* (Chapel Hill, University of North Carolina Press, 2005).
96 Ibid., p. 341.
97 Ibid., p. 335.
98 Ibid., p. 351.
99 Ibid.
100 Ibid.
101 Ibid.

Chapter 5

Social media, play and the rise of the sexual and transgressive child

The previous chapter addressed the emerging issues surrounding the control of young people's identity online. In doing so it took a broad view of what constitutes identity and how social media facilitates experimentation in respect of it by young people. Much of this experimentation is often seen as transgressive by the state or parents of the child. The law's role is often murky in this process, and in recent years it has been co-opted by various interests to bring to these debates both the need for the protection of children and young people by the law on the one hand and, at the same time and in tension with this role of law, the rights to autonomy of children and youth. The motives that lie behind the advancement of these differing roles for law are often unclear, and the law itself cannot sustain both roles in a consistent nor coherent fashion.

For that latter reason, analysis of the role of law often remains at the general level and ignores these tensions, especially with respect to terms which appear to be non-controversial. One such notion is that of 'play'. That children need to play and do play appears as self-evident. However, what presents as a simple notion has also become a legal concept which is embodied, as it is, in such documents as the UN Convention on the Rights of the Child. Article 31(1) sets out the child's right to play as a right to 'rest and leisure, to engage in play and recreational activities appropriate to the age of the child and to participate freely in cultural life and the arts'. The appearance of the right to play in such a document does require that it be defined as to its meaning and its boundaries. This is no easy task as the meaning of play is often contested.

The emphasis on seeking to prepare the child for a useful and productive life that has been identified in earlier parts of this book affects the notion that social media is or should be a context within which children play. Play can be regarded as 'down time' rather than serious business, and in the context of social media this sense of 'wasting time' online is often part of popular discourse. However, play can also be conceptualised as both serious and dangerous if it is part of a process of challenging accepted norms.

Stephen Flusty, in the context of youth contesting urban space in the city, writes that

> play becomes a stark refusal to disappear beneath the imperatives of spatial regulation that favours select target markets. In this refusal to disappear is an insistence on a right to claim, and remake, portions of the city. And in playing, this right is not merely asserted. It is acted upon in creative and highly visible ways.[1]

There are obvious parallels between urban spaces and cyberspace, as both have become places that are increasingly privatised and commodified, but yet they maintain a sense of being in the public sphere. As such they are both subject to ongoing struggles, often emanating from youth, as to how those spaces should be defined. These contests over the meaning of play arise most starkly in relation to sexual content in social media. The sexualisation of social media is perhaps one of the most debated aspects of online activity. It is not the intention to recount the detail all of those debates here, but they cannot be ignored as part of the discussion of young people's online play. Sexual matters are often associated with recreation and leisure, yet rarely debated as aspects of the right to play. It is to that point that much of this chapter is focussed.

5.1 The right of children to play with their identity online

We live in two worlds when it comes to children's play or leisure. On the one side sit child development experts who support play as crucial to the development of children and young people.[2] In that context play is often seen in romantic terms of children engaging in healthy activities with a range of benefits.[3] The other world of play is much darker and involves consideration of play as boundary pushing, challenging norms and engaging in 'dark leisure' pursuits.[4] As Rojek explains it, 'popular leisure activity seems to thrive on fragmentary, contrasting and fleeting experiences'.[5] Where do these different notions of play and leisure fit within children's right to play? And how does it all reside within the practice of social media?

In fact, official discussions of children's play share remarkably similar characteristics to debates about children and young people's activities online. At the level of general principle, there is a degree of emphasis on rights and inclusion of diversity. The definition of play current in England stems from the Department for Culture Media and Sport's review of children's play in 2004.[6] That definition of play is

> what children and young people do when they follow their own ideas and interests, in their own way and for their own reasons.[7]

On a first reading, this definition seems expansive as to what might be included within the meaning of 'play'. However, on closer analysis the 2004 review indicates a greater concern with the safety of children during play and no strong commitment to play as an activity that transgresses boundaries. Instead, there are parts of the review that seem to hold onto more romantic notions of children's play. For example, the review noted that '[t]he visible presence of children and young people making harmless and inoffensive use of public spaces is a sign of a healthy community'.[8] This seems to reflect concern with young people's use of public spaces and the fear of them engaging in anti-social behaviour in public spaces, which is clearly in a tension with a definition of play that speaks of young people following their own ideas and interests. The review did not engage with this tension, however, and instead referred to a public-opinion poll that adults identified 'activities for young people' above other concerns as something that needed to be improved at the local level.[9] The review commented that '[t]hese priorities no doubt reflected the long-standing recognition that "the devil makes work for idle hands" '.[10] In other words, the notion of play at work here was one that was consistent with the preservation of childhood innocence and purity. The review also commented on other surveys that had adults express the view 'that children today spend too much time watching TV or playing on computers. They would like them to get more physical exercise'.[11]

Thus, 'play' is more likely to be attached in the popular mindset with physical exercise, something that has a long historical connection with being good and pure. Yet this sense of play is not initially reflected in the basic definition given above. Nor is it reflected in the commentary by the UN Committee on the Rights of the Child on article 31 of the UN Convention on the Rights of the Child, which sets out the child's right to play. Indeed, that Committee explained at length the relevance of electronic communication for understanding the child's right to play:

> **Growing role of electronic media**: Children in all regions of the world are spending increasing periods of time engaged in play, recreational, cultural and artistic activities, both as consumers and creators, via various digital platforms and media, including watching television, messaging, social networking, gaming, texting, listening to and creating music, watching and making videos and films, creating new art forms, posting images. Information and communication technologies are emerging as a central dimension of children's daily reality. Today, children move seamlessly between offline and online environments. These platforms offer huge benefits – educationally, socially and culturally – and States are encouraged to take all necessary measures to ensure equality of opportunity for all children to experience those benefits. Access to the

> Internet and social media is central to the realization of article 31 rights in the globalized environment.[12]

Yet while this commentary places the use of social media at the centre of discussions about the child's right to play, it nevertheless retains the utopian and dystopian view of new technology referred to in an earlier chapter. This is particularly emphasised in the comment following the one above:

> Access to the Internet and social media is exposing children to cyberbullying, pornography and cybergrooming. Many children attend Internet cafes, computer clubs and game halls with no adequate restrictions to access or effective monitoring systems.[13]

Thus the 'good' versus 'bad' notions of new technology are at work even here, although at least there is some recognition of the role of social media as an aspect of play for children and young people. The problem is that such utopian/dystopian views of new technology get in the way of more analytical approaches to the term that would highlight the tensions within the term that make it difficult to come to one view as to what constitutes 'appropriate' play. The UN committee's legal analysis of 'play' illustrates how a more nuanced interpretation of the concept makes it much more difficult to have a clear view of what play is, and further, indicates how 'play' can create added tensions with the views often expressed that children's time on social media should be spent with one eye on their future reputation and status. The UN Committee also provided the following analysis of play under article 31 of UNCROC:

> Children's play is any behaviour, activity or process initiated, controlled and structured by children themselves; it takes place whenever and wherever opportunities arise. Caregivers may contribute to the creation of environments in which play takes place, but play itself is non-compulsory, driven by intrinsic motivation and undertaken for its own sake, rather than as a means to an end. Play involves the exercise of autonomy, physical, mental or emotional activity, and has the potential to take infinite forms, either in groups or alone. These forms will change and be adapted throughout the course of childhood. The key characteristics of play are fun, uncertainty, challenge, flexibility and non-productivity. Together, these factors contribute to the enjoyment it produces and the consequent incentive to continue to play. While play is often considered non-essential, the Committee reaffirms that it is a fundamental and vital dimension of the pleasure of childhood, as well as an essential component of physical, social, cognitive, emotional and spiritual development.[14]

What is striking in this definition is how it might actually justify computer hacking – where it does not cause any harm or damage to databases or computer systems – as play. It suggests that not all activities need have purpose, other than being 'for its own sake', yet at the same time recognises that type of activity as 'an essential component of physical, social, cognitive, emotional and spiritual development' or, in other words, the formation of identity. Although it does not use the term 'transgression', it does seem implicit in this explanation of play that the pushing and crossing of boundaries of 'acceptable' behaviour has a role in the pursuit of play as a right. In addition to this discussion of play, article 31 of course contains related rights, including a right to leisure. This right also indicates that it relates to activities that are unstructured:

> Leisure refers to time in which play or recreation can take place. It is defined as free or unobligated time that does not involve formal education, work, home responsibilities, performance of other life sustaining functions or engaging in activity directed from outside the individual. In other words it is largely discretionary time to be used as the child chooses.[15]

This immediately confronts adult comments about children spending too much time on computers (and perhaps social media), for example. Very simply, we may ask, who is to be the judge of that issue if children have this right?

However, the answer to that question must itself be messy from a legal perspective. There is still the problem of the child's best interests to consider, and how that connects with the vested interests that social media providers have in children and young people spending more and more time participating in the public sphere, which is presented by them as an opportunity to interact but which is a manipulative marketplace according to others. The UN committee does acknowledge the nature of media when discussing this right and its questionable ability at times to properly address the needs of children and young people. The Committee noted that much of the media 'fail to reflect the language, cultural values and creativity of the diversity of cultures that exist across society'.[16] This limits children's experience and also marginalises and devalues cultures that are non-mainstream.[17] In general, however, the commentary on article 31 of UNCROC by the Committee on the Rights of the Child does not explore in great depth the tensions within the stated right as it applies to the various forms of media in society, although it does so in relation to the issues surrounding children and young people's occupation of public physical places for play.

As has been observed in previous chapters, much has been made of cyberspace and social media as providing the new public sphere. What does not seem to have occurred alongside this conceptualisation of the online world as a spatial concept, where the citizenry meets and participates in democratic life, is an acknowledgment of the relevance of the large body of literature on law, human rights and the changing nature of public physical space.[18] In particular, much of that literature comments on the marginalisation of youth in those spaces.[19] For the most part, discussions of children in cyberspace fail to engage with that literature. When this does occur, it becomes apparent that children's and young people's place is constructed in cyberspace in a similar way to how they have been cast in urban spaces. The UN Committee on the Rights of the Child, in discussing the child's right to play, did engage with that body of thought in terms of how children claim space to play in urban environments, in terms which echo concerns about their activity in cyberspace and on social media. Under the heading 'Resistance to children's use of public space', the Committee observed:

> Children's use of public space for play, recreation and their own cultural activities is also impeded by the increasing commercialization of public areas, from which children are excluded. Furthermore, in many parts of the world, there is decreasing tolerance of children in public spaces. The introduction, for example, of curfews on children; gated communities or parks; reduced noise-level tolerance; playgrounds with strict rules for 'acceptable' play behaviour; restrictions on access to shopping malls builds a perception of children as 'problems' and/or delinquents. Adolescents, in particular, are widely perceived as a threat by widespread negative media coverage and representation, and discouraged from using public spaces.
>
> The exclusion of children has significant implications for their development as citizens. Shared experience of inclusive public spaces by different age groups serves to promote and strengthen civil society and encourage children to recognize themselves as citizens with rights. States are encouraged to promote dialogue between older and younger generations to encourage greater recognition of children as rights holders, and of the importance of networks of diverse community spaces in local areas or municipalities which can accommodate the play and recreational needs of all children.[20]

The committee continued to comment on the need to balance risk and safety in relation to children's use of public spaces. They noted that fear of physical harm to children has led to the increased monitoring of children in urban spaces, which constrains their play.[21] They noted that '[w]hile children must not be exposed to harm in the realization of their rights under article 31, some degree of risk and challenge is integral to play and recreational activities and is a necessary component of the benefits of these activities'.[22] In determining how much risk a child should be exposed to, the Committee said that '[t]he best interests of the child and listening to children's experiences and concerns should be mediating principles for determining the level of risk to which children can be exposed'.[23]

There are a number of points that arise from this discussion of children and young people's play in urban environments that relate to the play of children in social media. First, the observation that public spaces are becoming increasingly commercialised mirrors the nature of social media. As discussed earlier, Fuchs notes that while social media is presented as a democratic public sphere, it is a platform upon which large corporate interests seek to make revenue from advertising. In the physical realm, children and young people who 'congregate' in shopping malls get in the way of the use of the space for corporate profit. They then have a choice – move on or become consumers. In a similar fashion, young people's use of social media occurs within the context of a heavily commercialized space, albeit that the space is attractive because it is presented as a public sphere that appears to encourage diverse expressions of identity. But that appearance must be limited to the point that such expression undermines the commercial imperative. As we have seen, the surveillance, monitoring and control of children online is as much a reality in that space as it is in physical spaces.

The second point that arises here is the role of the rights of children. Again, we see the 'messiness' of law, as it does not lead inevitably to the conclusion that children's play is simply the romanticised version that has children playing happily in a playground as innocent and compliant individuals. The legal analysis of the right by the UN Committee indicates that it also has a 'darker' side that must contemplate children taking risks that many adults may feel uncomfortable with, or even threatened by. However, this is not to proceed to some new paradigm that asserts the rights of children to take risks without regard to competing considerations. If children and young people have the right to take risks in their play, then this needs to be mediated with regard to their best interests based on listening to their concerns but blending that with what must be the experience of their parents and their parents' concerns. Thus, in asserting the rights of children, the law still sees a role for parental involvement. In the commercialised space of social media we also have to consider the agenda of social media providers who may gain from having an audience who claim their independent rights to be in that space, but who do not benefit from having strong advocates to articulate their interests independent of that commercial aim. What we then have to consider is whether Google, Facebook and so on have an interest in children claiming their rights independent of their adult guardians and without the benefit of their independent oversight. In the age of social media is the real fear that young people will be encouraged to venture into that space independently, or is it with the possibility that parents have themselves absorbed the message that parental guidance means directing their children within the parameters that are designed by the social media providers?

The final point follows from the previous one. The UN committee, consistent with UNCROC, expressed that the role of states that are party to the Convention is to encourage the dialogue between younger people as rights holders and adults about the spaces needed for play. In the case of social media, the question that arises is what role the state plays vis-à-vis the social media providers, who are often powerful economically and politically. Clearly, governments themselves rely on and use social media for their messages and so are themselves dependent on those networks for their capacity to govern. As discussed above, there are many contradictions within the regulation of social media by the state. Calls for greater surveillance of individuals online are not usually matched by the acceptance of more transparency by government of its activities or by social media providers of their corporate intent. If children and young people claimed the right to play online in ways that test the boundaries of state and corporate tolerance of such transparency – such as in the nature of hacking culture – then how might we expect their best interests to be defined?

5.2 Sexualising and de-sexualising young people: social media and the lost romance of childhood

We turn then to an area that is perhaps one of the most debated yet highly contested areas of young people's online experiences. The role of social media in 'sexualising' children is one that preoccupies many commentators, scholars and politicians. The connection with 'play' is complex, for as has been suggested, to play is to challenge boundaries and test one's identity, although it is recognised that the use of the term 'play' here is not uncontroversial. Nevertheless, I do want to argue that understanding young people's sexualised behaviour on social media and online with some reference to it as 'play' is important to contextualise what is occurring.

It is important to first consider the very issue of young people and sexual rights before embarking further. David Archard argues that while many of the anxieties surrounding young people expressing their sexuality arise from the concern with the sexual abuse of children, he warns that while this concern is clearly justified, this 'should not blind us to either the possibility that children can engage in sexually non-abusive activities, or to the realities of any child's actual sexuality'.[24] To the extent that many of the views expressed about children and sex claim that preservation of the child's innocence and retention of their 'childhood' should be the aim of any law or policy, he remarks that

> [t]alk of the child's essential innocence is in danger both of being mythic and, ironically, of being sexualised. The child, like a virginal

> woman, can be the object of a male sexual desire to corrupt what is as yet uncorrupted.[25]

Others such as James Kincaid make similar points about childhood innocence. The innocent child is often said to be the reason for asserting that children are non-sexual, but that innocence can itself become eroticised.[26] The intense focus on defining children as non-sexual, of course, focuses on their sexuality nevertheless; as Kincaid writes,

> innocence was filed down to mean little more than virginity coupled with innocence: the species incapable of practising or inciting sex. The irony is not hard to miss: defining something entirely as a negation brings irresistibly before us that which we're trying to banish.[27]

Jenny Kitzinger also makes the point about the double standard at work when we claim that childhood is a time of innocence:

> The twin concepts of innocence and ignorance are vehicles for adult double standards. A child is ignorant if she doesn't know what adults want her to know, but innocent if she doesn't know what adults don't want her to know.[28]

Clearly, notions of childhood innocence get in the way of claims that children possess sexual rights. To hold a right of this kind, it is said, often assumes some capacity to prosecute it, and the legal test will always resort to notions of maturity and agency, in the vein of cases such as *Gillick*. Put simply, how can an innocent or ignorant child or young person possess that level of maturity to make informed decisions about sexual matters? However, this arguably misunderstands the nature of rights, what children and young people might be claiming here and the responsibility of adults, often parents, to children. We need to move away from the absolutist position that suggests that either parents will decide such matters on behalf of children and young people, or that children will decide. The latter may well suit certain interests who want to market their commodities directly to children, but they may not address the interests of the child to receive some guidance – based on their best interests – by adults without a commercial interest in them.

Judith Ennew explains this point in her discussion of the sexual rights of children in the context of anxieties about exposing children to sexual exploitation:

> The key to solving the problem lies not in denouncing repressive morality, but in denying the premise of childhood innocence. Recognizing

> childhood sexuality does not necessarily lead to absolute sexual anarchy. On the contrary, it implies another form of adult responsibility in which both rights and duties are acknowledged.[29]

Ennew then argues that as children develop, the responsibility of adults is to provide age-appropriate information about sexual matters to children, in a way which recognises different stages of children's development.[30] Ennew does proceed to suggest a narrow view as far as children's capacity to consent is considered. Having recognised that children's different stages of development mean that they 'possess differing information about the social rules surrounding intimacy and for judging the acceptability of sexual partners, as well as the social content of sexual activities and their physical and social consequences',[31] she concludes that '[c]hildren can thus rarely give informed consent to sexual intimacy and there is a case to be made for protecting them for any situation in which they consent because of lack of information or false information'.[32] This may be a product of the time in which she was writing, as it preceded cases such as *Gillick* and the creation of the UN Convention on the Rights of the Child. Nevertheless, there is value in the argument she makes for protection arising from the recognition of children's sexual rights. Just as assuming children's right to participate in, say, city design will be effective without any prior education about urban issues, so too to assume that a child inherently understands sexual matters and so can assert sexual rights ignores the prior need for education and guidance about such matters.

This suggests that what has been lost in claims for children's autonomous rights is consideration of how those rights are informed by the responsibility of parents and guardians to educate and guide their children in their best interests. This is not the same thing as making decisions for children and young people, but nor is it the same thing as assuming that children and young people have an inherent understanding of those matters. To do this is to construct an equally romanticised view of childhood as held by those who rely on childhood innocence to deny children their independent rights.

Of course, this continues to deliver us messy interpretations of laws that impact on children in sexual matters. Much of this is to do with the ideological bent of adults who are responsible for children's well-being. Carl Stychin places discussions of youth sexuality in the context of his analysis of law reform and the repeal of section 28 of the Local Government Act in the UK. This section prohibited the promotion of homosexuality by local authorities or teaching that promoted homosexuality in maintained schools.[33] As Stychin shows, law reformers utilised familial discourse to recentre heterosexual family life by arguing that as all heterosexual men and women come from a family, then laws that discriminate as did section 28 undermine traditional family life, as they promote negative attitudes towards gay family members.[34] As he explains:

> Discriminatory laws become an affront to the family, as it has been traditionally understood. And the family is itself chastised to the extent that it does not accept and love its gay children, who have been forced to leave their families in some cases. Of course, the possibility that gay youth may choose to reject their families is itself never seen as a possibility, nor is family seen as something from which you might want to escape.[35]

Stychin notes that while the debates on the reform of section 28 relied on 'family values', notions of gay youth sexuality were regarded as unproblematic.[36] Reformers adopted the progressive view that sexual identity is not a choice, and so this created a minority that required protection.[37] In disagreeing with conservatives who argue that there are two types of homosexuals, 'congenital and those converted by a homosexual experience during adolescence', reformers also accepted that only the first group exist – 'they seek to answer conservative claims that "youth" is a particularly vulnerable moment at which childhood innocence may be corrupted and perverted' as homosexual identity is fixed and a sign of 'maturity achieved and rational identity'.[38] Stychin also notes the various ways in which youth are constructed in these debates, ways which are at times in tension with each other. In constructing gay male youth, reformers accept they have no choice about who they are, but they do have choices about who they form relationships with. The reformers' aim is not to criminalise those they consent to form such relationships with.[39] Conservatives, on the other hand, invoke the imagery of 'the predator and wayward teenage boy' while reformers constructed a romanticised image of gay youth.[40] This led to a number of contradictory messages about youth:

> Youth are also seen as *knowing* – as saturated with information – but lacking in appropriate teaching on responsibility. They are no longer innocent children, devoid of knowledge (nor, therefore, should they be easily corruptible). For reformers, youth is a stage of development quite distinct from childhood, and much closer to adulthood. What is seen as necessary, then, is 'the cultivation of a more active subjectivity within young people who will be required to take more responsibility for their lives'.[41]

Stychin argues that gay male youth are desexualised in this process while heterosexual youth are constructed as hypersexualised, dangerous and out of control, with straight female youth in danger of becoming pregnant by them. Such youth are thus in need of greater regulation.[42] The desexualisation of gay male youth occurs as law reformers aimed to construct them as 'different', yet the 'same' in terms of relationship forms which are essentially non-hypersexualised, or in effect de-sexualised.[43]

The relevance of Stychin's discussion of the repeal of section 28 for social media and the law operates on various levels. One is the manner in which sexual imagery was used to construct youth in ways that met the political objectives of different sides of the debate. In the conservative mind, where homosexuality is a choice, one can also see the basis for the fear that social media can influence such choices. This perceived power of social media to create a certain type of youth seems to arise from this view of human behaviour and may well explain the current discourse around the role of social media in 'radicalising' youth. As we have seen, other commentators contest the notion that social media creates revolutions and sustains them – their argument is that there must already be in the community an impetus to support such views for social media to facilitate such challenges to authority.

In matters of sexuality, an online presence can affirm and make public a sexual identity which may not be possible in the young person's immediate real world. It may create a network of contacts and supports not otherwise available to them. The manner in which warnings about meeting online contacts in the real world are often made to young people reflects some of the points Stychin makes about romanticised notions of family life at work in the section 28 reform debates. It is rare, for instance, to acknowledge that the young person seeking contact with persons met online could be escaping from a violent or non-accepting family life. This does not reduce risks in meeting anyone, of course, but it places in context why young people might seek out others online. The law's focus seems so often fixated on harm that it is forgotten that there are other rights to claim in this space. As a result, the safest option is deemed to be the prevention of offline meetings rather than understanding them as an expression of identity that as a human right needs to at times be facilitated.

Ultimately, it is easier to regard the child that asserts rights that challenge these romanticised ideas about childhood innocence as transgressive and as the core of the problem rather than suggesting they might show the way to new solutions for old problems. As Mike Presdee wrote:

> Being 'young' is characterised by a culture created out of the tensions that emanate between regulation and rebellion; control and care; the civilised and the savage. The result is a contesting carnivalesque culture that forever pushed at the boundaries of transgression and where carnival becomes not the 'second life of people' but the first life of youth. Their culture, rather than being a search for the 'authentic' as in modern culture, is an endless search for the inauthentic; that is, a culture that is empty of the authority and the imperatives that come

> with authenticity. It is this perceived 'emptiness as protest' that prompts panic from 'adult' society.[44]

Although writing before social media became commonplace, Presdee also referred to the way in which new technology such as mobile phones allowed young people to 'carry their culture with them . . . with defiance'.[45] His utilisation of 'carnival' as a concept to explain and understand transgression seems worthy of revisiting in the age of social media, and perhaps especially as we come to consideration of sexual matters and social media. Presdee borrows Bakhtin's idea of the 'second life of the people',[46] which he explains:

> It is from the second life that the majority of transgressions emanate. It is here that we find the genesis and rationale for behaviour that anticipates the ability to destroy, disrupt and dissent. The second life of people is that part of life that is inaccessible and untouchable to the 'official' world of the scientific rationality of modernity and its politics, parties and politicians. It is the realm of resentment and irrationality *par excellence* and also the realm of much crime. It is that part of social life that is unknowable to those in power and which therefore stands outside their consciousness and their understanding. They cannot understand it or indeed even 'read' it as real life, but only as immoral, uncivilised, obscene and unfathomable social behaviour.[47]

As the state imposes on the population policies – presumably such as ones based on the need for austerity – the disconnect this creates between the 'official' world view and the reality for most people results in many people being pushed into the second life, resulting in, according to Presdee, 'no difference between carnival and true life, the second life, where the only laws are the laws of freedom with no possibility of any life outside of it'.[48] The second life is where people express their discontent and fears of official life, and so it is 'where everyday life resides and where the rationality of law loses its power'.[49]

Presdee opens our analysis to the way in which emotion, pleasure and irrational thoughts have come to govern our lives more and more. The commodification of social life, says Presdee, has led to 'the heightened pursuit of pleasure, which has become the necessary lubricant of everyday social life'.[50] In one passage Presdee writes of this in a way that could almost have been written today about young people's use of social media:

> This pursuit of popular pleasure contained within a culture of consumption becomes a continuing problem for legislators and moral reformers who endeavour to manage pleasure through legislation and control mechanisms that attempt to define particular desires and pleasure as

deviant and criminal. But there is, and has been in the past, a lack of any understanding of the dynamics of pleasure itself.[51]

In this way punishment defines one as the rebel; transgression is defined by the law's statement that this is prohibited behaviour. The message sent is, as Presdee remarks, not the intended one of what not do, but instead what you have to do.[52] It is the same as the police officer who tells teenage schoolchildren that posting embarrassing images of themselves is not a good idea because these images can stay on the Internet for a thousand years. Yet this immediately makes one think that for many young people, a thousand years of notoriety might be more than worth the risk, and even pleasurable.

This is not to suggest that such behaviour is intrinsically good or bad, for as Presdee notes, such outcomes represent the contradictions of modern life. As he says, 'irrational acts of destruction and violence intermingle with pleasure, fun, desire and performance'.[53] This also results in the breakdown of law and order, for the pursuit of punishment leads, as he says, to the need to 'riot for pleasure'.[54] Thus the London riots become a convergence of protest, transgression, excitement and performance – often played out on social media, which then enhances the excitement and performance aspects of the behaviour. The role of law in this is muddled and confused, and can even perpetuate disorder. Presdee notes the replacement of education with emotion in a world where anyone can be an 'expert' and traditional norms are inverted.[55] He wrote, 'truth and falsity become interposed as falsity becomes reality for all and lawmakers try desperately to make sense of the senseless world of commodities'.[56] In this new world, emotional responses such as hate and blame have replaced much rational thought as a response to perceived injustices and inequalities.[57] Law as a product of rational thought is replaced by law as an ideological construct. This may not be a new phenomenon, of course, but it challenges many views of law as a body of rationality based on evidence.

5.3 Social media and sexting: reinforcing sexual stereotypes or creating new boundaries

I think there is great value in the ideas expounded by Presdee for understanding young people's use of social media, particularly when it comes to sexual matters in that space. The example of sexting is particularly illustrative, as it contains all the elements of Presdee's analysis discussed above.

Sexting – a practice that includes such behaviour as the sending of sexualised 'selfies' using mobile technology – can be recognised as a form of play by young people, but which is regarded by many adults as inappropriate sexualised behaviour. Kath Albury notes this, and then proceeds to discuss the sexual rights of young people in this space.[58] Such discussions make perfect sense in that they raise issues of children's agency, the place of young women in digital spaces and the discourses on control of their bodies, and issues of ethical behaviour, particularly as it relates to the sending of sexualised images of others without their consent. It is an approach I also have taken to this area.[59] This leads to conclusions such as Albury's that imagine a new approach which contests what is to be regarded as 'appropriate' sexual conduct and suggests a shift away from whether one has sexted as a form of sexual expression towards a question of whether one has acted ethically in relation to sharing others' sexualised images.[60]

What seems to be lacking in this approach to sexting, though, is an examination of another right – the right to play. Although the behaviour was identified by Albury as a form of playing with digital technologies, the shift to constructing the phenomenon in terms of the sexual rights of young people fails to consider that right which is explicitly stated in the UNCROC. An exploration of the boundaries of the right to play will then come up against many of the points raised by Presdee, that play is more than, in this instance, using the technology to sext, but is itself an expression of identity and often will be regarded as transgressive and which in being so further embeds the individual's identity. Thus, calls for more ethical behaviour within the practice of sexting beg the question as to whether the message sent will be accepted or used as the new marker of what is unacceptable. To put it another way, Presdee's analysis raises an uncomfortable question for social scientists: Is young people's sexting behaviour an act of sexual expression of who they are that is worthy of protection as a sexual right? Or is it an act of pleasure or a performance that may be worthy of some protection as an aspect of the right to play but at its core is a self-absorbed action that has little intrinsic value other than the thrill and excitement it provides to the participants? Albury's analysis proposes a rational response to the reality of young people's behaviour online. Presdee's analysis suggests that the commodification of social life in fact underpins the practice and that without change at that level, transgression must continue as a response to the need for pleasure that that society encourages.

However, I do not understand Presdee as arguing against the need to articulate rational responses to social life. His approach is much more about being creative and imaginative in response to the realities of people's lives, which requires us to confront many uncomfortable understandings about those around us. In that vein, the pursuit of more positive rights for children and young people with respect to their sexual rights online in a way that attempts to understand youth culture and sub-culture is an advance on the negative and defensive approach which seems to rest on a given set of assumptions about what is 'good', 'bad', 'appropriate' and 'inappropriate'. It is also consistent with negotiating the meaning of the best interests of the child and young person with reference to their autonomous rights within a framework that also promotes a role for adults to participate in the process of reshaping the child's position.[61] This is a more nuanced approach than has prevailed until now. Yet because there is a great reliance on value judgments in this process, this does return us to the messiness of the law, which can undermine its legitimacy for those who are fixated on consistency in decision-making.

To address the many cultures of youth is confronting, as Presdee's work suggests. Many campaigners against sexting construct a narrative around the 'reality' of sexting that focuses on the quantity and prevalence of its practice. These works result in a wide degree of variance about the rate of sexting, and tend to often adopt a 'do you know what your children are doing' approach that seems designed to shock parents apparently ignorant to their child's activities.[62] Studies that suggest comparatively low rates of sexting[63] tend to be swept aside by the prevailing narrative that it is at a level, it is claimed, to concern us all.

Robbie Duschinsky explains the reason this data is generated by those concerned with youth sexting behaviour. He argues that debates about childhood sexualisation are a discussion about the loss of 'purity' or 'innocence' of the female child. In his analysis of the Home Office review of childhood sexualisation,[64] he argues that the review challenges any sense that young people who portray themselves to 'look sexy' are not doing so as an authentic expression of who they are but because they have been encouraged to do so by the current nature of society: 'young people have been displaced from their natural form of "who they are" by the intrusion of sexualisation.'[65] Thus this narrative relies on a series of assumptions about gender, children and young people's agency, and young people's sexuality. This leads its proponents to a position where they contend that it is the overwhelming nature of the social forces presently existent in society that endanger the purity of young females and hyper-masculinise young males.[66] In the context of sexting, this leads young females to take and send images of themselves that are sexual, while young males seek and cajole them to do so.

One can see in this view of the nature of sexting how it feeds into narratives such as the decline of civility in society. It also connects with notions of 'hidden truths', and as Duchinsky explains, the sexualisation narrative needs 'to search "behind" distorted appearances of the central truths, which take the form of quantifiable measures of the frequency of sexual harm'[67] and seek to expose the 'reality' of young people's lives. This is needed to correct for the distortions in public understanding of what is occurring in the treatment of children created by cultural representations.[68] One assumes that those who argue that children are being increasingly sexualised in order to feed the profits of corporations which sell merchandise that is fed on sexualised images of children, tend to an absolutist view in such matters and have great trouble with any sense of cultural relativism. This creates a group who understands the 'reality' of sexual harm, while those who differ in their position suffer from the 'unreality' of their position.[69]

Thus, the compilation of data on the extent of sexting always plays a large part in debates over law reform in this area. For those who regard the harm involved in sexting as self-evident, the only matter to focus on is to collect the empirical data to demonstrate how widespread the problem is, giving the issue political prominence as well as an ostensibly scientific basis for legal controls to be imposed. After all, they might ask, if the law does not seek to protect children from harm, then what is its purpose? The problem is that the frequency at which something occurs is of little assistance either in trying to understand the nature of the activity or in assisting us in defining 'harm'. A young person may send a photograph of themselves to another person, but whether it is 'appropriate' or 'inappropriate' will be a matter of how others read the image. In addition, even if the image is to be read as sexualised, there must be, then, another discussion about whether children should have the right to send such images. In both cases, important matters of values, rights and agency of children are operative. These are not matters in which a community consensus exists. Counter-narratives do exist. Karaian writes of the 'digital sexual expression rights of youth',[70] for example. Albury argues for a similar approach.[71]

The difficulty is in the legal implementation of these approaches. In the state of Victoria, Australia, reform of the law in response to sexting by youth further demonstrates the difficulty in addressing the various narratives that are at work in this area. The law was reformed after a Parliamentary Committee inquired into sexting following concerns that the law was overreaching and criminalising young people who sexted as being in possession of, or distributing, child pornography, leading to these young people's being registered as sex offenders.[72] The Committee received submissions from an array of individuals and organisations, many of which expressed concern about the harm caused by such practices as well as the sexualisation of childhood. That is, many submissions represented the dominant narrative that youth sexting is fundamentally wrong. On the other hand, a smaller number of submissions did speak to the agency of youth and their capacity to control their own body images.[73] The resultant changes to the law demonstrate well the messiness of law and the difficulty of 'balancing' between quite different conceptualisations of young people. A new offence of non-consensual sexting was recommended and subsequently created to address cases where sexting is done to harm others. The inquiry concluded that apart from punishing individuals who use sexting to cause harm, the new offence would also 'assist to inform the community on expectations around the appropriate use of communications technologies'.[74]

The offence of non-consensual sexting allows for a defence that the person depicted in the sexted image consented to its being sent. However, the consent of a person under 18 is irrelevant and cannot be used as a defence to the offence.[75] However, to find the offence proven, it is also required that 'the distribution of the image is contrary to community standards of acceptable conduct'.[76] In deciding that question, regard must be had to 'the nature and content of the image'; 'the circumstances in which the image was captured'; 'the circumstances in which the image was distributed'; 'the age, intellectual capacity, vulnerability or other relevant circumstances of a person depicted in the image' and 'the degree to which the image affects the privacy of a person depicted in the image'.[77] The requirement to make a number of judgments about the context in which the image was produced and distributed certainly reduces clarity about the expectations around the appropriate use of communications technologies as envisaged by the Law Reform Committee. Invoking 'community standards' is also fraught, and raises the question as to which 'community' one is to refer to here – tech-savvy young people, or conservative older people, for example? All this section does is once again stress the manner in which what is to be regarded as acceptable becomes a matter of values.

A more fundamental problem arising from the Victorian legislation is what the offence says about the concept of childhood that informed the reformers. The fact that the consent of a young person is deemed irrelevant to the commission of the offence denies those young people any agency with respect to their image. This is shown to be even more problematic when it is considered that a recent UK College of Policing briefing note on sexting refers to 'consensual sharing' by young people and identifies how sexting may 'range from consensual sharing to exploitation'.[78] The clear message of this note is that prosecution of young people in cases without any aggravating features and that are consensual may have harmful, long-term impacts on the child caused by labelling the child a 'sex offender', and it emphasises instead the 'need to work with schools to educate children on the risks of exchanging imagery'.[79] Removal and deletion of images is also discussed.[80] This represents a clear shift from constructing consensual sexting as a crime to regarding it as a child-welfare matter. To that extent, although the briefing note appears to accept that young people who are still minors may consent, the underlying message is that sexting is a practice that needs to be corrected, if not by the criminal law, then by other diversionary/child protection methods.

5.4 Legal responses to the sexual child online

The problem is that approaches to how sexting is perceived vary between and sometimes within jurisdictions. For some, the notion of 'consensual sexting' by youth is a nonsense, either on the basis that no mature person would consent to such a thing or, alternatively, that given their age it is unlikely that they would not have felt under some pressure to participate in the activity and so render any 'consent' void. This is the constant dilemma facing adults judging the capacity of the child to make their own decisions. If the decision of a child or young person is to do something regarded as against the best interests of that child or young person, then how can one say the person has the maturity to make such a decision?

Yet this seems to be where there is a need to further analyse and think about what the right to play means for children. The problem with claiming agency for children, or a right to sexual expression, is that these claims constantly throw us back to discussions about the child's maturity. But the right to play is not seen in this light. Play is intrinsically something regarded as what children and young people do as children and young people. On the other hand, the best-interests-of-the-child standard undermines autonomy rights because it seems to look to the future of the child; hence, when this standard is invoked in sexting debates, the concern is always on how the future reputation or interests of the child will be damaged by posting certain images of the child online. The attempts to reform the law in Victoria illustrate how that thinking can also damage the long-term interests of the child in other ways, particularly through criminalising or stigmatising the child in the present with the long-term implications of that record.

We know the benefits of play include learning about risks, understanding challenges and pushing boundaries. Play is often transgressive, and while this can have negative outcomes, as a society we also recognise that without transgression social change would never occur. Murray Lee et al. identified from their research on young people a number of motivations given by those young people for sexting.[81] When asked why they thought teenagers sent sexts, reasons given included 'to be fun and flirty', 'to feel sexy and confident', 'because he received one' and 'to get noticed or show off'.[82] Their work also identified that young people they interviewed had a good understanding of the legal consequences of their sexting.[83] Yet their conclusions were also that it was a common activity amongst young people, and even more so amongst gay and bisexual youth.[84] They commented on the reasons given for sexting (mentioned above):

> These motivations appear consistent with a system of mutual exchange where particular expectations are constructed in a digital economy of images and videos. The inherent risk of the activity, while obviously being something to be managed by most participants, is also part of the attraction.[85]

They also reported the views of youth focus groups who thought that young females were placed under pressure from young males to send sexts, which is consistent with literature on gender differences in sexting.[86] They also reported a view amongst young people that the law was out of step with new communication technologies.[87] Lee et al. conclude that a specific sexting offence (as now exists in Victoria) is preferred to prosecuting for child pornography distribution or possession, but that it may have net-widening impact and deter the use of diversionary or restorative approaches that would provide better outcomes, as well as consideration of non-criminal and non-legal options.[88] They also criticise education campaigns on sexting for preaching abstinence or responsibility for negative outcomes 'in the way early sexual assault prevention literature did'.[89] They comment:

> our data suggests that these messages do not equate with the lived experiences of young people engaged in these activities. Rather, a more realistic and effective approach to regulating such behaviour might be more aligned with 'harm minimisation'. That is, to recognise that young people who live lives on-line will almost inevitably experiment with sexting at some point, but that there is a need to attempt to minimise the potentially negative outcomes of the behaviour.[90]

While such conclusions have some rational basis, the problem, as Presdee might have said, is that the practice of sexting is also an act of pleasure or 'play', which Lee et al. themselves acknowledge has an attraction because of the risks which their recommendations seek to minimise. How does one put into the law a risk-minimisation approach that seeks to remove the risks from the behaviour that is engaged in because of those risks? This is where we are faced with the rejection of the law's rationality that Presdee notes. It seems that the 'voice of the young', which is often said to be absent from policy debates, is then heard in this research speaking to a quite different objective than the law reformers in such places as Victoria. In that State, we are left with young people unable to consent in law to practices they engage in on a 'consensual' basis in their reality, leaving the law to judge whether 'community standards' have been breached to finally determine whether their sexting is lawful. Yet clarity on which 'community' to draw on for this judgment is unclear. Is it any wonder that the law seems disconnected from the lives of young people and is more likely to have its 'rationality' rejected than embraced by the young?

Notes

1 Stephen Flusty 'Thrashing Downtown: Play as Resistance to the Spatial and Representational Regulation of Los Angeles' (2000) 17(2) *Cities* 149–158.
2 See e.g. Play England 'Why Play Is Important' www.playengland.org.uk/about-us/why-play-is-important/, accessed 16 July, 2017.
3 Ibid.
4 See e.g. Chris Rojek *Ways of Escape: Modern Transformations in Leisure and Travel* (London, MacMillan, 1993).
5 Ibid., p. 213.
6 Department for Culture Media and Sport *Getting Serious About Play: A Review of Children's Play* (Department for Culture Media and Sport, 2004).
7 Ibid., p. 6. This is also cited as the relevant definition of play today by Play England in their *Charter for Children's Play*, www.playengland.net, accessed 16 July, 2017.

8 Ibid., p. 10.
9 Ibid., p. 11.
10 Ibid.
11 Ibid.
12 United Nations Committee on the Rights of the Child General comment No. 17 (2013) on the right of the child to rest, leisure, play, recreational activities, cultural life and the arts (art. 31),CRC/C/GC17, 17 April, 2013.
13 Ibid.
14 Ibid.
15 Ibid.
16 Ibid.
17 Ibid.
18 See e.g. Don Mitchell *Social Justice and the Fight for Public Space* (New York, Guildford, 2003); Setha Low and Neil Smith (eds.) *The Politics of Public Space* (Oxford, Routledge, 2006); Anthony Maniscalco *Public Spaces, Marketplaces, and the Constitution: Shopping Malls and the First Amendment* (Albany, State University of New York Press, 2015); David Harvey *Rebel Cities: From the Right to the City to the Urban Revolution* (London, Verso, 2012); Susan S. Fainstein *The Just City* (Ithaca, Cornell University Press, 2010).
19 See e.g. Lia Karsten 'It All Used to Be Better? Different Generations on Continuity and Change in Urban Children's Daily Use of Space' (2005) 3(3) *Children's Geographies* 275–290; Gil Valentine 'Children Should Be Seen and Not Heard: The Production and Transgression of Adults' Public Space' (1996) 17(3) *Urban Geography* 205–220.
20 United Nations Committee on the Rights of the Child General comment No. 17 (2013) on the right of the child to rest, leisure, play, recreational activities, cultural life and the arts (art. 31), CRC/C/GC17, 17 April, 2013.
21 Ibid.
22 Ibid.
23 Ibid.
24 David Archard *Children: Rights and Childhood 2nd edn* (London, Routledge, 1993), p. 105.
25 Ibid.
26 James R. Kincaid *Erotic Innocence: The Culture of Child Molesting* (Durham and London, Duke University Press, 1998).
27 Ibid., p. 55.
28 Jenny Kitzinger 'Children, Power and the Struggle Against Sexual Abuse' in A. James and A. Prout, op.cit., pp. 145–166 cited in Judith Levine *Harmful to Minors: The Perils of Protecting Children from Sex* (New York, Thuder's Mouth Press, 2002), p. 3.
29 Judith Ennew *The Sexual Exploitation of Children* (New York, St Martin's Press, 1986), p. 61.
30 Ibid.
31 Ibid., p. 62.
32 Ibid.
33 *Local Government Act 1988* (UK), s.28.
34 Carl F. Stychin *Governing Sexuality: The Changing Politics of Citizenship and Law Reform* (Oxford and Portland, Hart, 2003), p. 34.
35 Ibid.
36 Ibid.
37 Ibid., p. 35.

38 Ibid., citing Debbie Epstein, Richard Johnson and Deborah L. Steinberg 'Twice Told Tales: Transformation, Recuperation and Emergence in the Age of Consent Debates 1998' (2000) 3 *Sexualities* 5.
39 Stychin, op.cit., p. 35.
40 Ibid.
41 Ibid., citing B. Vaughan 'The Government of Youth: Disorder and Dependence?' (2000) 9 *Social and Legal Studies* 347.
42 Stychin, op.cit., p. 36.
43 Ibid.
44 Mike Presdee *Cultural Criminology and the Carnival of Crime* (London and New York, Routledge, 2000), p. 114.
45 Ibid., p. 115.
46 Mikhail Bakhtin *Rabelais and His World* (Bloomington, Indiana University Press, 1984).
47 Presdee, op.cit., p. 8.
48 Ibid.
49 Ibid.
50 Ibid., p. 28.
51 Ibid.
52 Ibid.
53 Ibid., p. 29.
54 Ibid.
55 Ibid., p. 30.
56 Ibid.
57 Ibid., pp. 158–159.
58 Kath Albury 'Just Because It's Public Doesn't Mean It's Any of Your Business: Adults' and Children's Sexual Rights in Digitally Mediated Spaces' (2017) 19(5) *New Media and Society* 713–725.
59 See Brian Simpson 'Sexting, Digital Dissent and Narratives of Innocence – Controlling the Child's Body' in Sampson Lee Blair, Patricia Neff Claster and Samuel M. Claster (eds.) *Technology and Youth: Growing up in a Digital World* (Sociological Studies of Children and Youth, Vol. 19, Bingley, Emerald, 2015), pp. 315–349.
60 Albury, op.cit., pp. 721–722.
61 Ibid.
62 Simpson, op.cit., p. 321.
63 See e.g. Parliament of Australia *High-Wire Act: Cyber-safety and the Young: Interim Report*, Joint Select Committee on Cyber-safety (Commonwealth of Australia, 2011).
64 Home Office *Sexualisation of Young People Review* (London, UK Home Office, 2010).
65 Robbie Duschinsky 'The 2010 UK Home Office "Sexualisation of Young People" Review: A Discursive Policy Analysis' (2012) 41 *Journal of Social Policy* 715–731.
66 Ibid., p. 721.
67 Ibid., p. 726.
68 Ibid.
69 Ibid., p. 727.
70 Lara Karaian 'Lolita Speaks: "Sexting", Teenage Girls and The law' (2012) 8 *Crime Media Culture* 57–73.
71 Albury, op.cit.
72 Law Reform Committee, Parliament of Victoria *Inquiry into Sexting* (2013).
73 For a fuller analysis of the submissions see Simpson (2015), op.cit.

74 Law Reform Committee, Parliament of Victoria, op.cit., p. 149.
75 Summary Offences Act 1966 (Vic.), s.41DA.
76 Ibid., s.41DA(1)(b).
77 Ibid., s.40.
78 College of Policing Briefing Note *Police Action in Response to Youth Produced Sexual Imagery ('Sexting')* Version 1.0, November, 2016, www.college.police.uk
79 Ibid.
80 Ibid.
81 Murray Lee, Thomas Crofts, Alyce McGovern and Sanja Milivojevic *Sexting and Young People* (Report to the Criminology Research Council, November, 2015).
82 Ibid., pp. 34, 37
83 Ibid., p. 44.
84 Ibid., p. 72.
85 Ibid., p. 73.
86 Ibid., citing Kath Albury, Kate Crawford, Paul Byron and Ben Mathews *Young People and Sexting in Australia: Ethics, Representation and the Law,* ARC Centre for Creative Industries and Innovation website, 2013, www.cci.edu.au/sites/default/files/Young_People_And_Sexting_Final.pdf; Jessica Ringrose, Laura Harvey, Rosalind Gill and Sonia Livingstone 'Teen Girls, Sexual Double Standards and "Sexting": Gendered Value in Digital Image Exchange' (2013) 14(3) *Feminist Theory* 305–323; Lara Karaian, op.cit. (2012).
87 Ibid., p. 74.
88 Ibid., p. 76.
89 Ibid.
90 Ibid.

Chapter 6

Schools, young people and social media

Accountability, surveillance and control

An important issue is what role schools should play in the regulation, education and control of young people's use of social media. Given the significant focus on the risks and harms young people are thought to face on the Internet and in their use of social media, it should not surprise that the role of the school system is said by many to be that of providing education and warnings about those risks. In addition, the use of social media within the school setting itself is also said to present challenges, especially around relationships formed between students and between staff and students online. In this context, cyber-bullying, sexual harassment and sexualisation again are raised as matters that schools must confront and address. However, this concern about these aspects of schools and social media is ultimately grounded in a defensive reaction to the fear and harm that social media generates – not always without cause, certainly – but nevertheless a concern that only addresses social media as a 'problem' to be battled.

The other view of the role of schools in relation to social media is that it is one of preparing students for their future careers, which will inevitably involve the use of new communication technologies. This construction of the school's role relies heavily on the notion that children's time in school is to be spent on such preparation and therefore also fits neatly into the narrative that time spent on social media is either a distraction from such preparation or at least an aspect of recreational time that is justified only in terms of the respite it provides young people from their 'real' schoolwork. This claimed role of the school is thus also about learning boundaries when it comes to the use of social media.

The criticism of these roles of the school is that there seems little place for the teaching of the ambiguity of meaning when discussing social media, especially as it relates to the discourse of rights in the context of social media. The teaching of human rights to children and young people nearly always makes conservatives turn pale amid claims that youth need to learn about responsibilities ahead of rights. Yet as we have seen, the place of social media and the places it creates raises many and varied discussions about the rights of young people. Should schools be empowering young people with the tools to question and challenge the very boundaries that the school system is asked to create around social media in the first instance? This question cannot be properly answered without considering the social forces that social media operates within.

6.1 Educating young people for the new world of social media: public sphere or commercial space?

It seems readily accepted by education authorities that social media is part of the new landscape of work and that as a consequence young people must be educated in the use of social media applications if they are to function successfully in that terrain. For example, the social media policy of the Education Department of Western Australia notes in relation to the place of social media in the classroom:

> The competent and effective use of these technologies by students is now firmly on school curricula. Educational outcomes include preparing students to take their place in a modern technological workforce and being able to interact socially with their peers and the wider community.[1]

While the guidelines do also speak to the non-work applications of social media, the broader teaching of the context of social media carries a warning in the same guidelines:

> In using these legitimate applications, you must not place yourself or your students at risk. The context, purpose and potential impact of using these applications should always be considered. In brief, you must maintain a professional tone in all communications with students and these technologies should only be used for teaching and learning programs, and in accordance with school and/or Department policies.[2]

This risk-averse approach to teaching and teacher-student relationships is also reflected in other parts of the guidelines that warn teachers not to 'publish any material that is offensive, pornographic, obscene, defamatory, threatening, harassing, bullying, discriminatory, hateful, racist, sexist, or breaches copyright or a Court Suppression order, or is otherwise unlawful'.[3] Doing any of these things may result in disciplinary action, according to the guidelines.[4]

The problem with guidelines that warn teachers not to publish material that is 'otherwise unlawful' on social media is that it indicates little of substance yet suggests a breadth of concern that it must affect the preparedness of teachers to challenge their students' thinking about the nature of the public sphere that social media is said to create. It also potentially hampers the ability of teachers to speak to the students – through social media platforms – on the same level and thereby make their teaching more 'student centred' and engaging. Such 'personal' interactions will possibly be interpreted as unprofessional and inappropriate, which will worry teachers into avoiding such interactions altogether.

In the United States, such 'personal' social media publications by teachers directed at their students have been claimed to be inappropriate, resulting in the teachers claiming that their First Amendment right to free speech has been infringed when told to stop using social media in that way. Such claims have relied on the view that personal social media accounts are private spaces and so their right to free speech should be seen as that of a private citizen and protected.[5] As Russo et al. note, in the United States in two cases[6] involving teachers' claims that their free speech rights were infringed were unsuccessful because the social media postings only raised private matters, whereas the test for the protection of free speech rights for teachers relied on a finding that the speech 'touched on matters of public concern'.[7] Thus the schools in the cases cited by Russo were able to classify the private matters raised in the social media postings of the teachers as unprofessional and inappropriate.

In the United Kingdom, there is also reliance on guidance that teachers should refrain from posting 'inappropriate' material on their social media sites that are then seen by their students. For teachers, this creates doubt about exactly what they can and cannot do on social media, leading to unions asking for clarity; indeed, they desire to remove any 'grey' areas.[8] The problem, of course, is that the law cannot provide that degree of certainty, as it is a mixture of different value sets and definitions of what is 'appropriate' change over time. It also reflects the manner in which social media, as with family life, is recasting the nature of teacher-student relationships, given the ability of social media to allow for more personal actions at all times of the day and night. The General Teaching Council for Scotland recognises these aspects of social media in its professional guidance to teachers.[9] It places the guidance on social media in the following context:

> The ability to communicate in real time with others and access networks across the world brings with it great opportunities for teachers. It also offers great challenges as the boundary between teacher and pupil can quickly become blurred.
>
> These days all professions are subject to wide scrutiny and it can be hard to tell the difference between perception and reality. The views of teachers on their own profession are important and are at the centre of a self-regulating profession.

> However, the perspective of parents and the understandable fears of the wider public about inappropriate use of the internet also have to be considered; and these views can sometimes be shaped by sources which are unpredictable – including the media. Teachers therefore need to be alert to the risk that actions which might, on the face of it, seem quite innocent can be misunderstood and misconstrued by others.[10]

The interesting aspect of the principles expressed here is the emphasis placed on the need to respond to perceptions and misunderstandings of others with respect to the actions of teachers. It seems to be an admission that social media has the capacity to alter professional judgment in the sense of requiring teachers to think about the need for certain online interactions that may be pedagogically justified but regarded as 'inappropriate' by parents or the wider public. In such cases, the impact on the rights of children to receive an 'appropriate' education must be called into question, yet such discussions of children's rights rarely arise in relation to such matters, if at all.

The assumption in the Scottish guidance is that social media creates 'casual dialogue', leading to the possible misconstruing of otherwise innocent actions.[11] This is described as the way social media 'brings with it a new dimension and "feel" to a relationship' that affects how teachers and students interact when they become friends online.[12] The guidance then suggests that a teacher should never share online what they 'would not willingly or appropriately share in a school or school-related setting or in the community'.[13] The problem with such guidance is that again it ignores the value-based nature of such judgments and that different people will make different judgments about what they would or would not share. Of course, there may well be much information that most teachers or members of the public would agree is inappropriate to share. However, that does not mean the judgment is any less based on values. Indeed, the claimed high rate of teachers falling foul of misconduct allegations involving social media[14] would indicate that teachers are confused as to where the boundaries lie. The construction of the problem as one of 'lack of clarity' further denies the manner in which law often constructs ambiguity to avoid the pretence of certainty, which is impossible to achieve where values lie at the core of the matter.

As is often the case in such areas of ambiguity, the Scottish guidance then provides examples of how teachers can avoid risk when using social media. The examples either suggest a form of abstinence by not interacting online with students and parents, or they become circuitous to the question by suggesting that teachers should 'operate online in a way in which would not call into question your position as a professional'.[15] It also suggests that three questions can be asked by teachers before posting on social media:

> Might it reflect poorly on you, your school, employer or the teaching profession? Is your intention to post this material driven by personal

> reasons or professional reasons? Are you confident that the comment or other media in question, if accessed by others, (colleagues, parents etc.) would be considered reasonable and appropriate?[16]

Such questions, arguably, are not guidance at all but indicate both the difficulty in determining norms in the age of social media as well as the risk-averse nature of organisations, including schools. But there is an even more troubling aspect to such guidance, for given the lack of articulation about the nature of making professional judgments, it is far more likely that teachers will veer towards not posting online in may circumstances and so in effect self-censor themselves. The question that should then be asked is how healthy for a child's education rights is it for the people who are supposed to open their minds to critical and open thinking to feel constrained in how they use communication technologies?

The role of law, then, in such guidance documents is not portrayed as a dynamic institution that should be shaped by and respond to the opportunities presented by these new technologies. Instead it is presented as something to be feared. The Scottish guidance highlights the possibility of criminal prosecution or civil claims in the case of 'unwise behaviour online'.[17] Clearly, many guidance documents avoid detailed discussion of what is 'inappropriate' content and focus more on how to report it, why it is bad practice to discuss certain matters such as complaints about the school in the public space of social media or how privacy considerations should restrain public discussion of certain matters involving individuals including parents and the general community.[18] In some cases such documents, in relation to parents using social media to post comments about the school, includes as 'inappropriate' 'posting negative/offensive comments about specific pupils/staff at the School'.[19]

In emphasising the legal sanctions for posting what is vaguely defined 'inappropriate' content and proscribing 'negative' comments as also being inappropriate, such guidance suggests that schools may attempt to manage social media use to avoid criticism. This suggests that far from being understood as a public sphere where a free exchange of information takes place by a newly empowered citizenry, such spaces are being subjected to more and more control in order to create a quite different type of space. In this context, the way in which schools construct this space is likely to be the way in which young people taught within those schools come to understand it. The trends would suggest that the space created by social media is more and more that of a commercial space occupied by corporate and state interests to serve their needs.[20] While some open discussion will occur, it is marginalised by the messages contained in the guidance documents produced for and by schools. Parents, who may at times also speak for young people in a manner inconsistent with this corporatist agenda, are also constrained by such guidance documents as they are encouraged to follow certain forms of parental guidance issued by the state as discussed in earlier chapters.

6.2 Teaching the dark side of social media: new approaches to educating young people about online danger and cyber safety

Kath Albury suggests a wholly different approach to teaching about the risks associated with social media. Citing Dobson and Ringrose's approach,[21] Albury argues for an approach to the use of social media that is grounded in ethical approaches to online sharing rather than in 'gendered assumptions regarding appropriateness'.[22] By shifting the focus to positive rights to sexual expression, she asks a series of questions:

> What if a young woman's rights to digital participation did not imply an obligation to either (a) maintain absolute secrecy regarding her sexual desires or (b) abstain entirely from all forms of mediated sexual expression? What if being known as 'someone who gossips, and shares sexual images without consent' was the more shameful identity and was presented to young people as such? What if they were cautioned that inappropriate gossip and non-consensual picture sharing was a violation of others' rights, that it would potentially damage their 'reputation' and future employability?[23]

This is an important departure from current approaches where the 'risk' is in sharing sexualised images online, with the supposed negative consequences for future reputation. If we adopt Albury's suggestions, then we are acknowledging that current approaches to what schools should be educating young people about with respect to social media are based on a set of assumptions about how young women in particular should act to protect their sexual reputation by in effect denying their sexuality. In this regard, policies that look to schools to educate young people about online behaviour have to be examined for the assumptions they reveal that underpin the approach taken by educators within those schools to teaching about such matters.

An example of a school adopting gendered assumptions in their school policies occurred in Melbourne, Victoria in 2016 when a school told their female students that their legs exposed by short skirts distracted male students. They were told to stop wearing make-up and short skirts and sending sexy selfies. They were also told that if their skirts did not reach their knees they would be deemed inappropriate. A fifteen-year-old student made her own YouTube video in response that went viral. In it she said:

> I have self-respect, I look after myself. You can't tell me what self-respect is, you can't tell me what ladylike is. We don't live in the 50s anymore;

> I'm looking for equality, I'm looking forward to being able to show off my body without being sexualised. I am 15 years old. You do not get to sexualise me like that, you do not get to tell me that my body is sacred, because it isn't. Half the population is female all right. We're not sacred. We're not a new discovery, people know that I have legs, that I have knees, I have thighs, and I have a vagina. I don't want these girls to be growing up in a society where they need to believe that they have to be a certain way, because they can be however they want to be. They can be however makes them comfortable and confident.[24]

However, the less-reported school's response indicates the ongoing problems with official discourse about young people and the risks of social media. The principal of the school concerned was reported as saying that there was misunderstanding of the message the school was sending to students, and he said:

> It was stressed to students to be mindful of their digital footprint, and refrain from attempting to procure or disseminate inappropriate personal media which may be illegal . . . I want to be clear here and say that in no way did we suggest that what girls wear makes harassment or abuse acceptable. This is never the case . . . The enforcement of our uniform policy and the abuse and the recent exploitation of girls online are separate issues and should be treated as such . . . In public discussion about these two issues . . . they have, however, become linked. We regret this. It was never our intention that this should occur.[25]

However, it is hard to see how the two did not become linked and in doing so reinforced stereotyped views of gender roles. Of more significance is what this example says about expectations placed on schools to educate young people – and in this instance, young women – about digital citizenship. Certainly, there is a role for schools in alerting students to the risks associated with online interactions, but if young people's right to express their sexuality and to assert positive sexual rights is also to be an aspect of such education, then where do schools lie with respect to the capacity of young people to do so?

Marilyn Preston, writing in the United States, claims that teachers responsible for sexuality education often continue to adopt heteronormative and stereotyped views of gender roles in their own approach to their role.[26] She writes of one teacher she interviewed, saying that the teacher's

> belief that women are 'trying to follow in guys' footsteps' reinforces notions that men lack attachment in sexual interactions, as well as an essentialist understanding of men and women as naturally different. Lacey's words also support this particular discourse, in articulating

> that she believes girls are naturally more mature and thus 'can take on' the role of responsibility. This line of thinking echoes the societal stereotype of women as gatekeepers of sexuality and as in charge of, or responsible for, the policing of men's desires.[27]

She also found that some of the teachers she spoke with silenced the experience of LGBTQ students and downplayed violence against them, even suggesting that when it did occur it was due to the victim's 'flaunting' of their sexuality or questioning whether the student was gay.[28] Peterson's conclusions were that while the teachers regarded their classes as safe spaces to discuss sexuality, they still held to 'notions that reinforce problematic hierarchies and stereotypes of both men and women and preclude identities that sit outside of those categories'.[29] She concluded the following:

> This limits their ability to intervene or challenge the compulsory heterosexuality and peer regulation of gender that exist in schools. It also serves to work against the goal that the teachers maintain, of creating a space in schooling wherein sexuality can be discussed explicitly and in an affirming way.[30]

While there may have been some desire to teach these areas positively, they were hampered by a lack of guidance, resources and institutional support.[31] Whether this is the experience in other countries or jurisdictions may be questioned, but it does raise the question as to whether it is enough to assume that the recognition of a young person's rights to positive sexual expression will be part of school education. This will still depend on adequately trained teachers who possess the capacity to reflect on their own assumptions and value set to give effect to that kind of curriculum. At the very least one can see the gulf between those who assert that discussions of social media and the role of the school should embrace more diverse and positive notions of young people's sexual rights and those such as exemplified by the UK College of Policing briefing note on sexting, discussed in the previous chapter, and its comment that

> [p]olice should engage with schools to provide advice and information during investigations, and to educate children on the risks of exchanging imagery. Educational messages should highlight that once an image has been shared, its use is out of control.[32]

If schools are to educate young people about all their rights, including as digital citizens, then teachers have to become much more than channels for state and corporate discourses on what their relationship with social media should be.

6.3 Schools as sites of surveillance: social media and monitoring behaviour

Another area where schools are asked to play a role in young people's relationship with social media is in the surveillance of young people online. This seems to operate on a few levels. One is in a normalising manner, where the use of the technology to monitor young people is viewed as an accepted and proper part of the adoption of new communication technologies. The other level is much more direct although shifting in its manner. One way in which this takes place has been in the policing of young people's sexuality online, which continues to be a significant focus of concern. However, the use of monitoring online has also moved more recently to young people's online activity in relation to terrorism-related activity. This has resulted in the passage of anti-terrorism laws in Australia that allow for control orders to be placed on young people aged 14 and over.[33] In this area, the role of schools in the process of surveillance has also become more important.[34]

While some argue that such laws are counter-productive or do not attack the causes of terrorism,[35] what is less debated is how the assumption that the proper role of the school is to police this area fits with the place of education more generally to discuss critiques of society. The monitoring of children generally at school raises issues of young people's privacy. Some schools are said to be using applications that allow them to monitor whether students are accessing pornography or other material that places them at risk.[36] In support of such monitoring, it is claimed that schools have a duty of care to protect children from online risks, while against this form of surveillance sits the argument that it is intrusive and undermines young people's privacy rights.[37] What also needs to be added to such debates is that companies that develop such software to be placed on the mobile phones of students have a commercial interest in construing the legal concerns in a way that meets their interests in selling the applications to schools. The company mentioned in the above report, Family Zone, promotes itself heavily on social media. On their Twitter feed they claim they will have 120 schools signed up by the start of the 2018 school year.[38] They also claim to have 133 United States school installations, as well as partnerships with a New Zealand filtering platform and wholesale agreements in the Philippines and Indonesia.[39] The same tweet states their revenue to have grown from $A400,000 in 2016 to $A1 million in 2017 and a projected revenue of $14.5 million in 2019.[40] In effect, the aim of their technology is to enable parents (and schools) to control young people's access to social media and other sites while on mobile technology and so meet the challenge presented by it in terms of young people having access to the Internet beyond the home today.

Family Zone's website states that they have teamed up with 'cyber-experts' so that parents (and presumably schools, too) can choose an expert 'to provide settings that are custom-designed and age appropriate', thus freeing parents from having to keep up with 'technology, apps and online risks'.[41] One of the experts used by the company provides a statement that incorporates the utopian/dystopian view of the online world discussed earlier:

> I was an early adopter of digital technology and the internet for marketing online support communities and multi media, going back some 20 years. My attitude to the online world, video gaming, social media and online media is enthusiastic. My talks to students are often met with cheers, finally a grown up who isn't an old Fuddy Duddy about technology. I show students how to keep themselves safe online and provide them tips on how to grow into amazing digital citizens who can moderate their own online use, so that it is balanced and healthy. Not Just Fear Tactics! I offer a positive and common sense approach to cyber safety. I look forward to working with you on building a cyber safe generation.[42]

What has to be remembered about the various statements such as this from Family Zone's cyber-experts is that they are all part of their marketing strategy to sell their product. In constructing the issue as one of filtering out the 'bad' and keeping the 'good', they also feed the dominant narratives that abound in relation to social media. There is little if any mention of young people's rights in this space, other than to be protected online, while another expert asserts that '[p]arents have a right to know where their children go and who they communicate with'.[43] It also feeds into the narrative that the technology should be mastered by young people within this framework, as another cyber-expert on the site explains: 'as parents and teachers we need to teach them about the privacy that they have never had, stop saying no to using apps, enable them to use social media with awareness and understand that this is the world now.'[44]

Much of the critical response to companies such as Family Zone is that their applications are intrusive, place young people under surveillance and may undermine the parent/schoolchild relationship and create fear about the online world.[45] However, even more concerning is that such sites offer little information about how their cyber-experts define what is to be regarded as 'inappropriate' as would justify it being filtered out of a young person's online access. In some cases the qualification to judge such matters seems to derive from the expert being a parent, rather than from their professional expertise alone. However, while this reflects Presdee's comments on the demise of expertise and the rise of emotion in decision-making today, it also raises significant questions about how corporate interests begin to overlap with the education process in troubling ways. The dominance of those interests may tend to narrow rather than broaden discussions of what being a digital citizen means, and for young people it means that we may fail to embrace their rights in the fullest sense, moving beyond protection rights to also include positive rights to sexual expression and rights to transgress as an aspect of play. While many experts purport to seek a 'balanced' approach to young people's use of the online world, they often fail to engage with these areas that are confronting and so make such 'balanced' approaches extremely difficult.

Little mention is also made about the data on young people that is generated by such monitoring of them by parents or schools. There is a bitter irony in this, as many of those concerned about children 'over-sharing' such things as intimate images of themselves online promote monitoring software without apparently considering how much data is created about the child or young person's online habits and without considering how this data might be shared or used. In fact, much of the discussion about children sharing too much information online is directed towards the notion that the problem is sharing too much 'inappropriate' information. This explains the emphasis on sexualised images, material that might be construed as bullying or harassment and the like in this regard. The utopian/dystopian view of cyberspace that many of these commentators work with then leads them to suggest that sharing of 'appropriate' information is no bad thing, as it fits with the grand notion of cyberspace being the new public sphere. Privacy settings are often presented as the key here, as it is said those settings 'control' with whom the information is shared.

However, the lack of debate about what is appropriate and inappropriate online, and the simple binary of good and bad which underlies this, makes it easy for this debate to ignore the arguments of Fuchs that whatever one's privacy settings are, the social network provider has the personal information provided by the user and can access and use this to build profiles for its own commercial purposes. This qualifies the notion that privacy settings are so important to protect young people's privacy online. This may be true to an extent with other users they interact with, but, for example, as Facebook's data policy clearly indicates, they collect the information provided by users, including what they do on the platform; they use that information to 'provide, improve and develop services' and 'show and measure ads and services', and the information is shared within Facebook companies and with 'third-party partners and customers' who 'must adhere to strict confidentiality obligations in a way that is consistent with [Facebook's] Data Policy and the agreements [Facebook] enter into with them'.

What this opens up for the discussion is the manner in which algorithms and other analytics then process that information. Deborah Lupton and Ben Williamson regard that process as having the potential to undermine children's rights. They argue that

> people's life chances and access to opportunities are increasingly becoming shaped by the types of social sorting afforded by dataveillance. People have few opportunities to challenge the inferences and

predictions that are made by algorithmic calculations. They often have little knowledge about how corporations are exploiting their personal details and using them to construct detailed profiles on people used for decisions about their access to employment, insurance, social welfare, special offers and credit.[46]

While their comments extend beyond social media, the data collected on social media has many of these hallmarks. In addition, as a part of the education of young people within the school system, the normalisation of the 'proper' use of social media makes them more accepting of such datafication of their lives. Lupton and Williamson document the extent to which young people's lives are now monitored when they enter the education system in the UK and United States. This includes their educational progress, as well as such activity as their movements around the school, canteen purchases, personal health and well-being and mental health.[47] Of course, as they also note, young people have been monitored for centuries in order to make them into productive citizens.[48] However, it is the scope and intensity of data now collected on young people at school which has changed. They term this as a shift from the 'surveillance school' to the 'dataveillance school'.[49] One aspect of this shift is how the data can now be analysed by algorithms that predict future progress.[50] Lupton and Williamson remark:

> Such practices inscribe children within an ever-intensifying network of visibility, surveillance and normalization, in which their behaviours and bodies are continually judged and compared with others. One issue relates to the ways in which children come to be understood and portrayed via the algorithmic knowledge that such practices generate about them. The apparently scientific neutrality of digitized quantification of children's attributes obscures the reductionism that such processes inevitably produce. In any mode of information-gathering, certain features are ignored or neglected, while others are brought to the fore. Rendering children's behaviours, qualities and bodies into digital data, and relying principally on these data when making important assessments, judgements or inferences about them, may delimit what can be known about them and how they might be treated as a result. What is considered knowable or calculable about children and their lives becomes the outcome of the digital device and its software.[51]

Such comments suggest that schools' concerns with teaching the importance of privacy settings to students with respect to their use of social media miss the point and far more substantial problems with respect to their interaction with the digital world. Indeed, it further casts doubt on the relevance of and reasons why so many discussions of social media and digital technology default to legal issues to do with privacy. Emmeline Taylor and Tonya Rooney describe privacy rights in the context of surveillance debates as 'extremely slippery'[52] and 'the most equivocal of all human rights in terms of definition and circumscription'.[53] They further suggest that the established ways of understanding privacy in law fit less well into the ways that young people now construct privacy through their use of social networking sites, suggesting, for example, the need for new ways of thinking about privacy.[54]

However, there is a more fundamental need to question whether privacy rights should even be the main focus at all. Such rights seem particularly reactive in the age of social media, and in terms of the amount of data shared with the social media platform providers may well be in that instance at least a matter of shutting the door after the horse has bolted. Lupton and Williamson have identified the rather more troubling matter of how data collected about children is subject to algorithmic analysis that begins to predetermine their life choices. As they comment, 'information about children's bodies and behaviours becomes rendered into a form of biocapital, a digital mode of commercially exploiting human embodiment'.[55] Viewed in this context, the teaching of the virtues of social media (even if qualified by noting the risks and dangers) seems to be part of the larger process of 'recruiting children and their parents as contributors to the unpaid digital labour workforce'.[56] The problem is that the data-collection process within education systems seems both unavoidable and overwhelming, making issues of consent and privacy almost redundant, and the discussion of privacy settings on social media seems to be more of a smokescreen that obscures these larger issues.

In terms of the impact of rights, Lupton and Williamson draw on two developments that sit in tension with each other. On the one side, there is children's rights discourse that they claim is only just beginning to confront how those rights sit in relation to the digital age.[57] On the other side is the datafication and dataveillance of children and young people's lives.[58] They draw on various authors who have analysed the way in which children's right to free expression is problematic around issues of the capacity of children to form and express their own views.[59] Their concern is that analytics systems that process the data now held about children and young people exclude them from the process of expressing their views in matters that affect them, as the systems are automated and owned by interests that provide no place for children to express their views. Such systems 'consist of a range of embedded forms of knowledge and expertise, norms and values that originate with their designers and are encoded in the data the tools provide'.[60] These systems have the appearance of being objective and value free and so imply there is no need to hear the views of children and young people in this space. In this sense, granting young people the right to disrupt such systems supports the notion of the messiness of the law, as it would be perceived as getting in the way of scientific methods that claim to act for the best interests of the child or young person. As Lupton and Williamson note, such systems claim to 'speak on behalf of children'.[61]

These are valid concerns and should inform future discussions about how the rights of children and young people should be given effect within school systems that collect and analyse data. But there is a problem in the way in which Lupton and Williamson frame this debate. In part, this arises from the work of Sonia Livingstone which they draw on.[62] Her aim is to argue for a rights-based framework, which for media researchers represents new territory. This framework includes an approach to rights that engages with positive rights to free expression – of obvious importance for media researchers – and thus also asserts the agency of the child.[63] However, while broadly sympathetic, my criticism of some of this argument is that it fails to get into the detail of how children participate and become included in processes that affect them. Thus, Livingstone claims that

> [the UNCROC] legitimates children's agency. Although the [UNCROC] qualifies children's participation rights according to their capacity (or maturity) to express themselves, it also insists that decisions that affect children are taken in their best interests. Making children's voices heard is a task that many researchers of children and media are keen to undertake; those who have tried it know that children can indeed contribute to policy and practice that represents and meets their interests. . . . A case in point is a recent multinational consultation on children's rights in the digital age – grounded in participatory workshops held with children aged 6–18 living in 16 countries (and speaking eight languages) worldwide. This generated several messages from children to policy-makers. . . . Of these, two reveal children's conviction of the importance of the internet in their lives. To paraphrase, children stressed that:
>
> - The offline/online binary has been transcended by the diversity of communicative modes and settings that comprise children's daily lives.
> - Wherever or however they live, children's digital media uses are motivated by widely shared purposes and are mostly positive.[64]

She then proceeds to discuss the examples of children making their voices heard in Internet governance in terms that suggest they possess the capacity to do so, finally commenting that '[c]hildren understand that with rights come responsibilities, including being accountable for their own actions, and they want adults to support and trust them in using digital media wisely'.[65] She also offers that '[c]hildren wish to be involved in the policy deliberations that affect them, so they can offer their expertise and engage with processes that affect their rights'.[66]

While children and young people no doubt will often have the capacity to participate in these ways in relation to digital technology, the commentary potentially misconceives the nature of children's rights contained within the UNCROC and in the legal system more generally. First, it suggests that children's participation rights are qualified by their capacity. While this is often found in family and child law, the UNCROC asserts the child's right to freedom of expression, for example, as being subject only to restrictions that respect 'the rights or reputations of others', or 'for the protection of national security or of public order (ordre public), or of public health or morals'.[67] It may be in a practical sense that the child's maturity will determine the nature of their participation, but there is no such restriction apparent in relation to the child's freedom of expression in UNCROC. Under article 12 of UNCROC, the right of children to express views in matters that affect them is qualified by those views being 'given due weight in accordance with the age and maturity of the child'. But this does not mean a child is not heard who is perhaps immature; rather, it means that the weight to be given to their views may be reduced. This is an important point, because as children have often not been listened to in the past, how can we know whether their views should have weight unless we hear them?

However, there are other issues to raise with respect to Livingstone's comments on children and young people's participation rights. The tone of the examples she provides is that children should be listened to in relation to Internet governance because they are capable of acting responsibly and can make worthwhile contributions. This is also supported by her comments that children understand that they possess responsibilities as well as rights and that adults should be reassured that they can act wisely. This is problematic with respect to the nature of rights and their purpose. Judith Ennew quotes Paul Sieghart in her work on children and sexual exploitation:

> In all legal theory and practice, rights and duties are symmetrical. It is a popular fallacy that this symmetry applies within the same individual: that if I have a right, *I* must also have a correlative duty. This is not so: If I have a right, *someone else* must have a correlative duty; if I have a duty, *someone else* must have a corresponding right.[68]

The UNCROC makes it clear that states that are party to the Convention have the duty to ensure the rights granted to children are given effect. To require children and young people to act 'wisely' in relation to those rights could have the effect of seriously negating those rights, as it would allow adults to claim that, being conditional on a wise choice, the right would be inoperative if the child's choices are deemed to be so. As such judgments are matters of value it could also make the veto of the child's rights almost unaccountable. A conditional right in that sense is not a right. Such a view of the participation rights of children also contradicts Donnison's point that rights are valuable because they empower the rights holder to challenge those with power. In the case of the participation rights of children and young people, it is adult power over them that is often being challenged. Thus, such rights should empower children and young people to assert a viewpoint that does not always reassure adults that they can act wisely according to adults' views of what that might mean. The exercise of participation rights by children and young people must also contemplate the possibility that they will put a view that challenges current wisdom and may even be regarded as 'unwise' by adults. Rights can – and should – be used to challenge norms.

Finally, the view that UNCROC allows the child's 'voice' to be heard and that this is inherently positive runs the risk of romanticising both the child's understanding and the process. Livingstone's reassurance that children have worthwhile contributions to make may be so in the examples given, but the matter that goes to the rights of the child in her examples is not that the children have something positive to say but rather the question of how it came to be that this was so. It may well have been that such children were informed by their education about the matters they expressed views on. It is that education, and the states party to UNCROC who are obliged to ensure that children's right to express views are supported, that relates to UNCROC. Without an understanding of the issues, essential knowledge and information, as well as the powers of critical analysis necessary to put those views properly, being heard or having a voice may in fact be very hollow or even meaningless. The state's responsibility in ensuring that a child or young person is heard under article 13 of UNCROC is not simply that they are 'listened' to, but that the right embodied there is meaningful in that it is supported by an education system that provides the child with the fullest understanding of the relevant area. The concern in some of the commentary on the rights of children and young people in relation to digital media is that when listened to, they can bring a 'balanced' or 'responsible' approach to the use of the technology. This appears to be the result of an education system that has prepared children for the acceptance of digital technology for 'positive' purposes rather than one that has engaged with the commercial interests' manipulation of data, the debates over transgression and contest in the digital public sphere and the way in which the technology might be used to challenge and disrupt norms. It also suggests that children, if responsible, *should* participate in such discussions. Yet a right is something one can choose not to exercise; otherwise, it is an obligation. This all seems to be missing in the discussion of children's rights and digital technology.

6.4 Educating young people for social media: consumers or citizens?

It follows from the above that schools should do more than simply teach students about the risks of social media and the harm that can eventuate if they share too much information about themselves in the online world. But even more importantly, there is a clear disconnect between how many see the law in this area and what the law can be. The traditional role of law might be seen to be to assert the privacy rights of young people who use social media, for the protection of privacy has been associated with protecting the child from unwarranted intrusion into their lives, whether from sexual predators or corporate bodies seeking to sell their wares based on the child's consumption preferences. In the course of these claims for privacy rights in the digital world, there are vague references to the transformation of rights and new ways of thinking about the law in the context of digital technology, but the messiness of the legal principles that underpin much of rights discourse, as we have seen, seems to get in the way of more detailed articulation of such legal transformations.

However, new narratives are unfolding and start with the simple claim that schools could engage with the nuances of rights, transgression and the corporate hypocrisies over transparency and teach them as part of digital citizenry. The reason this may not currently be occurring would itself be an intriguing case study which would tell us much about who controls the digital spaces within which social media sits. Fuchs may argue that social media is ultimately a commercial space that qualifies so many of the rights children and young people may claim there. Yet I have also argued that viewed as a space, social media can learn much from the literature that narrates the ongoing struggle of young people to reshape the physical spaces within which they exist. The issue is whether schools are to meekly accept that their role is to teach young people how to acquiesce in the digital space of social media and accept its commercial purpose and where 'responsible' persons may participate in it within certain parameters, or whether their role will be to teach rebellion and transgression, thereby constructing those spaces as an ongoing struggle between competing interests for power in the new spaces that social media creates.

Notes

1 Department of Education, Western Australia *Guidelines for the Use of Social Media* (undated), p. 2.
2 Ibid.
3 Ibid.
4 Ibid.
5 See Charles J. Russo, Joan Squelch and Sally Varnham 'Teachers and Social Networking Sites: Think Before You Post' (2010) 5(5) *Public Space: The Journal of Law and Social Justice* 1–15.

6 Ibid., citing Spanierman v Hughes, 576 F Supp 2d 292 (D Conn 2008) and Snyder v Millersville WL 5093140 (ED Pa 2008).
7 Ibid., p. 5.
8 *BBC News* 'Teachers Need "Clearer" Social Networking Rules, Unions Say' 12 March, 2014, www.bbc.com/news/uk-wales-26539243, accessed 22 July, 2017.
9 The General Teaching Council for Scotland *Professional Guidance on the Use of Electronic Communication and Social Media* (undated), www.gtcs.org.uk/web/FILES/teacher-regulation/professional-guidance-ecomms-social-media.pdf, accessed 22 July, 2017.
10 Ibid., p. 2.
11 Ibid., p. 3.
12 Ibid.
13 Ibid.
14 See e.g. *BBC News* 12 March, 2014, op.cit.
15 Ibid., p. 4.
16 Ibid., p. 5.
17 Ibid., p. 3. See also e.g. Department of Education, Training and Employment, Queensland *Social Media and the School Community* (2013), http://behaviour.education.qld.gov.au/SiteCollectionDocuments/cybersafety/social-media-and-community-online.pdf, accessed 22 July, 2017, p. 3.
18 E.g. Department of Education, Training and Employment, Queensland (2013), p. 2.
19 E.g. Grahamvale Primary School No.3696 [Victoria, Australia] *Social Media Policy – Parents* (July, 2016), p. 2 www.grahamvaleps.vic.edu.au/documents/SocialMedia Parents.pdf, accessed 22 July, 2017.
20 Fuchs, op.cit.
21 Amy S. Dobson and Jessica Ringrose 'Sext Education: Pedagogies of Sex, Gender and Shame in the Schoolyards of Tagged and Exposed' (2016) 16(1) *Sex Education* 8–21.
22 Albury, op.cit., p. 722.
23 Ibid.
24 'Schoolgirl Hits Out at Unfair Expectations and Standards of Women' (August 23, 2016) www.youtube.com/watch?v=3I8TZV0L7WY, accessed 23 July, 2017
25 'Kambrya College Defends Assembly That Was Accused of "Slut-Shaming"' 23 August, 2016, news.com.au, accessed 23 July, 2017.
26 Marilyn J. Preston '"They're Just Not Mature Right Now": Teachers' Complicated Perceptions of Gender and Anti-queer Bullying' (2016) 16(1) *Sex Education* 22–34.
27 Ibid., p. 28.
28 Ibid., p. 29.
29 Ibid., p. 31.
30 Ibid.
31 Ibid., p. 32.
32 College of Policing Briefing Note, op.cit., p. 3.
33 Criminal Code (Cth), s.104.2(3) as amended by Counter-Terrorism Legislation Amendment Act (No. 1) 2016, Schedule 2, which lowered the relevant age from 16 to 14.
34 See e.g. Shaun Best 'Terrorism and the Role of the School in Surveillance' (2008) 2(2) *Education, Knowledge and Economy* 137–148; Amy Cook 'New Counter-terrorism Duties: What Schools Need to Know' *The Guardian* 3 March, 2015, www.theguardian.com/teacher-network/2015/mar/02/counter-terrorism-duties-schools-need-to-know, accessed 23 July, 2017.

35 See e.g. Emily Drefuss 'Blaming the Internet for Terrorism Misses the Point', 6 June, 2017, *www.wired.com*, accessed 23 July, 2017.
36 Henrietta Cook 'How Schools Are Tracking Students Using Their Mobile Phones' *The Age* 16 July, 2017, *www.theage.com.au*, accessed 17 July, 2017.
37 Ibid.
38 Family Zone Team, 19 July, 2017, https://twitter.com/familyzoneteam, accessed 23 July, 2017.
39 Ibid.
40 Ibid.
41 Family Zone: Cyber Experts, www.familyzone.com/au/cyber-experts, accessed 23 July, 2017.
42 Ibid.
43 Ibid.
44 Ibid.
45 Cook, op.cit.
46 Deborah Lupton and Ben Williamson 'The Datafied Child: The Dataveillance of Children and Implications for Human Rights' (2017) 19(5) *New Media and Society* 780–794.
47 Ibid., p. 784.
48 Ibid., p. 783.
49 Ibid., p. 784.
50 Ibid., p. 785.
51 Ibid., pp. 786–787.
52 Emmeline Taylor and Tonya Rooney 'Digital Playgrounds: Growing up in the Surveillance Age' in Emmeline Taylor and Tonya Rooney (eds.) *Surveillance Futures: Social and Ethical Implications of New Technologies for Children and Young People* (Oxford, Routledge, 2017), p. 9 citing Donald Madgwick and Tony Smythe *The Invasion of Privacy* (Oxford, Pitman, 1974), p. 9.
53 Ibid., p. 16 citing Emmeline Taylor (2010) 'I Spy With My Little Eye: The Use of CCTV in Schools and the Impact on Privacy', (2010) 58(3) *Sociological Review* 381–405.
54 Ibid., pp. 9–10.
55 Lupton and Williamson, op.cit., p. 787.
56 Ibid.
57 Ibid., p. 789.
58 Ibid.
59 Ibid., citing Sonia Livingstone 'Reframing Media Effects in Terms of Children's Rights in the Digital Age' (2016) 10(1) *Journal of Children and Media* 4–12; Nick Lee *Childhood and Society: Growing up in an Age of Uncertainty* (Maidenhead, Open University Press, 2001).
60 Ibid., p. 790.
61 Ibid.
62 Livingstone, op.cit., 2012.
63 Ibid., p. 10.
64 Ibid. (References omitted)
65 Ibid., p. 11.
66 Ibid.
67 UNCROC, art. 13(2).
68 Paul Sieghart *The Lawful Rights of Mankind* (Oxford, Oxford University Press, 1985), cited in Ennew, op.cit., p. 36.

Chapter 7

Working in the online society

Social media and the new workplace

The use of social media by young people in the workplace is no doubt a new frontier in debates about young people and their legal rights in relation to social media. Much of the discussion in previous chapters about how social media is constructed in relation to young people focussed on the utopian and dystopian views of social media. These views in effect suggest that when young people utilise the 'good' parts of social media they will become more productive citizens in the future, while becoming trapped by the 'bad' aspects of social media is likely to jeopardise that future. This is the space where it is said that online trashing of one's reputation by posting 'inappropriate' images on social media may result in difficulties in gaining employment, for example. The equation seems very simple at one level – harness while young the positive features of social media and become comfortable with the new communications technologies, and so become a reputable, skilled and productive employee as an adult. On the other hand, sliding into the abyss which is the dark side of social media is likely to make young people find life very hard as an adult. The dystopian view is as harsh and dramatic as that.

It is here that we see why it is considered that the role of schools in creating a curriculum that engages with social media becomes crucial in creating either of the above worlds. The simple path relies on narratives about social media that have already become well entrenched. The more complicated path is to engage with alternative narratives that engage with the messiness of law and the nuances of children and young people's rights to transgress, engage in uncomfortable acts of self-expression including sexual expression, and re-negotiate the position of young people in the family in the age of social media. However, these alternative paths also challenge powerful interests in the exercise of the rights mentioned, and they are heavily contested by the entrenched narratives that speak more to fear, risk aversion and the future productivity of young people. What I seek to do in this chapter is begin to explore whether the new workplace that social media facilitates is one that strengthens the power of corporate employers, or whether it allows young people to harness the new public sphere of social media to create a new workplace that recognises their rights as employees.

7.1 Social media and the culture of employee surveillance

Most workplaces now have a social media policy that guides employees on their use of social media during working hours. Notions that using social media at work wastes work time and obstructs workers in pursuing their workplace duties and tasks might lead one to think that employers would seek to ban the use of social media at work. In fact, for most workplaces the opposite is the case. Employers understand the value of social media for promotion of their business, and so allowing employees to use social media during work time may allow employees to become part of that marketing image and become comfortable in using it. There may also be practical matters of enforcing a proposed ban as well, but in any case, the use of social media in the workplace mirrors parental control of social media over their children's use of it. Employer guidance, in effect, is a soft form of control of what workers say online about their workplace, and it resembles the role of parental guidance within the family. The education of young people in the use of social media – whether by schools, parents or the state – becomes a crucial component in creating acceptance of the role of those with power to constrain how one behaves online. In the case of parental guidance, their role is to steer young people away from conducting themselves 'inappropriately' online, often understood to mean not engaging in sexualised behaviour or cyber-bullying. In the case of employers, what is 'inappropriate' shifts to criticism of the employer and damaging their reputation and that of their business. In other words, what we see here is the continuing of the narrative that sees the space created by social media as a space to be managed to meet the interests of powerful interests, in this case employers.

Examples of the text of some of these policies reveal much in this regard. Such policies are now commonplace in workplaces, particularly after early decisions in employment tribunals following the dismissal of employees for their social media posts that were considered objectionable by their employers. Those decisions preceded the creation of policies, and so a standard refrain from advisers was the need to establish policies to 'clarify' expectations of employees. The problem, of course, with this approach is that this then depends on whether such a policy is a negotiated document or one imposed on employees. Another problem is that the need for such policies has unfortunately evolved through some unfair dismissal cases that arose from situations that are cringeworthy, rather than shining examples of free expression. In this way they reflect the dystopian view of social media narrative that justifies the control and management of such behaviour, rather than referencing important human rights.

A good example of this in Australia is the decision of the Full Bench of Fair Work Australia (in effect an employment tribunal) in *Linfox Australia Pty Ltd v Stutsel.*[1] The facts in that matter were that Stutsel was a truck driver with the employer Linfox and had been dismissed on the basis of serious misconduct constituted by posting comments on Facebook about two of his managers. The comments were regarded as 'offensive, derogatory and discriminatory, and included suggestions of dishonest and underhanded conduct, and comments of sexual misconduct'.[2] The initial decision at first instance by a single commissioner was that the employee was not guilty of serious misconduct and should be reinstated. The commissioner made a number of comments about the Facebook posts which were the basis for the dismissal and found that while many were in poor taste, uncomplimentary or disgusting, the context within which they were made did not amount to sufficient grounds for dismissal. Commenting on some of the Facebook posts, the commissioner remarked that '[a]lthough the comments were distasteful, they were within the Applicant's right to free speech'.[3] In relation to the role of the company's social media policy, the commissioner said that '[t]he Company did not have a policy on the use of social media by employees. In an era in which many companies have detailed social media policies, the parts of the induction training material and handbook upon which the Company relied were not adequate to ground the action taken against the Applicant'.[4] The employer company then appealed to the Full Bench.

Part of the company's grounds of appeal was that the commissioner had 'placed undue emphasis on a purported right to free speech'.[5] The Full Bench dismissed the appeal on the basis that there was no significant error on the part of the commissioner to change that decision on appeal. However, in coming to that conclusion, the Full Bench did make a number of comments about the role of social media in the workplace. The Full Bench said on the matter of the employee's posting on Facebook:

> The posting of derogatory, offensive and discriminatory statements or comments about managers or other employees on Facebook might provide a valid reason for termination of employment. In each case, the enquiry will be as to the nature of the comments and statements made and the width of their publication. Comments made directly to managers and other employees and given wide circulation in the workplace will be treated more seriously than if such comments are shared privately by a few workmates in a social setting. In ordinary discourse there is much discussion about what happens in our work lives and the people involved. In this regard we are mindful of the need not to impose unrealistic standards of behaviour and discourse about such matters or to ignore the realities of workplaces.[6]

While this appears to provide some latitude to employees to engage in conversations on social media about their workplace, the Full Bench then qualified those remarks by the following:

> In the present case, the series of Facebook conversations in which the comments were made were described by the Commissioner as having the flavour of a conversation in a pub or cafe, although conducted in electronic form. We do not agree altogether with this characterisation of the comments. The fact that the conversations were conducted in electronic form and on Facebook gave the comments a different characteristic and a potentially wider circulation than a pub discussion. Even if the comments were only accessible by the 170 Facebook 'friends' of the Applicant, this was a wide audience and one which included employees of the Company. Further the nature of Facebook (and other such electronic communication on the internet) means that the comments might easily be forwarded on to others, widening the audience for their publication. Unlike conversations in a pub or cafe, the Facebook conversations leave a permanent written record of statements and comments made by the participants, which can be read at any time into the future until they are taken down by the page owner. Employees should therefore exercise considerable care in using social networking sites in making comments or conducting conversations about their managers and fellow employees.[7]

However, even these remarks were further qualified by the Full Bench's analysis of the actual Facebook posts. They described these as 'distasteful' but that '[s]ome of the comments were so exaggerated or stupid as not to amount to any credible threat against the managers'.[8] They also commented that '[o]ther comments were not of such a serious nature as was contended by the Company in the proceedings before the Commissioner and on appeal'.[9] Some of the comments about the managers had been posted by the employee's Facebook friends, and he did not understand that he could have deleted them. He also did not intend that the managers see the comments. He thought he was on maximum privacy settings.[10] When the Full Bench placed the posts in this wider context they were able to conclude:

> It is apparent from the recital of these matters that the findings of the Commissioner as to the Applicant's understanding about the use of Facebook were an important part of the circumstances taken into account in concluding that the dismissal was unfair. It is also apparent that, with increased use and understanding about Facebook in the community and the adoption by more employers of social networking policies, some of these factors may be given less weight in future cases.

> The claim of ignorance on the part of an older worker, who has enthusiastically embraced the new social networking media but without fully understanding the implications of its use, might be viewed differently in the future. However in the present case the Commissioner accepted the Applicant's evidence as to his limited understanding about Facebook communications. We have not been persuaded, having regard to the evidence and submissions presented, that such a finding was not reasonably open.[11]

They also commented:

> The postings on his Facebook page by the Applicant and others were appropriately a matter for concern and censure. The comments were childish and objectionable, and reflect poorly on those who participated in the conversations complained about. However, when the statements and comments posted on the Facebook page were objectively considered in their proper context they were not of such a serious or extreme nature as would justify dismissal for serious misconduct.[12]

The Full Bench did not specifically return to the matter of free speech. Such a right is not enshrined formally in Australian law, and so this is not surprising, even though it was mentioned at the outset of the decision. What does seem to have come out of the decision is the need for employers to formulate social media policies. But this is problematic if it is thought that employers can simply impose their terms under such a policy. The decision also made a number of comments about the postings, that while being distasteful they did not in themselves constitute grounds for termination of employment. The question is whether social media policies should also take that on board when being written. In effect, how much free speech should a social media policy embrace?

The relevance for young people and social media is that as a group they are perhaps less likely to challenge the terms of a social media policy written by an employer. This is partly because their access to resources to mount such a challenge are likely to be limited, but it is also a matter of their education and socialisation with respect to social media. In the absence of school curriculum that emphasises their right to speak online – even in terms that sometimes others have discomfort with – the policies they encounter when they enter the workplace will look much like what they have already encountered in the home and at school, and so will represent an approach to social media with which they are comfortable and accepting.

A brief examination of corporate social media policies would suggest that the main concern of those corporate employers is the potential for employees' online postings to damage the reputation or brand of their business. Thus, a social media policy that applies to three McDonald's franchises in

Australia specifies that while 'McDonald's supports free speech and encourages our people to embrace social media',[13] it also does 'not use social media to undermine the goodwill, reputation, development and/or operation of McDonald's, our products, our services and our people'.[14] It is stated that to do so may lead to 'disciplinary or other appropriate action up to and including termination of employment'.[15] It is also stated in the policy that this applies to the use of social media when the employee is not at work.[16] Another large Australian store, Target, has a similar policy that refers to employee obligations even when using social media in a personal capacity because 'these communications are frequently available to a larger audience than the author may realise', and employees must 'not communicate anything that might damage Target's reputation, brand image, commercial interests, or the confidence of our customers', for example.[17] In using social media, employees are also advised to 'use common sense and respect others in posts and discussions', and '[i]f a team member disagrees with the opinion of another, they should keep responses appropriate and inoffensive'.[18] Employees are also advised to 'adopt the simple practice of stepping back, re-reading and thinking about what they post before doing so'.[19]

In the United Kingdom, the supermarket chain Tesco addresses similar concerns in its social media policy for employees, including the protection of reputation and the avoidance of 'malicious, abusive, offensive, obscene, threatening, intimidating or contain nudity or images of a sexual nature, or that could be seen as bullying, harassment or discrimination' in a policy that is prefaced by the need for 'sound judgement, respect and common sense'.[20] The policy also begins with the statement, 'Whatever part of Tesco we work in we are ambassadors for our company'.[21] Such policies are often critiqued because they merge the workplace with the employees' personal lives in holding them accountable for social media postings when not at work. Tesco, for example, makes it clear that they scan social media sites for mention of Tesco, advising employees that '[i]nappropriate behaviour including posting confidential or sensitive information will be investigated' and could lead to disciplinary action and dismissal.[22] However, at an even more fundamental level they normalise surveillance of employees in the workplace in terms that are vague and difficult to define. If the expectation is that the provision of social media polices provides clear expectations to employees with respect to their use of social media and its relationship to their employment, then this appears to fail. Use of terms such as 'inappropriate' in this context further embeds a legal narrative around social media that uses language that disempowers the users of social media in its uncertainty.

For a generation of young people who have graduated from parental control and monitoring to state and school surveillance of their social media usage, their arrival in a workplace which is subject to further oversight of their use of social media will seem so commonplace as to be unremarkable.

These will also be workplaces where much of the work will be done by 'produsers', as Fusch calls them – customers who through the adoption of technology do the tasks previously done by employees, such as checking out their own groceries. Employers who seek to reconstruct their employees as 'ambassadors' appear to be replicating Fusch's example, as these employees in their own time post to social media positive stories about their employer. The question is whether an employee who posts criticism of an employer who adopts technology to reduce, say, the number of employees is posting 'inappropriate' comments that undermine the employer's brand. Such changes in the use of technology are usually presented as beneficial to customers rather than being about reducing the wage bill. This is where the vagueness of social media policies begins to impact on employees as an effective way to stifle dissent by labelling such statements as defamatory, damaging to the company's reputation or 'inappropriate'. The threat of possible dismissal is likely to make many employees afraid to test the meaning of the terms in the policy.

7.2 Controlling youth seeking employment: free expression *vs.* reputation protection

While the social media policies currently formulated apply to young people, they are not specifically addressed to them. However, there is little doubt that the greater take-up of social media by young people makes the wording of such policies even more relevant for present-day youth as they enter adulthood and take up employment. Young people have already been subject to strong messages at school and in society generally about the need to consider the protection of their reputation online when posting photographs of their social interactions, and of course in areas such as sexting. As we have seen, such conversations about using 'caution' when using social media rarely, if ever, take place in the context of young people's rights to express themselves. The need to form an identity and affirm that with others is also an important consideration. Also, the right to play has important functions in terms of well-being, boundary testing and social change. Clearly, the message that the preservation of 'reputation' is important in order to maximise employment opportunities is a conservative one, even if it is presented as the 'norm' for the whole society. However, the practice of young people on social media would often appear to challenge that assumption.

The problem, then, for scholars and commentators who do not wish young people's opportunities to turn on their exercise of identity rights is to formulate a way of acting within social media that does not prejudice the long-term interests of young people. One of the greatest concerns is that expressed to young people that sexting 'inappropriate' images of themselves may be on the Internet 'forever' and so be available for prospective employers to search and presumably take into account before offering employment to them. Such warnings are rarely interrogated because other than some vague notion of moral impropriety, what is it about posting an image of one's body that calls into question a person's employability? In particular, this seems often to be directed towards young women; thus, the suspicion is that underpinning such a warning is a conservative view of appropriate behaviour for females. As we have seen in the previous chapter, Albury opens this discussion to the question of conceptualising this behaviour around the positive rights of young people and focussing on criteria that may have a relationship with a person's employability.[23]

She then suggests that a workplace that truly embraced equity and diversity might in the future deem irrelevant online material that indicates a person has engaged in 'consensual, non-work-related sexual expression'.[24] It is also the manner in which warnings directed to young people about the possible impacts on future employment prospects are made that is disturbing. As Albury's work indicates, this not only denies young people their right to sexual expression; it also educates them that workplaces can take into account criteria for employment that may well be unlawful under anti-discrimination statutes. Lee et al. also report that many young people who were concerned that potential employers may check their digital identity use another name or identity on Facebook, or avoid posting altogether in acts of self-censorship.[25] The fact that law-enforcement agencies are not visiting employers to warn them about acting outside anti-discrimination laws when assessing social media posts of potential employees in the same way that they visit schools to warn young people about the dangers of sexting speaks volumes about relative power in society.

Rather than the legal lesson for young people being to be defensive in their online expression, it is important to consider how the law can frame a response to potential employers introducing irrelevant or unlawful considerations into the hiring process. This is clearly difficult in the absence of creative lawmakers and judges. A recent news item reporting on the prevalence of employers searching potential employees' social media presence commented that the aim is to '[cultivate] a positive online persona'.[26] While this report comments on how positive attributes about a person on social media may assist them in gaining employment, it also highlights that material that leaves a bad impression can lead to not being hired. The matters listed in this report were 'provocative or inappropriate photographs, videos or information'; 'information about them drinking or using drugs'; 'discriminatory comments related to race, gender, religion'; 'bad-mouthed their previous company or fellow employees'; 'lied about qualifications'; 'poor communication skills'; '[links] to criminal behavior'; 'shared confidential information from previous employers'; 'screen name was unprofessional'; 'lied about an absence'; 'posted too frequently'.[27]

The legal problem with all these examples of material that is said to leave a 'bad impression' is that most of them are not self-evident and require some value judgments to be made. How one judges what is a 'professional' screen name seems vexed, and to say that a person posts 'too frequently' begs the question of how much is just enough. Cultivating a positive online persona is also problematic in terms of how this might lead to individuals not expressing their real selves online, but instead a persona that meets their perceptions of what an employer values. For many, this seems beyond being a legal problem. It might be said that an employer must have some flexibility in determining whom they wish to employ. However, creating conditions within which individuals feel constrained in how they express themselves online may lead to a society that is less interesting, less diverse and less tolerant of differences. These are some of the reasons for the existence of human rights and anti-discrimination laws in the first place: to create that more open and tolerant society. In the Australian context, employers have been warned about possible 'adverse action claims'[28] where employment is denied, for example, because social media postings reveal union membership or sexual preference.[29] Both of these attributes are prohibited as reasons for not employing a person.[30] Indeed, the Australian Fair Work Act provides that 'an employer must not take adverse action against a person who is an employee or prospective employee of the employer because of the person's race, colour, sex, sexual orientation, age, physical or mental disability, marital status, family or carer's responsibilities, pregnancy, religion, political opinion, national extraction or social origin'.[31] However, if one takes the example of 'posting too frequently', does this mean that someone who chooses to place on social media many posts about their sexual identity could be declined employment for that reason and not offend the section?

This is not to suggest that social media postings should never justify the denial of employment to an individual. But while *Linfox Australia Pty Ltd v Stutsel* has been cited repeatedly as a case that underscores the need for employers to have a social media policy, it says much more about the need for judgment as to when speech in social media crosses the line as far as meeting the criteria for dismissal (as in that case) or is a reason for not employing a person. The comments in that case were regarded as 'childish and objectionable' and reflecting poorly on those involved; however, they were not regarded as sufficiently 'serious or extreme' to warrant dismissal. It is not sufficient to say that a post is 'unprofessional' or 'inappropriate'. What might be required by the law is a judgment about whether it is of such a degree that it justifies not employing the person. Albury maps an example of where that judgment might be made, that is, when the online behaviour involves non-consensual posting of sexualised images of others and so can be said to be unethical or even criminal. This, at least, seems a little more certain than the vague notion of being 'unprofessional', or posting 'provocative or inappropriate photographs'.

Another matter the law may consider is that young people may claim a right to make mistakes, as Eekelaar suggested following the *Gillick* decision. Instead of portraying the risk to reputation from social media postings as of the highest concern for future career prospects, and in doing so creating a culture of fear that limits young people's expression, it could be argued that posting material online that one subsequently regrets can have in the longer term much more positive consequences. Susannah Stern makes this point in her work that studied how young people presented themselves in social media. Where they did present themselves in ways that they later regretted in order to conform to peer expectations or to experiment, she found that the regret was not about the future impact on employment prospects but that they did not 'portray or convey an authentic self'.[32] This suggests the basis for a more ethical approach to behaviour online and underscores the importance of the right to self-expression and of the importance of playing online as part of learning about life. As Stern concludes:

> the idea that regretted self-presentations are both frequent and functional might wisely be considered by policy-makers, educators, and parents who hope to strengthen young people's online skills and choices. Encouraging young people to discuss their regret experiences can lead them to articulate what they might have done differently, and help them to construct and share strategies for pre-empting future regrettable situations. Recognizing that young people sometimes do not anticipate who might encounter their presentations and that they are keen to present themselves authentically, parents and educators can help young people develop techniques that enable them to be their real selves while accommodating multiple audiences. Finally, regretted self-presentations can be examined to consider what it means to be ethical and kind in families, friendships, and communities.[33]

Perhaps the law might encourage the right to expression as more central to the learning process of young people in a digital world than the stressing of a defensive practice that seeks to minimise risk. The need to take such risks may well lead to a much better standard of behaviour in the longer term.

7.3 Social media, workplaces and the new public sphere

Perhaps it is in the new workplace that one most starkly sees the myth of the new public sphere. The concurrent dystopian and utopian view of new technologies identified by Papacharissi is demonstrated by the Australian government's Department of Human Services social media policy for employees. This department administers the many social security payments made by the government and often receives criticism from welfare advocacy and other groups for the way in which it does so. In terms of open government, the policy begins in very utopian terms:

> We add value to customer communication with our active social media presence. With 14 social media accounts and close to 200,000 followers, we are building more meaningful relationships with customers, communities and other relevant stakeholders.[34]

Clearly, many companies and organisations regard social media as an effective marketing tool. This context for the above departmental policy reflects that type of usage. Social media is in effect a useful form of 'marketing' for this government department. However, the policy then proceeds to acknowledge the potentially more fraught domain of employees of the department using social media privately. On a positive note, it states:

> We support employees who choose to use social media in their capacity as private citizens, without intrusion. While acting as private citizens, APS employees enjoy most of the same rights to participate in the political life of the community as other citizens. That is, you need to be mindful that your online behaviour must be lawful, and you may still be bound by the APS Values, the Code and our policies.[35]

The last sentence does not follow structurally from the preceding sentence, which speaks to the free-expression rights of employees. The qualification in the last sentence is a reference to the standards of behaviour as a public servant and in effect the need to preserve the reputation of the department. A later section of the policy then comments more directly on such matters by prescribing what cannot be done by employees on social media. Two parts of this section relate in particular to material that may be seen as critical of the department:

When using social media, it is not acceptable at any time to:

- post comments or images that are so harsh or extreme in their criticism of the department, Government, a Member of Parliament from another political party, or their respective policies that they could be perceived to have an impact on your ability to work professionally, efficiently, impartially or apolitically in the APS.
- post comments or images that are, or could be perceived to be, so strong in their criticism of the department's administration, policies or programmes that it could seriously disrupt the workplace or compromise your ability to fulfil your duties as an APS employee in an impartial and unbiased manner – you are encouraged instead to resolve concerns in discussions with your manager or via the department's internal dispute or complaints resolution mechanisms.[36]

The policy does not therefore seem to exclude any criticism, only that which can be characterised as 'harsh or extreme' or 'strong'. The problem is again that this seems so vague in meaning that it makes it difficult for an individual to judge when the threshold is reached. In effect, the policy acts as a control on any criticism while giving the appearance of allowing some level of dissent. The reality for most employees is that they would not have the personal or financial resources to challenge through the courts an employer who claimed that the employee's social media posts were harsh or extreme. It may be that trade unions could fight the issue on behalf of an employee, but in an age of decreasing union membership, and with many young people in casual or part-time employment in industries where employers are not welcoming to unionised workforces,[37] this becomes problematic.

To consider this broader context, it is important to analyse the way in which social media policies operate within organisations. Such policies, whether written for government or corporate bodies, adopt the narrative that the problem with social media is that individuals must 'balance' between free expression and going 'too far' in speaking online such that it damages the organisation's brand or reputation. But the notion that one can 'balance' discussion in this way is clearly nonsense. If a government or corporation does not want certain matters discussed in the public sphere because they are matters that are politically uncomfortable for them, then how does one do so in a way that balances between the need to debate the matter and their discomfort? When the Australian government legislated to prevent workers in immigration detention centres from disclosing to the media evidence of human-rights abuses,[38] a group of workers issued a direct challenge to the government to prosecute them when they went public with their concerns.[39] There is no halfway house with respect to how to handle such information, especially when the limited exceptions to non-disclosure of information they were entitled to under the relevant legislation did not include disclosure to the Australian Human Rights Commission or the Commonwealth Ombudsman.[40]

In *Banerji v Bowles*[41] a commonwealth public servant employed in the Department of Immigration was disciplined for tweeting comments about the government's policies relating to immigration detention. The case came before the Federal Circuit Court on an interlocutory application to prevent the dismissal of the employee prior to the trial of the case. The employee argued that her tweets were constitutionally protected based on the implied right to political communication based on comments made by Kirby, J in the High Court of Australia in the case of *Australian Broadcasting Corporation v Lenah Game Meats Pty Ltd.*[42] That case itself draws on the principle that there is an implied right of political communication in the Australian constitutional context as stated in *Lange v Australian Broadcasting Corporation*,[43] implied essentially because the system of representative government established by the Australian Constitution could not work effectively if there was no right to political speech. While in *Banerji* the court was not deciding the substantive issues in the case, it declined to grant the interlocutory relief sought on the basis that there was no unqualified implied right to free speech under the principles in the earlier cases. This has much to do with the limited nature of the implied right to free speech in the Australian context articulated by the High Court in *Lange*, meaning that restrictions on political speech could be within the Constitution if they were not inconsistent with the system of government created by the Constitution.[44] Thus, the court was able to conclude that

> the unfettered right asserted by the Applicant does not exist. In the circumstances outlined in the current matter, and certainly only in the context of an interlocutory Application, I do not see that Ms. Banerji's political comments, 'tweeted' while she remains (a) employed by the Department, (b) under a contract of employment, (c) formally constrained by the APS Code of Conduct, and (d) subject to departmental social media guidelines, are constitutionally protected.[45]

While not a definitive ruling on the major issues, the decision does lend weight to the notion that social media policies – at least in Australia – limit the extent to which employees have the ability to express their views about their workplace.

Clearly, the notion that free speech is permissible but subject to some vague threshold as expressed in social media policies makes free speech conditional and thus not free. That the conditions are to be determined by the employer under their own policies makes them even more concerning. However, the answer cannot be in 'clearer' policies because this assumes that one can make clear what is never intended to be so. The aim of such policies is to fit within what Fuchs describes in the context of corporate social media use privacy policies, an 'ideology of corporate self-regulation'.[46] The issue here is not privacy, but the point is the same. The policies are by and large non-accountable and rest on a de facto regime of self-regulation, even if on occasion some do find their way into the court system. The focus on whether a social media post crosses the line between acceptable and unacceptable is a distraction. What needs to be considered is how social media will be viewed by those with power to define its content as problematic. As Fuchs says:

> Neither techno-optimism nor techno-pessimism is the appropriate method for analyzing social-media. Rather, one needs to decentre the analysis from technology and focus on the interaction of the power structures of the political economy of capitalism with social media.[47]

He regards social media as based on an ideology that 'overemphasizes novelty and democratic potentials'.[48] By constructing the 'bad' aspects of social media in terms of the behaviour of those individuals who cross the lines of 'taste' or 'decency', we trap ourselves in debates over fine points of difference in how to read vague terms in policies that are finally determined by those within the workplace with the power to apply them. The occasional reference to an outside tribunal legitimates this process, but the nuances that may be identified in such decisions with respect to the words in a policy or approach to free speech are, as we have seen, often lost in the chosen emphasis of corporate spin.

To adopt Fuchs's description of corporate social media use privacy policies, social media policies are not legal documents but ideological documents that embed a corporation's values and concerns within them and adopt language and terms that protect those interests. The vagaries of language, as much as broad rights to free expression, undermine the extent to which employees can claim the capacity to use social media to provide their views about their employer. It is somewhere in that evolving reality that we begin to understand why we presently teach young people about the perils of 'oversharing' via social media when its very reason for existing is to do just that. The point is that government and corporate social media policies demonstrate that the problem is not in sharing via social media – it is in what you share, who it is about and how it relates to their view of social media as a tool to communicate the messages they wish to send. It is, in other words, all about values, power and the contest over who is to control social media.

Notes

1 [2012] FWAFB 7097 (3 October 2012).
2 Ibid., para.2.
3 Ibid., para.9.
4 Ibid.
5 Ibid., para.14.
6 Ibid., para.25.
7 Ibid., para.26.
8 Ibid., para.27.
9 Ibid.
10 Ibid., para.33.
11 Ibid., para.34.
12 Ibid., para.35.
13 *McKeough Group Social Media Policy* www.mckeoughgroup.com/Documents/Social%20Media%20Policy.pdf
14 Ibid.
15 Ibid.
16 Ibid.
17 Target Australia, "Social Media Policy," www.target.com.au/company/careers/policies_and_procedures/social_media_policy, accessed 25 July, 2017.
18 Ibid.
19 Ibid.

20 *Tesco Social Media Policy*, 7 December, 2015: https://cdn.ourtesco.com/2015/11/Social-Media-Policy.pdf
21 Ibid.
22 Ibid.
23 Albury, op.cit., p. 722.
24 Ibid.
25 Lee et al., op.cit., p. 46.
26 Chad Brooks 'Keep It Clean: Social Media Screenings Gain in Popularity' *Business News Daily* June 16, 2017, www.businessnewsdaily.com/2377-social-media-hiring.html, accessed 27 July, 2017.
27 Ibid.
28 *Under Fair Work Act 2009* (Cth), s.342.
29 Veronica Siow 'The Impact of Social Media in the Workplace: An Employer's Perspective' (2013) 32(4) *Communications Law Bulletin* 12–14.
30 *Fair Work Act 2009* (Cth), ss.346, 351.
31 Ibid., s.351.
32 Susannah Stern 'Regretted Online Self-Presentations: U.S. College Students' Recollections and Reflections' (2015) 9(2) *Journal of Children and Media* 248–265.
33 Ibid., p. 261.
34 Australian Government Department of Human Services Social Media Policy for departmental staff: www.humanservices.gov.au/corporate/media/social-media-department/social-media-policy-departmental-staff, accessed 27 July, 2017.
35 Ibid.
36 Ibid.
37 See e.g. www.mcspotlight.org/campaigns/tactics/unionall.html, accessed 28 July, 2017. The CEO of McDonald's UK has been reported as saying 'I also want to be clear about our position towards the trade union movement in this country. There may well be some of our people that are in unions and importantly that's their choice and they are very welcome to do so. However, we are not going to arrange for union officials to come into our restaurants to recruit people.' Paul Pomroy 'McDonald's Serves the Needs of Its Loyal Workers' *The Telegraph* 23 April, 2016, www.telegraph.co.uk/business/2016/04/23/mcdonalds-serves-the-needs-of-its-loyal-workers/, accessed 28 July, 2017. This is not to suggest that McDonalds is alone in this regard of course, see e.g. Julie Gutman Dickinson 'Walmart's War Against Unions – and the U.S. Laws That Make It Possible' *Huffington Post*, The Blog, 6 May, 2013, www.huffingtonpost.com/julie-b-gutman/walmart-labor-laws_b_3390994.html, accessed 28 July, 2017.
38 *Australian Border Force Act 2015* (Cth).
39 Paul Farrell 'Detention Centre Staff Speak out in Defiance of New Asylum Secrecy Laws' *The Guardian* 1 July, 2015, www.theguardian.com/australia-news/2015/jul/01/detention-centre-staff-speak-out-in-defiance-of-new-asylum-secrecy-laws, accessed 28 July, 2017.
40 Ibid.
41 [2013] FCCA 1052, 9 August, 2013.
42 (2001) 208 CLR 199.
43 (1997) 189 CLR 520.
44 *Banerji v Bowles*, para.101.
45 Ibid., para.104.
46 Christian Fuchs *Social Media: A Critical Introduction* (Los Angeles, Sage, 2014), p. 256.
47 Ibid.
48 Ibid.

Chapter 8

The new Wasteland

Law, social media and myth

We have been here before, where the relationship of young people and new forms of media causes fear and anxiety in the minds of adults. When television broadcasting commenced, there were global debates around the role that the state should play in the 'public interest' to ensure that appropriate programming standards were adhered to, especially to address the educational and developmental needs of children. Newton Minow, a former Federal Communications Commission chair, was of the view that the 'public interest' concept was left vague in broadcasting law in the United States so as to encourage investment in broadcasting while allowing some capacity to reject licence applications in order to ration channels.[1] The consequence of the lack of clarity of the meaning of public interest in broadcasting was that there was little accountability of broadcasters for their programming content.[2] Other countries may have achieved slightly better outcomes with respect to aspects of television programming standards than the United States, but the commercial imperative of allowing private broadcasters to make profit, or state broadcasters to meet the needs of a plural society, will always blur the notion of public interest as a legal standard. Whether children and young people should be exposed to sex and violence on television was the commonly asked question in the golden age of television broadcasting. The same areas still concern us in the digital age.

The difference today is, of course, the interactive nature of the Internet and the manner in which young people are no longer simply the passive consumers of what they watch on broadcast media. They have become not only consumers but also the active creators of content on social media. The expanse of available information has been the other major shift in the digital age, which stokes fears of the 'knowing' child as well as increases young people's capacity for participation online and in the community, armed with the knowledge that this new media provides. In the earlier days of the Internet, the United Kingdom government recognised this in their communications policy vision in 2000:

> The explosion of information has fuelled a democratic revolution of knowledge and active citizenship. If information is power, power can

> now be within the grasp of everyone. No government can now rely on the ignorance of its population to sustain it. We are richer as citizens thanks to the expansion of modern media. This government wants to encourage this and give everyone access to all these riches as quickly as possible.[3]

This paragraph seems almost quaint, less than 20 years later, when it speaks of '[giving] everyone access to all these riches' in new media. The hallmark of social media has been the ability of users to control their own access and input, almost bypassing government in the process. Of course, it is now largely corporations that provide the social media platforms, and so in that sense there are in fact many forms of control over how access occurs, but the role of government is seriously diminished in terms of regulating standards and clearly has to rely on industry co-operation to achieve any form of regulation, other than when it practices outright blocking of Internet access, which is at least problematic in democratic nations. However, what the 2000 White Paper did not so readily envision is the extent to which new media would also contain material that falls well short of the description 'riches' – according to the dystopian narratives that have evolved since this time. Thus, while social media may open up a world of information and perspectives previously not heard or seen, it has also facilitated the proliferation of hate speech, misogynist utterings and narcissistic postings that might be classified as a 'wasteland' in Newton Minow's terms.

The problem for lawmakers is that even if much of social media can be characterised as a 'wasteland' in these terms, in a society of many competing views, how can a narrative that relies on emphatic views of what is worthwhile ever prevail in a media framework that is multi-jurisdictional, diverse and atomized? Even in the case of television regulation in the past, the upholding of one dominant view of what was in the public interest as far as content was concerned was always a difficult task.[4] In the case of social media, given its nature, this seems impossible to achieve. However, as we have seen, where government does still play a role is in the way it is able to create a narrative around social media and so encourage various forms of control of its use through parental guidance, corporate regulation and self-censorship. Legal responses are muted and tend to mainly operate in more extreme and less controversial areas such as extreme child pornography or violence. But even here they must be qualified by notions of, and debates over, the meaning of 'extreme'. As experience in areas such as cyberbullying demonstrates, attempts to legislate to control such social media activity continually come up against problems of definition that are underpinned by competing values as to what is to be permitted online and what is not. For this reason, the law is often recruited to perform a symbolic function. This is not to suggest that this means the law has no impact, for this would be to accept the orthodox view of law that it is only law because it is enforceable and has legal consequences. In being part of a narrative, law can create a cultural context for certain outcomes to occur, although this is nevertheless often a 'messy' process with no guarantees as to those outcomes.

8.1 Law and the competing narratives of youth and social media

Law is then shaped as much by ideology, myth and romance as it is by science and evidence, perhaps even more so in the case of young people and social media. The demonization of young people leads us to pass laws to address the threats we fear from them. At the same time, the romanticisation of the young leads to laws designed to protect their innocence. When we insist on including the voice of young people in debates on law and policy, those people who romanticise youth are not expecting to hear challenging and uncomfortable opinions from them, nor for that matter do they expect to hear little of any value. Adults charged with acting in the 'best interests' of children and young people use the term as if it is self-evident as to what it means, and in the process those adults fail to see how their own interests, values and expectations begin to colour how they view young people and their needs.

In the middle of these narratives of childhood the law becomes a messy attempt to make all of it cohere in some way. The language of children's rights merges with the needs of children and young people for protection, and soon we are then speaking of 'protection rights' as distinct from 'autonomy rights', while acting in the child's best interests becomes a process under which almost any action can be justified in relation to children and young people. It then no longer makes sense to simply advance the 'rights of the child' in relation to social media or digital technology unless one also makes clear precisely which version of rights one is speaking to. This ambiguity and lack of clarity about the nature of the rights of children and young people is important to analyse. It might be thought that such ambiguity in the law serves to provide some scope for the exercise of discretion, for competing values to operate and for plurality in parental choices about how to raise children. This may be true to some extent, but the ambiguity of children's rights also serves to qualify and undermine them to the point where the rights of children and young people are seen to be substantively different in scope than the rights accorded to adults.

The ambiguous nature of law was explored by Carson in his work on factory legislation in the United Kingdom.[5] The broader application of his work has been widely explored and written about in relation to how 'ambiguity about legal categories can serve a range of interests'.[6] Though Carson was a criminologist and primarily interested in exploring the ambiguity around white-collar criminal offences, there are some useful insights that arise from his work when thinking about young people, law and social media and matters to do with the rights of young people in that context. Many who come to law expect there to be an underlying rationale that is coherent and consistent. Thus, when we come to discussions of social media and young people and begin to speak of their legal rights in that context, there is the same expectation. Carson had a similar project with respect to the criminal law, but as Freiberg explains, Carson demonstrated that this was 'doomed because . . . the outcomes are politically, economically and socially contingent and not grounded in immutable logic or defensible doctrine'.[7] Instead, as Freiberg observes, by the 1980s much of what the law criminalised in areas such as Internet pornography, computer crime and crimes against children seemed to be more about governments wanting 'to deliver strong symbolic moral messages that they are maintaining social order'[8] than any coherent approach to what constitutes crime. The notion that the law performs symbolic functions only in some areas has significance for any discussion of children's rights. It may be said that children and young people have a right to free expression under UNCROC, for example, but this right is overridden by local statutes in the name of the protection of, or from, young people. However, this looks at the matter as one mediated by the interests of children and for children. An alternative narrative is that to grant young people such rights threatens the power of adults, and so the law in such contested areas is subject to a process of 'negotiation, resistance and compromise'[9] that accommodates the interests of power holders, in this case adults.

In all of this we can also assume too readily that the actions of the various interests groups are performed according to some rationale. However, as Presdee argues, there is also an emotional and irrational aspect to the actions of those denied power. In the case of young people, and especially those who are marginalised in society, this often surfaces in actions that challenge boundaries, including what is lawful to do. These are not simply the acts of 'wicked' or 'evil' youth but are done in response to the limitations placed upon them by society. Presdee adopts the concept of carnival to explain this:

> It is at this moment that the need for the carnivalesque, the search for the carnivalesque, becomes an essential element within the culture of everyday lived life as we seek to find solace in transgression in order to free ourselves from the rules, regulations and regimentation of rational contemporary life. In some way the carnivalesque promises freedom.[10]

Applied to young people's use of social media, Presdee's example of the carnival challenges many of the views that young people can become better citizens online in the new public sphere that social media provides. While this may occur in some cases, for other young people the simple and spontaneous act of engaging on social media is itself the act that constitutes freedom. Warned that sexualised images posted on social media may be there 'forever' or render them guilty of child pornography offences, adults may then ask why so many young people still engage in sexting. The answer may be because their images will be there forever, a testament of their capacity to break the rules. If so, then law's purpose for young people may be to set the markers for transgression, not lay down the parameters within which they must behave.

This is where the utopian and dystopian views of new technology also invade the debate. But if only it was as easy to identify the 'good' and the 'bad' aspects of social media. When social media advocates speak of 'empowerment' and 'resilience' of children and young people as they move online, it is the language of rights they invoke, but the purpose seems to be to ensure that those young people are able to withstand the 'bad' aspects of social media in order that they are able to utilise the 'good' – the riches – available on social media and the Internet more generally. In doing so, they avoid engaging with the question of whether those same children and young people have the right to be annoying online and to use it to break the rules that regulate their lives. The short answer to this question can too readily be 'no' because to 'annoy' online is often only thought of as in terms of bullying or harassment of vulnerable people, even if under the guise of free speech.[11] A proper engagement with this question would consider whether young people need to be educated about the use of social media to challenge, question and annoy those with power in society as well as consider the ethical issues in using it against the weak and powerless.

In other words, the brevity of the rights often claimed to be possessed by young people becomes the vagueness and ambiguity that protects the powerful from scrutiny. As Fuchs contends, we cannot analyse social media outside consideration of the political economy we operate within. It is only then we can understand the many contradictions within the narratives of social media and how the law responds to them. We see this in the example of privacy, which is said to matter when young people go online and interact with other users, yet there is little discussion of how the social media platform providers themselves collect and use data provided by users – often by simply using the platform – to turn their profits. Likewise, the transparency that the state now wants in respect of what users are doing online, in the name of national security, is not reciprocated with respect to its own use of the new media. And while social media is portrayed as a new democratic space, it is seen to be more and more a convenient marketing tool by commercial and political interests than a space where citizens seek information. In this context, the 2000 UK White Paper referred to above may have been more of a warning than a prediction about the future, in the sense that those interests may well prefer a less well-informed citizenry happily consuming the wares being marketed on social media and reviewing them or 'liking' their usefulness rather than active social media users critiquing those same interests in more fundamental ways. Within capitalism, social media is itself a commercial space, while it also struggles with being used to undermine that economic system.

8.2 Reconstructing children and young people's rights in social media

For the above reasons, while it is recognised that there are severe limitations with the concept of rights within the economic system we operate within, this does not mean that they cannot be harnessed at times to question the legitimacy of the position of powerful interests. Human rights, including children's rights, are often expressed in terms so general and vague as to be capable of being interpreted in ways that undermine any efficacy they do possess. However, they can also be more imaginatively written and be creatively interpreted where lawyers or judges with equal amounts of imagination hold sway. As Donnison argues, rights can be valuable commodities that challenge the powerful and allow the powerless to claim space – be it physical, psychological or economic. Of course, so too can transgression that is spontaneous, as it too disrupts the comfort of the powerful by mocking or simply refusing to behave as they expect. This is where law and its practitioners must be imaginative. If the purpose of a right is to allow for proactive challenge to the established order so as to reduce power inequalities, does this also imply a right to transgress?

There are risks in being imaginative in reading rights in this way. The rise of political populism and a new authoritarianism in public life creates the risk that the right to be annoying will be used by some to be hateful, harassing or misogynistic. But we rarely assess the risk of silencing young people. We are more aware today than ever of the consequences of not listening to children after many inquiries into past cases of institutional abuse of children. However, we should not see that knowledge as of historical relevance only; contemporary research indicates that children and young people continue to be anxious about the extent to which they are listened to by adults.[12] The research by Tim Moore et al. for Australia's Royal Commission into Child Sexual Abuse found that the children they surveyed 'felt it was important for adults to take time to really listen to them':[13]

> They felt that even caring adults often unwittingly stopped them from talking, focusing more on what they would do rather than taking the time to understanding children's feelings, validating them and finding out what they needed in the moment.[14]

They also found that adults often downplayed children's concerns instead of assisting them in understanding the risks they faced and learning from the adults' experience.[15] In terms of building their resilience, young people reported to them that they wanted 'frank conversations about what risks existed and how to best deal with them' but that this should not be simply about telling them what not to do such as not sexting or taking risks 'but also how to manage issues if they emerged'.[16] However, they also wanted realistic strategies that took into account the realities of their position:

> children and young people did note that sometimes adults' strategies for dealing with their concerns made them feel worse when they were unsuccessful. Telling children that they needed to stand up for themselves or to act confidently were seen as unhelpful when they didn't take into account that children might be smaller or less confident than their attacker. Participants reported that instead, such strategies made them feel weaker and the issues less resolvable because of their limitations.[17]

Of course, this research had a particular focus on physical world encounters such as bullying or abuse (although young people's online and offline worlds can often merge), but the usefulness of the messages in the research transcend that context. In effect, the children were asking adults to act in their best interests, and what it suggests is required of adults is that they have to reflect more carefully on what the best interests of the child mean in situations where children feel unsafe or affected in some way. It is simply not enough to 'listen'; what the young people are asking adults to do is *really* listen. As in so many matters relevant to law and social media, it comes down to this matter of emphasis and nuance.

In this context, one would think that social media, open and freely accessible to young people without constraint, might be an effective way for children and young people to communicate their fears, anxieties, hopes and aspirations to adults. Social media also offers young people with access to others who can empower them through knowledge and help them to protect themselves. As Archard says, 'any strategy to protect children from abuse will be inadequate if it maintains children in their ignorance and powerlessness'.[18] We may fear whom young people interact with on social media, but can we assume that relying for such knowledge on schools, churches or governments, which have failed young people so often in the past, will result in their suddenly turning away from their previous approach to children and young people? Archard also notes that the modern conception of children is that of 'incompetent innocents',[19] which then justifies denying them various rights, especially to decide matters for themselves. While we may have moved on slightly from that conception of children and young people since the time that Archard first wrote it, there is much in debates about social media and the law today to suggest that it remains a strong narrative of young people. If anything, we can add to that conception a fear of young people given access to the knowledge that the digital word opens to them and making them now 'knowing rebels' as much as 'incompetent innocents'. We move constantly between the need to shield the innocent child from harm and controlling the youth who 'knows too much'.

Where does this leave the law and rights discourse? One question often asked is whether the law should compromise the ability to speak openly in the new public sphere provided by social media so as to prevent harm to others. A more confronting way to state this is to ask whether the right to be annoying online should be qualified in any way. While cyber-bullying is a real problem, another problem is in agreeing a universal definition for it. The same problem arises in relation to other forms of harassment and 'inappropriate' behaviour online. It has been argued that these are not legal technical problems, but matters of values that will and should be made. Nevertheless, they should not deter us from also being uncomfortable about the constraints such legal definitions place upon young people's ability to voice criticism of their parents, governments, employers or corporations when they act in ways that do not take account of their best interests. While we should be concerned about protecting children from various harms online in relation to sexual predators or misogynists, we are also right to be concerned about encouraging them to become active citizens in wider public debates about their immediate and long-term welfare interests. We need to be wary about how conceptions of young people as innocents to be protected or youths to be feared online deflects attention from the harm done to young people by those with real political and economic power in society. Social media can be a device to make their decisions more transparent, and young people have a right to learn about how to do that effectively, too.

As Archard says, the possession of rights is not a cure-all for all the matters that confront young people,[20] and that applies also in relation to social media. But they do, as he says in relation to the UNCROC, represent 'a public and palpable affirmation of the standing and worth of children'.[21] Having said that, they also might be another part of symbolic law that give the impression of state recognition while in their ambiguity and vagueness allow the powerful to re-define their scope constantly in ways that minimise their effect. While rights, as Donnison suggests, are powerful, we do also need to be suspicious of the motives of those who grant them. I also agree with the sentiment of Fuchs that we cannot understand any of what we have discussed about law, social media or young people outside matters of political economy. However, the contradictions and tension in the system we live within also provide some scope to consider how a restatement of children's and young people's digital rights might re-cast their digital futures.

8.3 A radical charter of children's and young people's digital rights

Where I have arrived at is a modest restatement of young people's digital rights having regard to the discussions in this book. I do not expect any of these to be implemented; they are my contribution to 'boundary pushing', in the hope that we must push boundaries in order to see the possibilities open to us. With that qualification, I would suggest that the following rights are some that are important for young people in relation to how they use social media. I also attempt to state each right's purpose as an aid to interpretation of the ambit of the right rather than a limitation on the right.

- Young people have the right to free expression on social media without qualification or conditions. The purpose of this right is to enhance the young person's capacity to be heard about matters that affect them, to bring to the attention of relevant adults, who must act in their best interests, information and views they should consider before acting and to remind those who exercise political and economic power that they should listen to young people before exercising that power.
- Young people have the right to play on social media. The purpose of this right is to engage in transgression with respect to their identity, viewpoints and opinions as a means of better understanding who they are and who they might become. It is an unconditional right and cannot be reduced for any reason. No one shall use such social media posts of a young person to reduce or minimise their future employment, educational or other options that might otherwise be affected by drawing reputational conclusions based on those posts.
- Young people have the right to be annoying online. The purpose of this right is to challenge those with power in ways that make them feel uncomfortable. This right limits the capacity of those who exercise power in society to classify such postings as 'inappropriate'. This right may not be exercised to cause upset or harm to vulnerable individuals, or to engage in online activity that exploits others or embarrasses them without their consent.
- Young people have the right to be educated about the way in which social media is constructed, controlled and profited from by social media platform providers. This right includes the right to know how privacy settings operate in social media but also the right to know how social media platform providers use the data they collect about young people. The purpose of this right is to enhance the knowledge that young people have about those who exercise power over their lives.
- Young people have the right to expect adults to always act in their best interests in relation to their use of social media. The purpose of this right is to ensure that adults acknowledge their responsibilities towards children and young people online and to respect their rights online. This does not mean that adults must always accept the views of young people. Adults have a responsibility to *really* listen to children and young people about how they wish to participate in digital spaces, to reflect on their views and to take them seriously, but they have a duty to finally

act according to what their experience and maturity tells them is best for the child or young person, and within the limits of the fundamental rights expressed in this charter.

- Young people have the right to take risks when using social media. The purpose of this right is to grant to young people the most precious right: the right to make mistakes. This enables young people to learn from their mistakes, but it also enables young people to learn from adults who care about their best interests, not from a position of control over their lives but from a position of love and concern. This right should be held dear by young people and exercised only after listening to adults that care about them.
- These rights are based on the need for adults to take children seriously, and on the need for children to accept that many adults care about them and that those adults are also to be listened to before exercising their rights.

Such a charter must of course be interpreted, and this is where the creativity of lawyers, judges and others must come to the fore to ensure that other laws and regulations reflect its spirit. Ultimately, the proper observance of children and young people's rights in social media depends on the cultural recognition of their place in society, which in turn is a response to the various narratives that occupy the relevant discourse. Within that discourse law plays a small but important, if often messy, role.

Notes

1 Newton N. Minow and Craig L. LaMay *Abandoned in the Wasteland: Children. Television and the First Amendment* (New York, Hill and Wang, 1995), p. 4.
2 Ibid., pp. 20–21.
3 United Kingdom Department of Trade and Industry and Department of Culture, Media and Sport *A New Future for Communications* (Communications White Paper, Command 5010, 12 December, 2000), para.1.1.15.
4 Simpson (2004), op.cit., p. 49.
5 See e.g. Wesley G. Carson 'The Institutionalization of Ambiguity: Early British Factory Acts' in Gilbert Geis and Ezra Stotland (eds.) *White Collar Crime: Theory and Research* (London, Sage, 1980), pp. 142–173.
6 Arie Freiberg 'Jurisprudential Miscegenation: Strict Liability and the Ambiguity of Law' in Augustine Brannigan and George Pavlich (eds.) *Governance and Regulation in Social Life: Essays in Honour of W.G. Carson* (Oxford, Routledge, 2007, Kindle Edition), p. 75.
7 Ibid., p. 80.
8 Ibid., p. 81.
9 Ibid., p. 83.
10 Mike Presdee 'Young People, Fire and Arson as Resistance' in Brannigan and Pavlich, op.cit., pp. 171–172.
11 See e.g. Laura Beth Nielsen *License to Harass: Law, Hierarchy and Offensive Public Speech* (Princeton, Princeton University Press, 2004). Though not written in the

context of social media, its relevance is on the point that it is often the powerless that bear the brunt of harassment on them and dine under the banner of free speech.

12 See e.g. Tim Moore, Morag McArthur, Debbie Noble-Carr and Deborah Harcourt *Taking Us Seriously: Children and Young People Talk About Safety and Institutional Responses to Their Safety Concerns: A Report for the Royal Commission into the Institutional Responses to Child Sexual Abuse* (Institute of Child Protection Studies, Australian Catholic University, August, 2015).
13 Ibid., p. 59.
14 Ibid.
15 Ibid., pp. 60–61.
16 Ibid., p. 62.
17 Ibid., p. 63.
18 David Archard *Children: Rights and Childhood 2nd edn* (London, Routledge, 1993), p. 206.
19 Ibid., p. 218.
20 Ibid.
21 Ibid.

Bibliography

Abbott, Kenneth and Duncan Snidal 'Hard and Soft Law in International Governance' (2000) 54 *International Organization* 421–456

Abiala, Kristina and Patrock Hernwall 'Tweens Negotiating Identity Online – Swedish Girls' and Boys' Reflections on Online Experiences' (2013) 16(8) *Journal of Youth Studies* 951–969

Albury, Kath 'Just Because It's Public Doesn't Mean It's Any of Your Business: Adults' and Children's Sexual Rights in Digitally Mediated Spaces' (2017) 19(5) *New Media and Society* 713–725

Albury, Kath, Kate Crawford, Paul Byron and Ben Mathews *Young People and Sexting in Australia: Ethics, Representation and the Law*, ARC Centre for Creative Industries and Innovation website, 2013, www.cci.edu.au/sites/default/files/Young_People_And_Sexting_Final.pdf

Archard, David *Children: Rights and Childhood 2nd edn* (London, Routledge, 1993)

Aroldi, Piermarco and Nicoletta Vittadini 'Children's Rights and Social Media: Issues and Prospects for Adoptive Families in Italy' (2017) 19(5) *New Media and Society* 741–749

Australian Government, Department of Human Services *Social Media Policy for Departmental Staff*, www.humanservices.gov.au/corporate/media/social-media-department/social-media-policy-departmental-staff, accessed 27 July 2017

Bakhtin, Mikhail *Rabelais and His World* (Bloomington, Indiana University Press, 1984)

Ball, James and Symeon Brown 'Why BlackBerry Messenger Was Rioters' Communication Method of Choice' *The Guardian*, 8 December, 2011, www.theguardian.com, accessed 30 July 2017

BBC News 'Teachers Need "Clearer" Social Networking Rules, Unions Say' 12 March, 2014, www.bbc.com/news/uk-wales-26539243, accessed 22 July 2017

Benkler, Yochai *The Wealth of Networks* (New Haven, Yale University Press, 2006)

Best, Shaun 'Terrorism and the Role of the School in Surveillance' (2008) 2(2) *Education, Knowledge and Economy* 137–148

Borden, Iain *Skateboarding Space and the City: Architecture and the Body* (Oxford and New York, Berg, 2001)

boyd, danah *It's Complicated: The Social Lives of Networked Teens* (Yale University Press, Kindle Edition, 2014)

Braidotti, Rosi *Nomadic Subjects: Embodiment and Sexual Difference in Contemporary Feminist Theory* (New York, Columbia University Press, 1994)

Brewer, Holly *By Birth or Consent: Children, Law and the Anglo-American Revolution in Authority* (Chapel Hill, University of North Carolina Press, 2005)
Bridgman, Rae 'Criteria for Best Practices in Building Child-Friendly Cities: Involving Young People in Urban Planning and Design' (2004) 13(2) *Canadian Journal of Urban Research* 337–346
Brooks, Chad 'Keep It Clean: Social Media Screenings Gain in Popularity' *Business News Daily*, June 16, 2017, www.businessnewsdaily.com/2377-social-media-hiring.html, accessed 27 July 2017
Burgess, Jean and Joshua Green *You Tube* (Cambridge, Polity Press, 2009)
Carson, Wesley G. 'The Institutionalization of Ambiguity: Early British Factory Acts', in G. Geis and E. Stotland (eds.), *White Collar Crime: Theory and Research* (London, Sage, 1980) 142–173
Castells, Manuel *Communication Power* (Oxford, Oxford University Press, 2009)
Chalfen, Richard '"It's Only a Picture": Sexting, "Smutty" Snapshots and Felony Charges' (2009) 24(3) *Visual Studies* 258–268
Chambers, Paul 'My Tweet Was Silly, but the Police Reaction Was Absurd' *The Guardian*, 11 May, 2010
Children's Commissioner for England *Growing Up Digital: A Report of the Growing Up Digital Taskforce* (London, Children's Commissioner for England, January, 2017)
Cohen, Stan *Visions of Social Control* (Cambridge, Polity Press, 1985)
College of Policing Briefing Note *Police Action in Response to Youth Produced Sexual Imagery ('Sexting')* Version 1.0, November, 2016, www.college.police.uk
Commonwealth of Australia *Report of the Royal Commission on Television* (Canberra, Government Printing Office, 1954)
The Conservative and Unionist Party Manifesto *Forward Together: Our Plan for a Stronger Britain and a Prosperous Future* (Conservative Party, 2017)
Cook, Amy 'New Counter-Terrorism Duties: What Schools Need to Know' *The Guardian*, 3 March, 2015, www.theguardian.com/teacher-network/2015/mar/02/counter-terrorism-duties-schools-need-to-know, accessed 23 July 2017
Cook, Henrietta 'How Schools Are Tracking Students Using Their Mobile Phones' *The Age* 16 July, 2017, www.theage.com.au, accessed 17 July 2017
Crown Prosecution Service *Guidelines on Prosecuting Cases Involving Communications Sent via Social Media*, www.cps.gov.uk, accessed 12 June 2017
Davey, Melissa '"What Is the Evidence?" Commissioner Questions Victoria's Youth Justice Crackdown' *The Guardian* (Australia), 4 July, 2017, www.guardian.com, accessed 4 July 2017
Department for Culture Media and Sport (UK) *Getting Serious About Play: A Review of Children's Play* (Department for Culture Media and Sport, 2004)
Department of Education, Training and Employment, Queensland *Social Media and the School Community* (2013), http://behaviour.education.qld.gov.au/SiteCollectionDocuments/cybersafety/social-media-and-community-online.pdf, accessed 22 July 2017
Department of Education, Western Australia *Guidelines for the Use of Social Media* (undated)
Dickinson, Julie Gutman 'Walmart's War Against Unions – and the U.S. Laws That Make It Possible' *Huffington Post*, The Blog, 6 May, 2013, www.huffingtonpost.com/julie-b-gutman/walmart-labor-laws_b_3390994.html, accessed 28 July 2017

Dobson, Amy S. and Jessica Ringrose 'Sext Education: Pedagogies of Sex, Gender and Shame in the Schoolyards of Tagged and Exposed' (2016) 16(1) *Sex Education* 8–21

Donnison, David 'Rethinking Rights Talk', in Lionel Orchard and Richard Dare (eds.), *Markets, Morals and Public Policy* (Sydney, The Federation Press, 1999) 219–231

Douglas, Mary *Purity and Danger* (London and New York, Routledge and Kegan Paul, first published 1966)

Drefuss, Emily 'Blaming the Internet for Terrorism Misses the Point' 6 June, 2017, www.wired.com, accessed 23 July 2017

Duschinsky, Robbie 'The 2010 UK Home Office 'Sexualisation of Young People' Review: A Discursive Policy Analysis' (2012) 41 *Journal of Social Policy* 715–731

Dyer, Gwynne 'Class at Root of Rioting in London' *Toronto Sun*, 10 August, 2011, www.toronto.sun, accessed 30 July 2017

Eekelaar, John 'The Emergence of Children's Rights' (1986) 6 *Oxford Journal of Legal Studies* 161

Ennew, Judith *The Sexual Exploitation of Children* (New York, St Martin's Press, 1986)

Epstein, Debbie, Richard Johnson and Deborah L. Steinberg 'Twice Told Tales: Transformation, Recuperation and Emergence in the Age of Consent Debates 1998' (2000) 3 *Sexualities* 5

Fainstein, Susan S. *The Just City* (Ithaca, Cornell University Press, 2010)

Farrell, Paul 'Detention Centre Staff Speak out in Defiance of New Asylum Secrecy Laws' *The Guardian*, 1 July, 2015, www.theguardian.com/australia-news/2015/jul/01/detention-centre-staff-speak-out-in-defiance-of-new-asylum-secrecy-laws, accessed 28 July 2017

Federal Trade Commission *Complying with COPPA: Frequently Asked Questions*, www.ftc.gov, accessed 10 July 2017

Federal Trade Commission *FTC Facts for Consumers: Social Networking Sites: A Parent's Guide*, September, 2007 http://www.ictliteracy.info/rf.pdf/FTC%20Social%20Networking%20Guide%20for%20Parents.pdf

Federal Trade Commission *Protecting Consumer Privacy in an Era of Rapid Change: Recommendations for Businesses and Policymakers*, FTC Report, March, 2012

Flusty, Stephen 'Thrashing Downtown: Play as Resistance to the Spatial and Representational Regulation of Los Angeles' (2000) 17(2) *Cities* 149–158

Freeman, Michael D.A. *The Rights and Wrongs of Children* (London, F. Pinter, 1983)

Freiberg, Arie 'Jurisprudential Miscegenation: Strict Liability and the Ambiguity of Law', in Augustine Brannigan and George Pavlich (eds.), *Governance and Regulation in Social Life: Essays in Honour of W.G. Carson* (Oxford, Routledge, 2007, Kindle Edition) 74–90

Fuchs, Christian *Culture and Economy in the Age of Social Media* (New York and London, Routledge, 2015)

Fuchs, Christian *Social Media: A Critical Introduction* (Los Angeles, Sage, 2014)

The General Teaching Council for Scotland *Professional Guidance on the Use of Electronic Communication and Social Media* (undated), www.gtcs.org.uk/web/FILES/teacher-regulation/professional-guidance-ecomms-social-media.pdf, accessed 22 July 2017

Gillis, Wendy 'Rehtaeh Parsons: A Family's Tragedy and a Town's Shame' *thestar.com*, April 12, 2013, accessed 12 June 2017; 'Rehtaeh Parsons, Canadian Girl, Dies After Suicide Attempt; Parents Allege She Was Raped by 4 Boys' *thestar.com*, April 12, 2013, www.huffingtonpost.com.au, accessed 12 June 2017

Gladwell, Malcolm 'Small Change: The Revolution Will Not Be Tweeted' *The New Yorker*, 4 October, 2010

Grahamvale Primary School No.3696 [Victoria, Australia] *Social Media Policy – Parents*, July, 2016, p. 2, www.grahamvaleps.vic.edu.au/documents/SocialMedia Parents.pdf, accessed 22 July 2017

Graves, Lucas 'Everyone's a Reporter' *Wired.com*, January 9, 2005, accessed 12 June 2017

Greenfield, Charlotte 'Should We "Fix" Intersex Children?' *The Atlantic*, 8 July, 2014, www.theatlantic.com, accessed 30 July 2017

Groskop, Viv 'Children and the Internet: A Parent's Guide' *The Guardian*, 3 November, 2013, www.theguardian.com/technology2013/nov/03/internet-children-parents-safety, accessed 20 June 2017

The Guardian and London School of Economics and Political Science *Reading the Riots: Investigating England's Summer of Disorder* (The Guardian and London School of Economics, 2011)

Halliday, Josh 'UK Riots 'Made Worse' by Rolling News, BBM, Twitter and Facebook' www.guardian.com, 28 March, 2012, accessed 30 July 2017

Haraway, D. *Simians, Cyborgs, and Women: The Reinvention of Nature* (London, Routledge, 1991)

Harvey, David *Rebel Cities: From the Right to the City to the Urban Revolution* (London, Verso, 2012)

Holt, John C. *Escape from Childhood: The Needs and Rights of Children* (Harmondsworth, Penguin, 1975)

Home Office *Sexualisation of Young People Review* (London, UK Home Office, 2010)

James, Alison and Alan Prout 'Re-presenting Childhood: Time and Transition in the Study of Childhood', in A. James and A. Prout (eds.), *Constructing and Reconstructing Childhood: Contemporary Issues in the Sociological Study of Childhood* (Classic Edition, Routledge, Oxford, 2015) 202–219

Jenkins, Henry *Participatory Culture in a Networked Era: A Conversation on Youth, Learning, Commerce, and Politics* (Cambridge, Wiley, 2016, Kindle Edition)

Jenkins, Lyndsey, Ruoyun Lin and Debora Jeske 'Influences and Benefits of Role Models on Social Media', in Yogesh Dwivedi, Matti Mäntymäki, M.N. Ravishankar, Marijn Janssen, Marc Clement, Emma L. Slade, Nripendra P. Rana, Salah Al-Sharhan and Antonis C. Simintiras (eds.), *Social Media: The Good, the Bad, and the Ugly* (I3E 2016, Lecture Notes in Computer Science, vol. 9844. Springer, Cham, 2016) 673–684

Karaian, Lara 'Lolita Speaks: "Sexting", Teenage Girls and the Law' (2012) 8 *Crime Media Culture* 57–73

'Kambrya College Defends Assembly That Was Accused of "Slut-Shaming"' news.com.au, 23 August, 2016, accessed 23 July 2017

Karsten, Lia 'It All Used to Be Better? Different Generations on Continuity and Change in Urban Children's Daily Use of Space' (2005) 3(3) *Children's Geographies* 275–290

Kennedy, Helen, 'Beyond Anonymity, or Future Directions for Internet Identity Research' (2006) 8(6) *New Media Society* 859–876

Kincaid, James R. *Erotic Innocence: The Culture of Child Molesting* (Durham and London, Duke University Press, 1998)

King, Michael and Christine Piper *How the Law Thinks About Children 2nd edn* (Aldershot, Ashgate, 1995)

Kitzinger, Jenny 'Children, Power and the Struggle Against Sexual Abuse', in Alison James and Alan Prout (eds.), *Constructing and Reconstructing Childhood: Contemporary Issues in the Sociological Study of Childhood* (Classic Edition, Routledge, Oxford, 2015), 145–166

Klabbers, Jan 'The Redundancy of Soft Law' (1996) 65(2) *Nordisk Journal of International Law* 167–182

The Law Commission *Computer Misuse* (Working Paper No. 110) (London, HMSO, 1988)

Law Reform Committee, Parliament of Victoria *Inquiry into Sexting* (Parliament of Victoria, 2013)

Lee, Murray, Thomas Crofts, Alyce McGovern and Sanja Milivojevic *Sexting and Young People* (Report to the Criminology Research Council, November, 2015)

Lee, Nick *Childhood and Society: Growing up in an Age of Uncertainty* (Maidenhead, Open University Press, 2001)

Levine, Judith *Harmful to Minors: The Perils of Protecting Children from Sex* (New York, Thuder's Mouth Press, 2002)

Livingstone, Sonia 'Reframing Media Effects in Terms of Children's Rights in the Digital Age' (2016) 10(1) *Journal of Children and Media* 4–12

Livingstone, Sonia and Amanda Third 'Children and young people's rights in the digital age: An emerging agenda' (2017) 19 (5) *New Media and Society* 657–670

Low, Setha and Neil Smith (eds.) *The Politics of Public Space* (Oxford, Routledge, 2006)

Lupton, Deborah and Ben Williamson 'The Datafied Child: The Dataveillance of Children and Implications for Human Rights' (2017) 19(5) *New Media and Society* 780–794

Madgwick, Donald and Tony Smythe *The Invasion of Privacy* (Oxford, Pitman, 1974)

Maniscalco, Anthony *Public Spaces, Marketplaces, and the Constitution: Shopping Malls and the First Amendment* (Albany, State University of New York Press, 2015)

McAfee *A Parent's Guide to Social Networking Sites* (McAfee, 2009)

McCullagh, Declan 'From WarGames to Swartz: How U.S. Anti-Hacking Law Went Astray' *CNET news*, 13 March, 2013, https:www.cnet.com/au/news/from-wargames-to-aaron-swartz-how-u-s-anti-hacking-law-went-astray, accessed 7 July 2017

McKenzie, Iain 'Is Technology to Blame for the London Riots?' *BBC News*, 8 August, 2011, www.bbc.com, accessed 30 July 2017

Minow, Newton N. and Craig L. LaMay *Abandoned in the Wasteland: Children, Television and the First Amendment* (New York, Hill and Wang, 1995)

Mitchell, Don *Social Justice and the Fight for Public Space* (New York, Guildford, 2003)

Moore, Tim, Morag McArthur, Debbie Noble-Carr and Deborah Harcourt *Taking Us Seriously: Children and Young People Talk About Safety and Institutional Responses to Their Safety Concerns: A Report for the Royal Commission into the Institutional Responses to Child Sexual Abuse* (Institute of Child Protection Studies, Australian Catholic University, August, 2015)

Mordue, Tom 'Tourism, Urban Governance and Public Space' (2007) 26(4) *Leisure Studies* 447–462

New Zealand Law Commission *Computer Misuse* (Report no. 54, Wellington, New Zealand Law Commission, 1999)

Nielsen, Laura Beth *License to Harass: Law, Hierarchy and Offensive Public Speech* (Princeton, Princeton University Press, 2004)

Nikken, Peter and Marjon Schols 'How and Why Parents Guide the Media Use of Young Children' (2015) 24 *Journal of Child and Family Studies* 3423–3435

Office of the e-Safety Children's Commissioner *Parent's Guide to Online Safety* (Australian Government, undated)

Oldenburg, Ray *The Great Good Place: Cafes, Coffee Shops, Bookstores, Bars, Hair Salons and Other Hangouts at the Heart of a Community 2nd edn* (New York, Marlowe, 1999)

Olsen, Frances E. 'The Myth of State Intervention in the Family' (1985) 18 *University of Michigan Journal of Law Reform* 835–864

Oswell, David *The Agency of Children: From Family to Global Human Rights* (Cambridge, Cambridge University Press, 2013)

Ovadia, Dana 'The Birth of an Intersex Infant: Exploring the Options and Ethics Behind Decision-Making' (2013) 6(1) *Journal of Student Nursing Research* 17–20

Papacharissi, Zizi A. *A Private Sphere: Democracy in a Digital Age* (Cambridge, Polity Press, 2010)

Papacharissi, Zizi A. *Affective Publics: Sentiment, Technology, and Politics* (OUP, USA, Oxford Studies in Digital Politics, 2015)

Papacharissi, Zizi A. 'The Virtual Sphere 2.0: The Internet, the Public Sphere, and Beyond', in Andrew Cahdwick and Philip N. Howard (eds.), *Routledge Handbook of Internet Politics* (New York, Routledge, 2009), 230–245

Parliament of the Commonwealth of Australia *High-Wire Act: Cyber-Safety and the Young: Interim Report*, Joint Select Committee on Cyber-Safety, June, 2011

Paus-Hasebrink, Ingrid, Philip Sinner and Fabian Prochazka *Children's Online Experiences in Socially Disadvantaged Families: European Evidence and Policy Implications* (London, EU Kids Online/EU Kids III/ Reports/Disadvantaged_children.pdf)

Play England 'Why Play Is Important', www.playengland.org.uk/about-us/why-play-is-important/, accessed 16 July 2017

Pomroy, Paul 'McDonald's Serves the Needs of Its Loyal Workers' *The Telegraph*, 23 April, 2016, www.telegraph.co.uk/business/2016/04/23/mcdonalds-serves-the-needs-of-its-loyal-workers/, accessed 28 July 2017

Pornwasin, Asina 'With Social Media, Everyone's a Reporter!' *The Nation*, 29 November, 2015, www.nationmultimedia.com, accessed 12 June 2017

Presdee, Mike 'British Sociological Association Conference' *Unpublished Paper*, 6–9 April, 1992

Presdee, Mike *Cultural Criminology and the Carnival of Crime* (London and New York, Routledge, 2000)

Presdee, Mike 'Young People, Fire and Arson as Resistance', in Augustine Brannigan and George Pavlich (eds.), *Governance and Regulation in Social Life: Essays in Honour of W.G. Carson* (Oxford, Routledge, 2007, Kindle Edition) 164–178

Preston, Marilyn J. ' "They're Just Not Mature Right Now": Teachers' Complicated Perceptions of Gender and Anti-Queer Bullying' (2016) 16(1) *Sex Education* 22–34

The Report of the Nova Scotia Task Force on Bullying and Cyberbullying (A. Wayne MacKay, Chair) *Respectful and Responsible Relationships: There's No App for That*, February 29, 2012

Reynolds, Louis and Ralph Scott *Digital Citizens: Countering Extremism Online* (Demos, London, 2016)

Ringrose, Jessica, Laura Harvey, Rosalind Gill and Sonia Livingstone 'Teen Girls, Sexual Double Standards and "Sexting": Gendered Value in Digital Image Exchange' (2013) 14(3) *Feminist Theory* 305–323

Rojek, Chris *Ways of Escape: Modern Transformations in Leisure and Travel* (London, MacMillan, 1993)

Russo, Charles J., Joan Squelch and Sally Varnham 'Teachers and Social Networking Sites: Think Before You Post' (2010) 5(5) *Public Space: The Journal of Law and Social Justice* 1–15

Schulte, Stephanie Ricker *Cached: Decoding the Internet in Global Popular Culture* (Critical Cultural Communication) (New York, New York University Press, Kindle Edition, 2013)

Shah, Saqib 'Instagram Is Set to Turn a Huge Profit for Facebook This Year' 16 April, 2016, www.digitaltrends.com, accessed 26 June 2017

Shelton, Dinah, ed. *Commitment and Compliance: The Role of Non-binding Norms in the International Legal System* (Oxford, Oxford University Press, 2000)

Sieghart, Paul *The Lawful Rights of Mankind* (Oxford University Press, Oxford, 1985)

Simpson, Brian *Children and Television* (London and New York, Continuum, 2004)

Simpson, Brian 'Sexting, Digital Dissent and Narratives of Innocence – Controlling the Child's Body', in Sampson Lee Blair, Patricia Neff Claster and Samuel M. Claster (eds.), *Technology and Youth: Growing up in a Digital World* (Sociological Studies of Children and Youth, Vol. 19, Bingley, Emerald, 2015), pp. 315–349

Siow, Veronica 'The Impact of Social Media in the Workplace: An Employer's Perspective' (2013) 32(4) *Communications Law Bulletin* 12–14

Smart, Carol *Feminism and the Power of Law* (New York, Routledge, 1989)

Smith, Phillip, Timothy L. Phillips and Ryan D. King *Incivility: The Rude Stranger in Everyday Life* (Cambridge, Cambridge University Press, 2010)

Sørensen, Holm B. 'Chat – identitet, krop og kultur' [Chat – Identity, Body and Culture], in B. Holm Sørensen (ed.), *Chat: Leg, identitet, socialitet og læring* [Chat: Play, Identity, Sociality, and Learning] (Ko¨penhamn, Gads forlag, 2001), pp. 15–36

Stanley, Christopher *Urban Excess and the Law: Capital, Culture and Desire* (London, Cavendish, 1996)

Steinberg, Stacey 'Sharenting: Children's Privacy in the Age of Social Media' (2017) 66 *Emory Law Journal* 839

Steinmetz, Kevin F. *Hacked: A Radical Approach to Hacker Culture and Crime* (New York, New York University Press, 2016)

Stern, Susannah 'Regretted Online Self-Presentations: U.S. College Students' Recollections and Reflections' (2015) 9(2) *Journal of Children and Media* 248–265

Stevens, Robin, Stacia Gilliard-Matthews, Jamie Dunaev, Marcus K. Woods and Bridgette M. Brawner 'The Digital Hood: Social Media Use Among Youth in Disadvantaged Neighborhoods' (2017) 19(6) *New Media and Society* 950–967

Stychin, Carl F. *Governing Sexuality: The Changing Politics of Citizenship and Law Reform* (Oxford and Portland, Hart, 2003)

Sullivan, Colin and Mike Lyons 'Social Networks in the 2011 London Riots' *Civic Media*, 11 December, 2014, www.medium.com, accessed 30 July 2017

Synott, Anthony 'Little Angels, Little Devils: A Sociology of Children' (1983) 20 *Canadian Review of Sociology and Anthropology* 79–95

Taylor, Astra *The People's Platform: Taking Back Power and Culture in the Digital Age* (London, Fourth Estate, 2014)

Taylor, Emmeline 'I Spy with My Little Eye: The Use of CCTV in Schools and the Impact on Privacy' (2010) 58(3) *Sociological Review* 381–405

Taylor, Emmeline and Tonya Rooney 'Digital Playgrounds: Growing up in the Surveillance Age', in Emmeline Taylor and Tonya Rooney (eds.), *Surveillance Futures: Social and Ethical Implications of New Technologies for Children and Young People* (Oxford, Routledge, 2017) 1–16

Toffler, Alvin *The Third Wave* (New York, Bantam, 1980)

Travis, Alan 'Online Antisocial Behaviour Complaints "Becoming a Real Problem for Police"' *The Guardian*, 24 June, 2014, guardian.com, accessed 12 June 2017

Turkle, Sherry *Life on the Screen: Identity in the Age of the Internet* (London, Weidenfeld and Nicolson, 1995)

United Kingdom Department of Trade and Industry and Department of Culture, Media and Sport *A New Future for Communications* (Communications White Paper, Command 5010, 12 December, 2000)

United Nations Committee on the Rights of the Child, General comment No. 17 on the *Right of the Child to Rest, Leisure, Play, Recreational Activities, Cultural Life and the Arts* (art. 31), CRC/C/GC17, 17 April, 2013

Valentine, Gil 'Children Should Be Seen and Not Heard: The Production and Transgression of Adults' Public Space' (1996) 17(3) *Urban Geography* 205–220

Valentine, Gil 'Theorizing and Researching Intersectionality: A Challenge for Feminist Geography' (2007) 59(1) *The Professional Geographer* 10–21

Valkenburg, Patti, Marina Krcmar, Allerd Peters and Nies Marseille 'Developing a Scale to Asses Three Styles of Television Mediation: "Instructive Mediation", "Restrictive Mediation" and "Social Coviewing"' (1999) 43 *Journal of Broadcasting and Electronic Media* 52–66

Vaughan, Barry 'The Government of Youth: Disorder and Dependence?' (2000) 9 *Social and Legal Studies* 347

Verdoodt, Valerie 'Children's Access to Social Media and the GDPR – "Please Mom, Can I Go on Facebook?"' *KU Leuven Centre for IT & IP Law*, www.law.kuleuven.be/citip/blog, accessed 19 June 2017

Wiggins, Kaye 'Should Children Ban Their Parents from Social Media?' *BBC News*, 2 November, 2016, www.bbc.com/news/business-37834856, accessed 19 June 2017

Zelizer, Viviana A. *Pricing the Priceless Child: The Changing Social Value of Children* (New York, Basic Books, 1985)

Index